Cuchulain, the hound of Ulster

Eleanor Hull

CUCHULAIN
THE HOUND OF ULSTER

The Raven of Ill-omen

CUCHULAIN
THE HOUND OF ULSTER

BY

ELEANOR HULL

AUTHOR OF
"THE CUCHULLIN SAGA IN IRISH LITERATURE"
"PAGAN IRELAND" "EARLY CHRISTIAN IRELAND"
ETC.

WITH EIGHT ILLUSTRATIONS BY
STEPHEN REID

"Bec a brig liomsa sin," ar Cuchulaind, "gen
go rabar acht aonlá no aonoidchi ar bith acht go
mairit m'airdsgeula dom és."
Stowe MS., C. 6, 3.
R. Irish Academy.

"Though the span of my life were but for a
day," Cuchulain said, "little should I reck of
that, if but my noble deeds might be remembered
among men."

NEW YORK
THOMAS Y. CROWELL COMPANY
PUBLISHERS

Printed in Great Britain
by Turnbull & Spears, Edinburgh

Contents

		PAGE
Introduction		9

CHAP.

I. How Conor became King of Ulster . . .	15
II. Queen Meave and the Woman-Seer . . .	18
III. The Boy-Corps of King Conor	25
IV. How Cuchulain got his Name	33
V. How Cuchulain took Arms	40
VI. Of Cuchulain's First Feats of Championship .	47
VII. Cuchulain's Adventures in Shadow-land . .	57
VIII How Cuchulain wooed his Wife	68
IX. Meave demands the Brown Bull of Cooley and is refused	78
X. The Plucking out of the Four-pronged Pole .	88
XI. The Deer of Ill-Luck	94
XII. Etaroomal's well-deserved Fate . . .	104
XIII. The Fight with Spits of Holly-Wood .	113
XIV. The Combat with Ferdia	118

CHAP.		PAGE
XV. THE FALL OF FERDIA		128
XVI. ULSTER, AWAKE!		143
XVII. THE END OF THE BOY-CORPS		151
XVIII. THE "RISING OUT" OF ULSTER		160
XIX. THE HUMBLING OF QUEEN MEAVE		167
XX. THE FAIRY SWAN-MAIDENS		171
XXI. HOW CUCHULAIN WENT TO FAIRY-LAND		182
XXII. DEIRDRE OF CONTENTIONS		194
XXIII. THE UP-BRINGING OF DEIRDRE		201
XXIV. THE SLEEP-WANDERER		208
XXV. THE WILES OF KING CONOR		217
XXVI. THE SORROWFUL DEATH OF USNA'S SONS		224
XXVII. THE FIGHT OF CUCHULAIN WITH HIS SON CONLA		241
XXVIII. THE HOUND AT BAY		252
XXIX. FAME OUTLIVES LIFE		264
XXX. THE RED ROUT		270
NOTES ON THE SOURCES		275

Illustrations

	PAGE
THE RAVEN OF ILL-OMEN	*Frontispiece*
QUEEN MEAVE AND THE DRUID	18
CUCHULAIN SETS OUT FOR EMAIN MACHA . . .	28
CUCHULAIN DESIRES ARMS OF THE KING. . . .	42
MACHA CURSES THE MEN OF ULSTER	80
FERDIA FALLS BY THE HAND OF CUCHULAIN . . .	140
"THE MOMENT OF GOOD-LUCK IS COME"	160
CUCHULAIN COMES AT LAST TO HIS DEATH . . .	268

Introduction

THE events that circle round King Conor mac Nessa and Cuchulain as their principal figures are supposed to have occurred, as we gather from the legends themselves, about the first century of our era. According to one of the stories, King Conor is said to have died in a paroxysm of wrath and horror, brought on by hearing the news of the crucifixion of our Lord by the Jews. Though this story is evidently one of the few interpolations having their origin in Christian times (the main body of the legends being purely pagan), the probability that they took shape about this period is increased almost to certainty by the remarkable agreement we find in them with the accounts derived from classical writers who lived and wrote about this same period, and who comment on the habits of the Gauls of France, the Danube valley and Asia Minor, and the Belgic tribes who inhabited South-eastern Britain, with whom the Roman armies came into contact in the course of their wars of aggression and expansion. The descriptions given by Poseidonius, a century before Christ, or Diodorus, Cæsar and Livy half a century later, agree remarkably with the notices found in these Irish stories of social conditions, weapons, dress, and appearance. The large wicker shields, the huge double-bladed swords lifted above the head to strike, the courage amounting to rashness of the Celt in attack, the furious onset of the scythed war-chariots, the disregard of death, the habit of rushing into battle without waiting to don their clothes, the single combats, the great feasts, the " Champion's Bit " reserved as a mark of distinction for the bravest warrior ; these, and many other characteristics found in our tales, are commented upon in the pages of the Roman historians. The culture represented in them is that known to archæologists as " late Celtic," called on the Continent the La Tène period, *i.e.* the period extending from about 400 B.C. to the first century of the Christian era ; and the actual remains of weapons, ornaments, and dress found in Ireland confirm the supposition that we are dealing with this stage of culture.

We may, then, take it that these tales were formed about the beginning of our era, although the earliest written documents that we have of them are not earlier than the eleventh and twelfth century. Between the time of their invention for the entertainment of the chiefs and kings of Ireland to the time of their incorporation in the great books which contain the bulk of the tales, they were handed down by word of mouth, every bard and professional story-teller (of whom there was at least one in every great man's house) being obliged to know by heart a great number of these romances, and prepared at any moment to recite those which he might be called upon to give. In the course of centuries of recitation certain changes crept in, but in the main they come to us much as they were orginally recited. In some tales, of which we have a number of copies of different ages, we can trace these changes and notice the additions and modifications that have been made.

Over a hundred distinct tales belonging to this one cycle alone are known to have existed, and of a great number of them one or more copies have come down to us, differing more or less from each other.

The old story-tellers who handed down the romantic tales of Ireland handled their material in a very free manner, expanding and altering as suited their own poetic feeling and the audience they addressed. A reciter of poetic power fearlessly re-arranged, enlarged or condensed. As a general rule, the older the form of a story the shorter, terser, and more barbaric is its character. In the long tale of the Táin bó Cuailgne, which forms the central subject of the whole cycle, the arrangement of the episodes and the number of incidents introduced is quite different in the oldest copy we have of it, that found in the compilation called (from the particular piece of parchment on which it was written) the " Book of the Dun (or Brown) Cow," compiled in 1100 in the monastery of Clonmacnois on the Shannon, from the version in the Book of Leinster, a great vellum book drawn up and written for Dermot mac Morrough, the King of Leinster who invited Strongbow and the Normans to come over from Wales half a century later. The oldest form of the story is often the more manly and self-restrained ; there is a tendency, as time goes on, not only to soften down the more barbarous and rougher portions, but to emphasise the pathetic and moving scenes, and to add touches of symbolism and imagination. Though they lack the brief dignity of the older versions, the more recent copies are often more attractive and full of poetry. For instance, we have in this book drawn largely on some comparatively recent (seventeenth-eighteenth century) MSS. in the British Museum, not hitherto translated, for the details (many of them full of poetic imagination) of the history of Cuchulain's journey into Shadowland to learn feats of bravery,[1] and in the account of his death and the incidents that immediately follow it.   In the different versions of the former story, the name of the country to which Cuchulain went is variously given as Alba or Scotland, Scythia, and the "Land of Scáthach," *i.e.* the home of the woman-warrior from whom he learned. It is evident that Scythia is only a mistake for Scáthach, made by some scribe and copied by others. Scáth means a "Shadow," and probably the original idea was purely symbolic, meaning that the hero had passed beyond the bounds of human knowledge into an invisible world of mystery called Shadowland.   The writer of the copy that I have used returns to this original idea, and the whole story, in his hands, becomes symbolic and imaginative.   So also, in the account of Cuchulain's death, the modern scribe introduces new details which add to the beauty and striking effect of this most touching episode.   To my mind the scribes, in making these additions, acted in a perfectly legitimate manner, and I have not hesitated in this book, which does not aim at being a text-book, but a book written for the pleasure of the young, to follow their example.   I have freely, in minor points, re-arranged or pruned the tales, adding details from different sources as suited my purpose, and occasionally expanding an imaginative suggestion indicated, but not worked out, by the scribe. But I have seldom allowed myself deliberately to alter a story, or to introduce anything not found somewhere in the tales as they have come down to us.   An exception is the story of Cuchulain's visit to fairy-land, commonly known as the "Sickbed of Cuchulain," which

---

[1] This story has been published by Dr Wh. Stokes in *Rev. Celt.* xxix. (1908), since the above was written.

required a slight modification of the central situation in order to make it suitable reading for any children into whose hands the book might chance to fall; it was too poetic and touching an episode to be altogether omitted without loss to the conception of the cycle as a whole.

It is, after all, the human interest of these old stories, and not primarily their importance as folklore and the history of manners, that appeals to most of us to-day. As the Arthurian legend all through the Middle Ages set before men's minds an ideal of high purpose, purity of life, and chivalrous behaviour in an age that was not over-inclined to practise these virtues, so these old Irish romances, so late rescued from oblivion, come to recall the minds of men in our own day to some noble ideals.

For, rude as are the social conditions depicted in these tales, and exaggerated and barbaric as is the flavour of some of them, they nevertheless present to us a high and often romantic code of natural chivalry. There is no more pathetic story in literature than that of the fight between the two old and loving friends, Cuchulain and Ferdia; there is no more touching act of chivalry to a woman than Cuchulain's offer of aid to his enemy Queen Meave, in the moment of her exhaustion; there is no more delightful passage of playful affection than that between the hero and his lady in the wooing of Emer. These tales have a sprightliness and buoyancy not possessed by the Arthurian tales, they are fresher, more humorous, more diversified; and the characters, more especially those of the women, are more firmly and variously drawn. For Wales and for England Arthur has been for centuries the representative " very gentle perfect knight "; for Ireland Cuchulain represented the highest ideal of which the Irish Gael was capable. In these stories, as in Malory's " Morte D'Arthur," we find " many joyous and pleasant histories, and noble and renowned acts of humanity, gentleness and chivalry "; and we may add, with Malory, " Do after the good and leave the evil, and it shall bring you to good fame and renommée."

ELEANOR HULL

Cuchulain

CHAPTER I

How Conor became King of Ulster

THERE was a great war between Connaught and Ulster, that is, between Conor, King of Ulster, and Meave, the proud and mighty Queen of Connaught. This was the cause of the war between them. When Conor was but a lad, his mother was a widow, and there was no thought that Conor would be king. For the King of Ulster at that time was Fergus mac Roy, a powerful and noble king, whom his people loved; and though Conor was of high rank and dignity, he stood not near the throne. But his mother, Ness, was ambitious for him, and she used all her arts to bring it about that he should be called to the throne of Ulster. Ness was a handsome woman, and a woman of spirit, and in her youth she had been a warrior; and Fergus admired her, and she wrought upon him so that in the end he asked her to be his wife. She made it a condition that for one year Fergus would leave the sovereignty, and that Conor should take his place; " for," said she, " I should like to have it said that my son had been a king, and that his children should be called the descendants of a king." Fergus and the people of Ulster liked not her request, but she was firm, and Fergus all the more desired to marry her, because he found it not easy to get her; so, at the last, he gave way to her, and he resigned the kingdom for one year into the hands of Conor.

But, as soon as Conor was king, Ness set about to win away the hearts of the people of Ulster from Fergus, and to transfer them in their allegiance to Conor. She supplied her son with wealth, which he distributed secretly among the people, buying them over to his side; and she taught him how to act, so that he won over the nobles and the great men of the province. And when, the year being out, Fergus demanded back the sovereignty, he found that the league formed against him was so strong that he could do nothing. The chiefs said that they liked Conor well, and that he was their friend, and they were not disposed to part with him; they said, too, that Fergus having abandoned the kingdom for a year, only to gain a wife, cared little for it, and had, in fact, resigned it. And they agreed that Fergus should keep his wife, if he wished, but that the kingdom should pass to Conor. And Fergus was so wrath at this, that he forsook his wife, and went with a great host of his own followers into Connaught, to take refuge with Queen Meave and with Ailill, her spouse. But he swore to be revenged upon Conor, and he waited only an opportunity to incite Meave to gather her army together that he might try to win back the sovereignty, or at least to revenge the insult put upon him by Conor and by Ness.

Now Fergus mac Roy was of great stature, a mighty man and a famous warrior, and his strength was that of a hundred heroes. And all men spoke of the sword of Fergus, which was so great and long that men said that it stretched like a rainbow or like a weaver's beam. And at the head of his hosts was Cormac, the Champion of

the White Cairn of Watching, a son of Conor, who liked
not the deed of his father; for he was young, and he had
been one of the bodyguard of Fergus, and went with
Fergus into exile to Connaught. And that was called
the Black Exile of Fergus mac Roy.

CHAPTER II

Queen Meave and the Woman-Seer

CRAFTILY Fergus wrought upon Queen Meave that she should espouse his cause and lead an army into Ulster's coasts, to win the kingdom back for him again. And Meave was no way sorry to make war, for Connaught and the North at all times were at strife, and frays and battle-raids were common between them. So with light heart Queen Meave sent heralds out and messengers through Connaught to collect her armed bands, bidding them meet her within three months' space before her palace-fort of Cruachan. And in three months a goodly host was gathered there, and tents were pitched, and for awhile they tarried round the palace-courts, eating and drinking, so that with good heart and strength they might set forth to march towards Ulster's borders.

Now, in the dark and dead of night before the break of day when all the host should start their forward march, Meave could not sleep; and stealthily she rose and bid them make her chariot ready, that she might seek a Druid whom she knew, and learn from him the prospects of the expedition and what should be the fate before her hosts.

Far in the depths of a wide-spreading wood the Druid dwelt. An old and reverend man was he, and far and wide men knew him for a prophet and a seer. The " Know-

1ᵒ

Queen Meave and the Druid

18

ledge that enlightens " he possessed, which opened to his
eyes the coming days and all the secret things the future
held.   Gravely he came out to meet the troubled Queen,
and he from her chariot handed her, as proudly she
drew up before his door.

" We have come to thee, O Druid and magician,"
said the Queen, " to ask of thee the fate and fortune of
this expedition against Ulster which we have now in
hand, whether we shall return victorious or not."

" Wait but awhile in patience," said the aged man,
" and I will read the future, if the gods allow."

For two long hours Meave waited in the hut, while on
the hearth the fire of peat burned low, and a strange
dimness spread about the house as though a mist had
risen between herself and the magician, who, on his
palms performed his curious rites, and in a slow and
solemn chant sang charms and incantations ; by strange
and magic arts known to his craft seeking the " Knowledge that enlightens."   And, at the last, when all was
still, he rose to his full height, stretched out his arms,
and called upon the gods of fire, and air, and wind,
and light, to open up and lay before his gaze the
future things that were in store for Meave and for her
hosts.

Then he made total darkness in his hut, and ate a
curious food, concocted by magicians ; and when he had
eaten, he fell into a sleep, his servant watching over him,
his two palms laid upon his cheeks.   Then in a minute,
or two minutes, he uttered sounds, but like one talking
in his sleep, and the servant bade Meave question him,
for his sleep of inspiration was upon him.   So Meave
said : " In mine host this day are many who do part
from their own people and their friends, from their

country and their lands, from father and from mother.
Now, if these all return not safe and sound, upon me will
be the anger of their friends, and me they will upbraid.
Tell me, then, will these return alive ? "

And the magician said : " These might return ; but
yet I see a little boy who stands upon the way to hinder
them.   Fair he is and young and but a boy ; and yet on
every path I see him, holding back thy hosts, slaughter-
ing and pursuing, as though the strength of the gods
were in his arms.   On every path they fall, in every
battlefield the ground is strewn with dead, and in the
homes of Connaught men and women weep the sons and
husbands who return no more.   Who this youth may be
I know not, but I see that he will bring trouble on thy
hosts."

Then Meave trembled at the saying of the Druid ; but
she asked again, " Among all those who will remain
behind and those who go, there is none dearer to
us than we are to ourselves ; inquire therefore of
thy gods if we ourselves shall come alive out of this
hosting ? "

The wizard answered : " Whoever comes or comes not,
thou thyself shalt come."

Then Meave mounted her chariot again, and turned
her horses' heads towards Cruachan.   But heaviness was
at her heart, and deep dejection lay upon her mind, and
moodily she thought of what the Druid prophesied to
her.

They had not driven far when suddenly the horses
swerved aside and reared and snorted with affright.
Meave started up, and shaking off her reverie, in the dim
twilight of the breaking dawn, close up beside her
chariot-shaft, she saw a woman stand.   Red as a fox-

glove were her cheeks and blue as the spring hyacinth beneath the forest trees her sparkling eyes. Like pearls her teeth shone white between her lips, and all her skin was fair as the white foam that dances on the wave. Around her fell, in waving folds of green, a cloak such as the fairy women wear, which hides them from the eyes of mortal men.

But while she looked in wonder on the maid, astonished at her lovely face and mien, Meave saw her garment change to dusky red. And in the dimness, she perceived the maiden held a sword, point upward, in her hand, a massive sword, such as a mighty man-of-war might wield. And from the point blood dripped, and one by one the drops fell on the Queen, till all her cloak, and garments, and the chariot-floor ran red with streams of blood.

And terror came on Meave, and all in vain she sought to force her horses forward, but still they reared and curvetted, but would not advance. " Girl," cried the Queen at last, "what doest thou here, and who and what art thou ? "

" I am a woman of the fairy race," the maid replied ; " I come to-night to tell thee of thy fortunes, and the chance that shall befall thee and thy hosts upon this raid that thou dost make on Ulster."

" What is thy name, and wherefore thus, without my will, hast thou presumed to come and speak with me?" replied the angry Queen.

" Great cause have I to come ; for from the fairy-rath of thine own people, near to Cruachan, am I here ; and Feidelm the prophetess my name."

" Well, then, O prophetess Feidelm," said Queen Meave, " how seest thou our host ? " but yet she trembled as she spoke. And Feidelm said, "I see thy hosts all red, I see them all becrimsoned."

"Thou seest ill, O prophetess," said Meave; "for in the courts of Emain now the King lies sick and ill; my messengers have been to him, and nought there is that we need fear from Ulster. Therefore, O Feidelm, woman-prophet Feidelm, tell us now but the truth; how seest thou our hosts?"

"I see them all dyed red, I see them all becrimsoned," said the girl again.

"It cannot be," said Meave. "For many months my spies have been in Ulster, and this well I know; that in Ulster they dream not of the coming of a host. Now tell us this time true, O Feidelm, O woman-prophet Feidelm, how seest thou our host?"

But again the maiden answered as before: "I see all red on them, I see them all becrimsoned."

Then Meave grew angry, and fury came upon her, and she called on her charioteer to slay the fairy maid. But the man was afraid to touch her, so strange and formidable did she stand there, holding the dripping sword upright.

Then once again Meave answered her: "Girl, I care not for thy threats, for well I know, that when the men of Ulster come together, frays and quarrels will arise among themselves, either as regards the troop which shall precede the host, or that one which shall follow; or about precedence among the leaders, or about forays for cattle and for food. Therefore, I conclude that they will fall upon each other, and that it will be but a little matter for me to disperse them, and return again with spoils to Cruachan."

Then the maiden's face grew grave, and she spoke as

though she saw a vision, and Meave trembled as she listened to her words. "I see thy host," she said, "crimson and red, fall back before the men of Ulster, Yet the host of Ulster seems not a mighty host, but faint and weak through sickness, and the King of Ulster lies on his bed. Through all my dreams there comes a lad, not old in years, but great in weapon-feats. Young though he is, the marks of many wounds are on his skin, and round his head there shines the ' hero's light.' A face he has the noblest and the best, and in his eyes sparkle the champion's gleams; a stripling, fair and modest in his home, but in the battle fierce and tough and strong, as though he wore a mighty dragon's form. In either of his hands four darts he holds, and with a skill before unknown, he plies them on your host. A formidable sword hangs by his side, and close beside him stands his charioteer, holding his pointed spear. A madness seems to seize him in the fight; by him your hosts are all hewn down, and on the battle-field the slain, foot laid to foot and hand to hand, do thickly lie. Before the hosts of Ulster all unmoved he stands as if to guard them from the fight; all on himself the burden of the uneven contest falls. Strong heroes -cannot stand before his blows, and in the homes of Connaught women weep the slain who come not back. This is the vision that I see, and this the prophecy of Feidelm, Cruachan's woman-seer."

Then all her pride and courage fled from Meave, and fearfully she asked the woman-seer, " What is the name by which this youth is known ? "

And Feidelm said : " To all the world the youth's name will be known, Cuchulain son of Sualtach, of the Feats; but in the North, because he guards their homes as a good watch-dog guards the scattered flocks upon the mountain-side, men call him lovingly, 'The Hound of Ulster.'"

Then to her fairy-dwelling Feidelm returned, and Meave went to her tent again.

CHAPTER III

The Boy-Corps of King Conor

NOW all that she had heard that night so troubled Meave that she thought not well to proceed upon her hosting at that time. She lay upon her bed and pondered long upon the fairy woman's words, and more and more she wondered who this youth might be, the lad of mighty feats whom all men called "The Hound of Ulster." When daylight came, she sent a message to the captains of her host, commanding them to tarry yet a day, till she should learn further about the youth who stood upon her path and seemed a threatening terror to her hosts. Then like a king and queen they robed themselves and sat within their tents, Ailill and she, and sent a herald forth commanding Fergus and the chief of Ulster's exiles to appear before them, to tell them of Cuchulain.

When they were gathered, Fergus, Cormac son of Conor and the rest, Ailill addressed them. "We hear strange tales of one of Ulster's chiefs, a youthful hero whom men call the "Hound." From you, O chiefs of Ulster, we would learn all you can tell about this famous lad. What age hath he ? and wherefore hath he gained this name ? and have his deeds become known to you ? "

"His deeds are known to us, indeed," Fergus replied, "For all the land of Ulster rings with this young hero's renown."

" Shall we find him hard to deal with ? " then said Meave. " Last night I met a fairy-maid, who told me to beware, for among the warriors of the North, this lad would trouble us the most."

" He will trouble you the most, indeed," said Cormac and Fergus with one voice. " You will not find a warrior in your path that is so hard to deal with, not a hero that is fiercer, nor a raven more greedy of prey, nor a lion that is more dangerous than he. You will not find another man to equal him, whether of his age or of a greater age, so strong and terrible and brave is he, nor is his match in Erin either for his beauty or his prowess or in all deeds and feats of skill."

" I care not for all this," said haughty Meave ; " not these the things I fear ; for, after all, whatever you may say, Cuchulain, like another, is but one ; he can be wounded like a common man, he will die like any other, he can be captured like any warrior. Besides, his age is but that of a grown-up girl ; his deeds of manhood come not yet."

" Not so indeed," said Fergus and they all. " It would be strange if he to-day were not the equal of any grown-up man or many men ; for even when he was in his fifth year, he surpassed all the chieftain's sons of Emain Macha at their play ; when he was but seven he took arms, and slew his man ; when he was a stripling he went to perfect himself in feats of championship with Scáth, the woman-warrior of Alba ; and now to-day when he is nearly seventeen years old, his strength must be equal to the strength of many men."

" Tell us," said Meave, " who is this warrior-lad ; tell us also of his boyish feats and how the name of ' Ulster's Hound ' came to be his."

"I will tell you," said Fergus; "for Cuchulain is my own foster-son and Conor's; though they say, and I myself believe it, that he is of the offspring of the gods, and that Lugh of the Long Arms, God of Light, is guardian to the boy. But Sualtach is his father, a warrior of Ulster, and the child was reared by the sea-side northward on Murthemne's plain, which is his own possession. At my knees he was brought up, and Amergin the poet was his tutor; the sister of King Conor nourished him with Conall the Victorious in her home. For at his birth Morann the judge prophesied of his future renoun. 'His praise,' he said, 'will be in all men's mouths, his deeds will be recounted by kings and great men, warriors and charioteers, poets and sages. All men will love him; he will give combat for Ulster against her enemies; he will decide your quarrels; he will avenge your wrongs. Welcome the little stranger who is here.'"

And Meave and Ailill said, "That is a brave account to give of a young child; no wonder is it that Ulster prides herself in him; but tell us now, Fergus, for eager are we all to hear, the feats of Cuchulain as a little boy."

"I will tell you that," said Fergus. "When he was yet a tiny boy, not much past four years old, some one in passing by Murthemne told him a long tale of the boy-corps of King Conor in Emain Macha; that the King had established it for all the sons of nobles and of chiefs, to train them up in strength and bravery. He told him that the King had set apart a playing-ground for the boys, close to his own fort, and there every day they practised games of skill, and feats of arms, and wrestled and threw each other. He told him, too, that the King took so much interest in the boy-corps, that scarce a day passed by that he did not spend some time in watching the pastimes of the lads, for he looked to them to be his future men-of-war and leaders of his hosts. He told the little boy that when they had proved themselves fit by skill and aptness for a higher grade, the King bestowed on them a set of war-gear suited to their age, small spears and javelins, a slender sword, and all equipment like a champion. Now when the boy heard this, a great longing arose within his little mind to see the boy-corps and join in their sports and practising for war. 'I would wrestle, too,' he said, 'and I am sure that I could throw my fellow.' But I and his guardians,'' said Fergus, '' objected that he was yet too young, and that when he was ten years old it would be soon enough to test his strength against the older boys. For to send a boy of four years old or five to take his part among lads of ten or twelve we thought not well, for we feared that harm would come to him, knowing that he must ever, since his babyhood, be in the midst of all that was going on. Therefore, we said, 'Wait, my child, until some grown warrior can go with thee, to protect thee from the rough practice of the elder boys and bid them have a care for thee, or else till Conor the King, thy fosterer, himself calls thee hither under his proper charge.' But the lad said to his mother, that it was too long to wait, and that even on this instant he would set off; 'And all you have to do, mother, is to set me on my way, for I know not which way Emain lies.' 'A long and weary way for a young boy it is to Emain,' said his mother, 'for the range of the Slieve Fuad Mountains must be crossed.' 'Point me but out the general direction,' he replied. 'Over there, to the

Cuchulain sets out for Emain Macha

north-west, lies the palace of the king.' ' Let me but get my things, and I am off,' he said.

"These were the things that the child took in his hand. His hurley of brass and his ball of silver in one hand, his throwing javelin and his toy spear in the other. Away he went then, and as he went, this would he do to make the way seem short. He would place his ball on the ground and strike it with his hurley, driving it before him ever so far; then he flung the hurley after it, driving that as far again; then, always running on, he threw his javelin, and last of all his spear. Then he would make a playful rush after them, pick up the hurley, ball, and javelin as he ran, while, before ever the spear's tip touched the earth, he had caught it by the other end. Thus on he ran, scarce feeling tired, so engrossed was he in the game.

" At last Cuchulain reached Emain, and sought out the palace of the King and the playing-field where the boys were practising, three times fifty in number, under the charge of Follaman, one of Conor's younger sons; the King himself being present, watching the game.

" The youths had been practising martial exercises, but when Cuchulain came up they were hurling on the green. Without waiting for anyone, the little fellow dived in amongst them and took a hand in the game. He got the ball between his legs and held it there; not suffering it to travel higher up than his knees or lower than his ankle-joints, so making it impossible for any of them to get a stroke at it, or in any way to touch it. In this way he got it gradually nearer and nearer the end of the field; then with one effort he lifted it up and sent it home over the goal. In utter amazement the whole corps looked on. But Follaman their captain cried—'Good now, boys, all together meet this youngster who has come in we know not whence, and kill him on the spot as he deserves. The boy insults us that he comes amongst us without placing himself under the protection of some chief's son in order that his life should be preserved; for it is not allowed to the son of any private person or common warrior to intrude upon your game, without first having asked permission and taken a pledge of the chiefs' sons that his life shall be respected; we admit not common men to the boy-corps save under the protection of some youth of higher rank.' For they did not know Cuchulain, neither did he know the rules of the boy-corps. 'Have at him, all of you,' cried Follaman, 'and give him what he deserves; no doubt he is the son of some private man, who has no right to intrude into your play without safe conduct. Defend your honour and the honour of the corps.' Then the whole of the lads gathered round Cuchulain and began to threaten him, and together with one throw they hurled at him their toy spears, on every side at once. But Cuchulain stood firm, and one and all he parried them and caught them on his little shield. Then all together they threw at him their hurley-sticks, three fifties at a time; but all of them he parried, catching a bundle of them on his back. Then they tried their balls, throwing them all together, but he fended them off with arms and fists and the palms of his hands, catching them into his bosom as they fell. After a long while of this his 'hero-fury' seized Cuchulain. His hair rose upright on his head, and in his wrath and fierceness it seemed as though a light poured forth from each single hair, crowning him with a crown of fire. A strong contortion shook him, and he grew larger and taller as he stood before the lads, so that they shrank terrified before him. He made for them like a young lion springing on his prey, and before they could reach the door of the fort fleeing from him for safety, he had stretched fifty of them on the ground.

"Now it happened that the King and I," said Fergus, "were playing chess together at a table in the open air, on the borders of the playing field, amusing ourselves while the boys' games were going on. Five of the boys, not seeing in their haste where they were running, rushed past the place where Conor and I were sitting, and nearly overturned the table with the chess. Cuchulain was in full pursuit, and he seemed about to leap the table to make after them, when the King caught him by the arm.

"'Hold, my little fellow,' said the King, restraining him, 'I see this is no gentle game thou playest with the boy-corps.'

"'What could I do?' replied the lad. 'I came to-day, O King, from a far land to join myself with them, and they have not been good to me; I have not had the reception of a welcome guest.'

"'What is your name, little one?' said the King. 'Setanta, son of Sualtach, is my name; your own foster-son am I, and the foster-son of Fergus,' said the boy. 'It was not fitting that I should have had this rough reception.' 'But knewest thou not the rules of the boy-corps, that a new-comer must go under their protection, so that they will respect his life?' said the King. 'That I knew not,' said the boy, 'otherwise I should have conformed to their rules; do thou thyself undertake my protection, I pray thee, O King.' The King liked the fine spirit of the lad, and his open face and bravery in his self-defence, and he said, ' I will do that, my boy.' Then he called the boy-corps together, and said, ' I, myself, have taken upon me the protection of this little boy; promise me now that he shall play amongst you safely.' ' We promise it,' they said. Then all made off to play again; but Setanta does just what he will with them, wrestling and throwing them, and soon fifty of them are stretched upon the ground. Their fathers think that they are dead, and raise a cry against Setanta. But no such thing; merely had he with his charges, pulls, and pushes so frightened them, that they fell down at last through terror on the grass.

" ' What on earth is the lad at with them now ? ' asks Conor.

" ' You bound them over to protect me,' said the boy, ' but you never bound me over to protect them; and I avow that until they place themselves under my protection, as I am placed under theirs, I will not lighten my hand from them.' ' I place them under thy protection then,' said Conor. ' And I grant it,' said the lad.

" And now," said Fergus to Queen Meave and Ailill, " I submit that a youngster who, at the age of four or five years did all this, need not excite your wonder, because now being turned seventeen years, he prove a formidable foe to Connaught in time of war."

" I think not indeed," said Ailill; and sulkily Meave said, " Perhaps, indeed, he may,"

CHAPTER IV

How Cuchulain got his Name

THAT evening at supper, Meave sat silent, as though she were revolving matters in her mind. When supper was ended and she and her husband and Fergus, with one or two others of her chief captains, sat in the tent-door around the fire, looking out on the hosts who rested at close of day by the forest fires, singing and telling tales, as was their wont after the evening meal, Meave said to Fergus, " Just now you spoke of that little boy as Setanta, but I have heard him called Cuchulain, or Culain's Hound ; how did he get that name ? "

And Cormac, Conor's son, answered eagerly, " I will tell you that story myself, for I was present, and I know the way of it."

" Well, tell us now," said Meave and Ailill both at once.

And Cormac said—" In Ulster, near Cuchulain's country, was a mighty artificer and smith, whose name was Culain. Now the custom is, that every man of means and every owner of land in Ulster, should, once in a year or so, invite the King and his chiefs to spend a few days, it may be a week or a fortnight, at his house, that he may give them entertainment. But Culain owned no lands, nor was he rich, for only the fruit of his hammer, of his anvil and his tongs, had he. Nevertheless he desired to entertain the King at a

C

33

banquet, and he went to Emain to invite his chief. But he said, ' I have no lands or store of wealth ; I pray thee, therefore, to bring with thee but a few of thy prime warriors, because my house cannot contain a great company of guests.' So the King said he would go, bringing but a small retinue with him.

" Culain returned home to prepare his banquet, and when the day was come, towards evening the King set forth to reach the fort of Culain. He assumed his light, convenient travelling garb, and before starting he went down to the green to bid the boy-corps farewell.

" There he saw a sight so curious that he could not tear himself away. At one end of the green stood a group of a hundred and fifty youths, guarding one goal, all striving to prevent the ball of a single little boy, who was playing against the whole of them, from getting in ; but for all that they could do, he won the game, and drove his ball home to the goal.

" Then they changed sides, and the little lad defended his one goal against the hundred and fifty balls of the other youths, all sent at once across the ground. But though the youths played well, following up their balls, not one of them went into the hole, for the little boy caught them one after another just outside, driving them hither and thither, so that they could not make the goal. But when his turn came round to make the counter-stroke, he was as successful as before ; nay, he would get the entire set of a hundred and fifty balls into their hole, for all that they could do.

" Then they played a game of getting each other's cloaks off without tearing them, and he would have their mantles off, one after the other, before they could, on their part, even unfasten the brooch that held his cloak.

When they wrestled with each other, it was the same thing: he would have them on the ground before all of them together could upset him, or make him budge a foot.

"As the King stood and watched all this, he said: ' 'Tis well for the country into which this boy has come! A clever child indeed is he; were but his acts as a grown man to come up to the promise of his youth, he might be of some solid use to us; but this is not to be counted upon.'"

"Then," Fergus said, breaking in upon the tale, "I was vexed because the King seemed to doubt the child, whether his after deeds would equal the promise of his youth; and I spoke up and said, 'That, O King, I think not wisely said; have no fear for this boy, for as his childish deeds outstrip the acts of childhood, so will his manly feats outshine the deeds of heroes and great men.' Then the King said to me, 'Have the child called, that we may take him with us to the banquet.'

"So when Setanta came, the King invited him; but the boy said, 'Excuse me now awhile; I cannot go just now.' 'How so?' said the King, surprised. 'Because the boy-corps have not yet had enough of play.' 'I cannot wait until they have,' replied the King: 'the night is growing late.' 'Wait not at all,' replied the child; 'I will even finish this one game, and will run after you.' 'But, young one, knowest thou the way?' asked the King. 'I will follow the trail made by your company, the wheels of their chariots and hoofs of the horses on the road,' he replied."

"Thereupon,"—continued Cormac,—"Conor starts; and in time for the banquet he reaches Culain's house, where, with due honour, he is received. Fresh rushes had been strewn upon the floor, the tables all decked out, the fires burning in the middle of the room. A great vat full of ale stood in the hall, a lofty candlestick gave light, and round the fires stood servants cooking savoury viands, holding them on forks or spits of wood. Each man of the King's guests entered in order of his rank, and sat at the feast in his own allotted place, hanging his weapons up above his head. The King occupied the central seat, his poets, counsellors, and chiefs sitting on either hand according to their state and dignity. As they were sitting down, the smith Culain came to Conor and asked him, ' Good now, O King, before we sit at meat I would even know whether anyone at all will follow thee this night to my dwelling, or is thy whole company gathered now within ? ' ' All are now here,' said the King, quite forgetting the wee boy; ' but wherefore askest thou ? '

" ' It is only that I have an excellent watch-dog, fierce and strong; and when his chain is taken off, and he is set free to guard the house, no one dare come anywhere within the same district with him; he is furious with all but me, and he has the strength and savage force of a hundred ordinary watch-dogs. This dog was brought to me from Spain, and no dog in the country can equal him.' ' Let him be set loose, for all are here,' said Conor; ' well will he guard this place for us.'

" So Culain loosed the dog, and with one spring it bounded forth out of the court of the house and over the wall of the rath, making a circuit of the entire district; and when it came back panting, with its tongue hanging from its jaws, it took up its usual position in front of the house, and there crouched with its head upon its paws, watching the high road to Emain. Surely an extraordinarily cruel and fierce and savage dog was he.

" When the boy-corps broke up that night, each of the lads returning to the house of his parent or his fosterer or guardian, Setanta, trusting to the trail of the company that went with Conor, struck out for Culain's house. With his club and ball he ran forward, and the distance seemed short on account of his interest in the game. As soon as he arrived on the green of Culain's fort, the mastiff noticed him, and set up such a howling as echoed loud through all the country-side. Inside the house the King and his followers heard, but were struck dumb with fear, nor dared to move, thinking surely to find the little lad dead at the door of the fort. As for the hound himself, he thought with but one gulp to swallow Setanta whole. Now the little lad was without any means of defence beyond his ball and hurley-stick. He never left his play till he came near. Then, as the hound charged open-jawed, with all his strength he threw the ball right into the creature's mouth ; and as for a moment the hound stopped short, choking as the ball passed down its throat, the lad seized hold of the mastiff's open jaws, grasping its throat with one hand and the back of its head with the other, and so violently did he strike its head against the pillars of the door, that it was no long time until the creature lay dead upon the ground.

" When Culain and the warriors within had heard the mastiff howl, they asked each other, as soon as they got back their voices, ' What makes the watch-dog cry ? ' ' Alas ! ' the King said, ' 'tis no good luck that brought us on our present trip.' ' Why so ? ' inquired all. ' I mean that the little boy, my foster-son and Fergus's, Setanta, son of Sualtach, it is who promised to come after me ; now, even now, he is doubtless fallen by the hound of Culain.' Then, when they heard that it was Conor's foster-son who was without, on the instant to one man they rose; and though the doors of the fort were thrown wide they could not wait for that, but out they stormed over the walls and ramparts of the fort to find the boy."

"Quick they were," said Fergus, interrupting, "yet did I outstrip them, and at the rampart's outer door I found the child, and the great hound dead beside him. Without a pause I picked up the boy and hoisted him on my shoulder, and thus, with all the heroes following, we came to Conor, and I placed him between the monarch's knees."

"Yes, so it was," said Cormac, taking up the story again where he had left it; "but let me tell of Culain. The smith went out to find his dog, and when he saw him lying there, knocked almost to pieces and quite dead, his heart was vexed within him. He went back to the house, and said, ' 'Twas no good luck that urged me to make this feast for thee, O King; would I had not prepared a banquet. My life is a life lost, and my substance is but substance wasted without my dog. He was a defence and protection to our property and our cattle, to every beast we had and to our house. Little boy,' said he, ' you are welcome for your people's sake, you are not welcome for your own; that was a good member of my family thou didst take from me, a safeguard of raiment, of flocks and herds.' ' Be not vexed thereat,' replied the child, ' for I myself will fix on my own punishment. This shall it be. If in all Ireland a whelp of that dog's breed is to be found, 'tis I myself will rear him up for thee till he be fit to take the watch-dog's place. In the meantime, O Culain, I myself will be your hound for

defence of your cattle and for your own defence, until the
dog be grown and capable of action ; I will defend the
territory, and no cattle or beast or store of thine shall
be taken from thee, without my knowing it.'

" ' Well hast thou made the award,' said they all,
' and henceforward shall your name be changed ; you
shall no longer be called Setanta ; Cu-Chulain, or the
" Hound of Culain," shall your name be.

" ' I like my own name best,' the child objected. ' Ah,
say not so,' replied the magician, ' for one day will the
name of Cuchulain ring in all men's mouths ; among the
brave ones of the whole wide world Cuchulain's name
shall find a place. Renowned and famous shall he be,
beloved and feared by all.' ' If that is so, then am I
well content,' replied the boy.

" So from that day forth the name Cuchulain clung
to him, until the time came when he was no longer
remembered as the Hound of Culain's Fort, but as the
guardian and watch-dog of defence to the Province
against her foes ; and then men loved best to call him
' The Hound of Ulster.'

" Now," continued Cormac, " it would be reasonable
to expect that the little boy, who, at the age of six or
seven years slew a dog whom a whole company would
not dare to touch when he was at large, would, at the age
of a grown youth, be formidable to Ulster's foes."

And Meave was forced to admit that it was likely that
he would.

CHAPTER V

How Cuchulain took Arms

WHEN Meave had thought awhile, she said, "Are there yet other stories of this wondrous boy?" "Indeed," cried Fiacra, one of the companions of Cormac, who came with him when he went from Ulster into exile, "the story of his taking arms is not told yet, and I think it more than all the other stories you have heard." "How so?" said Meave; "tell it to us now."

Then Fiacra said, "The very year after Cuchulain got his name, he was playing outside the place where Caffa the magician sat with eight of his pupils teaching them his lore. It chanced that he was telling them, as the magicians and Druids are wont to believe, that certain days were lucky for special acts and other days unlucky. 'And for what,' asked one of the boys, 'would this day at which we now are be counted lucky?'"

"This is the day," said Caffa, "on which any youth who should assume arms, as became a champion of war, should attain eternal fame; beside him, no warrior's name in Ireland should ever more be named, or spoken in the same breath with it, for his glory would transcend them all. For such a youth, however, no happy thing were this, for he should die at an early age, no long-lived warrior he; his life shall be but fleeting, quickly o'er."

40

Outside the house Cuchulain overheard the conversation of the teacher with his boys. Instantly and without a moment's pause he laid aside his hurley and his ball, and put off his playing-suit. Then, donning his ordinary apparel, he entered the sleeping-house of the King. " All good be thine, O King," said he. " Boy, what hast thou now come to ask of me ? " replied the King. " I desire," said he, " to take arms as a warrior and champion to-day." " Who told thee to ask for this ? " said the King, surprised. " My master Caffa, the magician," answered he. " If that is so, thou shalt not be denied," replied the King, and he called on those who were about him to give the lad two spears and sword and shield : for in Emain the King had always ready seventeen complete equipments of weapons and armature ; for he himself bestowed weapons on a youth of the boy-corps when he was ready to bear arms, to bring him luck in using them. Cuchulain began to try those weapons, brandishing and bending them to try their strength and fitness to his hand ; but one after another they all gave way, and were broken into pieces and little fragments. " These weapons are not good," said he ; " they are but the equipment of a common warrior, they suffice me not." Then when he had tried them all, and put them from him, the King said : " Here, my lad, are my own two spears, my own sword and shield." Then Cuchulain took these weapons, and in every way, by bending them from point to hilt, by brandishing them, by thrusting with them, he proved their strength and mettle. " These arms are good," said he, " they break not in my hand. Fair fall the land and country whose King can wield armour and weapons such as these ! "

Just at the moment Caffa came into the tent. Won-

dering, he asked : " Is the little boy so soon assuming
arms ? "   " Ay, so it is," said the King.   " Unhappy
is the mother whose son assumes arms to-day," said
the magician.   " How now ? " cried the King; " was
it not yourself who prompted him ? "   " Not so, indeed," said Caffa.   " Mad boy, what made you then
deceive me, telling me that Caffa it was who prompted
you to ask for arms ? "   " O King of Heroes, be not
wrath," replied the lad.   " No thought, indeed, had I
to deceive.   When Caffa was instructing his pupils in the
house to-day, I overheard, as I was playing with my ball
outside, one of the lads asking him what special virtue
lay in this day, and for what it was a lucky day.   And
he told them that for him who should assume arms this
day, his luck should be so great that his fame would
outstrip the fame of all Ireland's heroes, and he would
be the first of Ireland's men.   And for this great re-
ward no compensating disadvantage would accrue to
him, save that his life should be but fleeting."

" True is that, indeed," said Caffa, " noble and famous
thou shalt be, but short and brief thy life."   " Little
care I for that," replied the lad, " nor though my life
endured but for one day and night, so only that the
story of myself and of my deeds shall last."

" Then get thee into a chariot, as a warrior should,
and let us test thy title to a future fame."

So a chariot of two horses was brought to Cuchulain,
and every way he tried its strength, driving it furiously
round and round the green, goading the horses and turning suddenly.   But for this usage the chariot was not fit,
and it broke beneath him.   Twelve chariots were brought
to him, and he tested them all in this manner, but all of
them he reduced to fragments.   " These chariots of

Cuchulain desires Arms of the King

42

thine, O Conor, are no good at all, they serve me not, nor are they worthy of me, thy own foster-son."

Then the King cried : " Fetch me here Ivar, my own charioteer, and let him harness my steeds into the kingly chariot, and bring it here to serve Cuchulain." Then the kingly chariot of war was brought and Cuchulain mounted, testing it every way ; and well it served him at every test. " The chariot is good, and the steeds are good, they are worthy of me," said the boy ; " it is my worthy match."

" Well, boy, it is time that thou wert satisfied at last ; now I will take the horses home and put them out to graze," said Ivar.

" Not yet awhile," said Cuchulain. " Drive but the horses round the kingly fort." Ivar did so, and then he said again : " Be satisfied now, my lad ; I go to turn the horses out to grass." For it was but seldom that King Conor went forth in his war-chariot, because the men of Ulster willed not that the King should expose his person in battle ; so Ivar was grown idle, and fat through his idleness, and he liked not at all the un- wonted exertion that the wee boy asked of him.

" Not yet awhile," said Cuchulain again ; " too early is it to turn in ; drive now towards the playing-fields that the boy-corps may salute me on this the first day of my taking arms." They did so, and the boy-corps gathered round. " These are a warrior's arms that thou hast taken ! " cried they all, surprised to see him thus equipped in the King's own warrior-gear, and driving in the chariot of the King. " Just so, indeed," replied the boy. Then they wished him well in his warrior- career. " May success in winning of spoils, and in blood- drawing, be thine," they cried. " But all too soon it is thou leavest us and our boyish sports for deeds of war." " In no way do I wish to part with the beloved boy-corps," replied the lad; " but it was a sign of luck and good fortune that I should take arms to-day; therefore I thought not well to miss my luck."

Then Ivar urged the child again, for he was growing tired of the thing, to let him take the horses out to graze. " 'Tis early yet, O Ivar," said the boy; " whither then goes this great High-road I see?" " That is the High-road to the borders of the Province, and to the Ford of Watching or the Look-out Ford," replied the charioteer. " Why is it called the Look-out Ford?" asked then the boy. " Because there, on the extreme limits of the Province, a watcher who is a prime warrior of Ulster always stands, prepared to challenge any stranger, before he pass the ford, of his business in the Province: if he who comes be a bard or peaceful man, to grant him protection and entertainment; but if he be a foe, to challenge him to combat at the ford. And seldom," said the charioteer, " does a day pass, but at the ford some enemy is slain. As to the bards who pass in peace, no doubt it is the kindness of that warrior they will praise when once they come to Emain, and stand before the King." " Who guards the ford this day, if thou dost know?" inquired Cuchulain. " Conall the Victorious, Ulster's foremost man of war, it is who holds the ford this day." " Away then," cried the lad, " goad on thy steeds, for we will seek the ford and Conall."

" The horses are already tired, we have done enough for this one day," quoth Ivar. " The day is early yet, and our day's labours hardly yet begun," replied the youth; " away with you along this road."

They come at last to the ford's brink, and there beside
the Ford of Watching stood young Conall, at that time
Ulster's foremost man of war.

When he saw the lad driving fully equipped for war
in the chariot of the King, he felt surprise. "Are you
taking arms to-day, small boy?" he said. "He is
indeed," said Ivar. "May triumph and victory and
drawing of first blood come with them," answered
Conall, for he loved the little lad, and many a time he
had said to his fellows: "The day will come when this
young boy will dispute the championship of Ireland
with me." "Nevertheless," said he to Cuchulain, "it
seems to me that oversoon thou hast assumed these arms,
seeing that thou art not yet fit for exploits or for war."
The boy heeded not this, but eagerly asked, "What is it
thou doest at the Ford of Watching, Conall?" "On
behalf of the Province I keep watch and ward, lest
enemies creep in."

"Give up thy place to me, for this one day let me
take duty," said Cuchulain. "Say not so," replied the
champion, "for as yet thou art not fit to cope with a
right fighting-man."

"Then on my own account must I go down into the
shallows of yon lake, to see whether there I may draw
blood on either friend or foe." "I will go with thee,
then, to protect thee, to the end that on the border-
marshes thou run not into danger." "Nay, come not
with me, let me go alone to-day," urged the lad. "That
I will not," said Conall, "for, were I to allow thee all
alone to frequent these dangerous fighting grounds, on
me would Ulster avenge it, if harm should come to thee."

Then Conall had his chariot made ready and his horses
harnessed; soon he overtook Cuchulain, who, to cut

short the matter, had gone on before. He came up abreast with him, and Cuchulain, seeing this, felt sure that, Conall being there, no chance for deed of prowess would come his way; for, if some deed of mortal daring were to be done, Conall himself would undertake the same. Therefore he took up from the road a smooth round stone that filled his fist, and with it he made a very careful shot at Conall's chariot-yoke. It broke in two, and the chariot came down, Conall being thrown forward over his horses' heads.

"What's this, ill-mannered boy?" said he.

"I did it in order to see whether my marksmanship were good, and whether there were the makings of a man-at-arms in me." "Poison take both thy shot and thyself as well; and though thy head should now fall a prize to some enemy of thine, yet never a foot farther will I budge to keep thee."

"The very thing I asked of thee," replied the boy, "and I do so in this strange manner, because I know it is a custom among the men of Ulster to turn back when any violence is done to them. Thus have I made the matter sure." On that, Conall turned back to his post beside the Look-out Ford, and the little boy went forward southward to the shallows of the marshy loch, and he rested there till evening-tide.

CHAPTER VI

Of Cuchulain's First Feats of Championship

THEN Ivar said, " If one might venture to make a suggestion to such a little one, I should rejoice if we might now turn back and find our way home to Emain again. For at this moment in the hall supper is being carved and the feast has just begun ; and though for you your appointed place is kept at Conor's side until you come, I, on the contrary, if I come late must fit in where I may among the grooms and jesters of the house. For this reason I judge it now high time that I were back to scramble for my place."

" Harness the horses and prepare the chariot," Cuchulain said, and thinking that they now were going home, the charioteer most gladly hastened to obey. " What mountain is that over there ? " inquired the boy. " Slieve Mourn," replied the driver. " Let us go thither," said the lad. They reach the mountain's foot, and, " What is that cairn I see upon the top ? " said he again. " The White Cairn is its name," quoth Ivar sulkily. " I would like to visit the White Cairn," said the boy. " The hill is high, and it is getting late," replied the charioteer. " Thou art a lazy loon," Cuchulain says, " and the more so that this is my first day's adventure-quest, and thy first day's trip abroad with me." " And if it is," cried Ivar, " and if ever we get home again, for ever and for ever may it be my last ! "

They gained the topmost peak, and far away descried a stretch of level country. "Come now, driver," said the lad, "describe to me from here the whole of Ulster's wide domain; its forts and dwellings, fords and meadow-lands, its hills and open spaces. Name every place in order, that thus I may the better know my way about.

"What is yon well-defined plain with hollow glens and running streams before us to the south?" "Moy Bray," replied the charioteer. "The names, again, of all the forts and palaces scattered over it?" Then Ivar pointed out the kingly dwelling-places of Tara and Taillte, and the summer palace of Cletty on the river Boyne; the Fairy Mound of Angus Og, the god of Youth and Beauty, and the burial-tomb of the Great God or Dagda Mór. And at the last he showed beneath the hill where lay the fort of the three fierce and warlike sons of Nechtan the Mighty.

"Are those the sons of Nechtan of whom I heard it said that the Ulstermen who are yet alive are not so many as have fallen by their hands?" "The same," said Ivar. "Away then, with us straight to Nechtan's fort," Cuchulain cried. "Woe waits on him who goes to Nechtan's fort," replied the charioteer; "whoever goes or goes not, I for one will never go." "Alive or dead thou goest there, however," said the boy. "Alive I go then, but sure it is that dead I shall be left there," replied the charioteer.

They make their way then down the hill and reach the green before the fort at the meeting of the bog-land and the stream; and in the centre of the green they saw an upright pillar-stone, encircled by an iron collar on its top. Words were engraven on the collar forbidding any man-at-arms or warrior to depart off the green, once

he had entered it, without challenging to single combat
some one of those living within the fort. Cuchulain read
the writing, and he took the collar off the pillar-stone, and
with all his strength he hurled it down the stream, for
it was thus the challenge should be made.

" In my poor opinion," said the charioteer, " the collar
was much safer where it was, and well I know that this
time, at all events, thou wilt find the object of thy careful
search, a quick and violent death."   " Good, good, O
driver, talk not over much, but spread for me the chariot
coverings on the ground, that I may sleep a while."

Now the charioteer was frightened, for he knew the
fierceness and ill-fame of the sons of Nechtan, and he
grumbled that Cuchulain should be so rash and foolhardy in a land of foemen as to sleep before their very
door ; but for all that he dared not disobey, and he took
the cushions out of the chariot and spread them on the
ground, and covered Cuchulain with the skins ; and in
a moment the little fellow was asleep, his head resting
peacefully on his hand.   Just then Foll, son of Nechtan,
issued from the fort. Ivar would well have liked to
waken up Cuchulain, but he did not dare, for the child
had said before he fell asleep : " Waken me up if many
come, but waken me not for a few;" and Foll mac Nechtan
came alone. At sight of the chariot standing on his
lands, the warrior thundered forth, " Driver, be off at
once with those horses ; let them not graze upon our
ground ; unyoke them not." " I have not unyoked
them," said the charioteer. " I hold the reins yet in my
hands, ready for the road." " Whose steeds and chariot
are they ? " enquired the man. " The steeds of Conor,
King of Ulster," said Ivar. " Just as I thought," said
Foll; " and who has brought them to these borders ? "

D

"A young bit of a little boy," said Ivar, hoping to hinder Foll from fighting him. "A high-headed wee fellow, who, for luck, has taken arms to-day, and come into the marshes to show off his form and skill as though he were a grown champion." "Ill-luck to him, whoever he is," said Foll; "were he a man capable of fight, I would send him back to the King dead instead of alive." "Capable of fight he is not, indeed, nor a man at all," said Ivar, "but only a small child of seven years, playing at being a man."

Cuchulain in his sleep heard the affront that the charioteer put upon him, and from head to foot he blushed a rosy red. His face he lifted from the ground and said: "I am not a child at all, but ripe and fit for action, as you will see; this 'small child' here has come to seek for battle with a man." "I rather hold that fit for action thou art not," replied Foll, surprised to find the little fellow rising from his sleep and speaking with such boldness. "That we shall know presently," replied the boy; "come down only to the ford, where it is customary in Ireland that combats should take place. But first go home and fetch your arms, for in cowardly guise come you hither, and never will I fight with men unarmed, or messengers, or drivers in their cloaks, but only with full-weaponed men-of-war."

"That suits me well," said Foll, and he rushed head-long for his arms. "It will suit you even better when we come to the ford," said Cuchulain. Then Ivar warned Cuchulain that this Foll was no ordinary foe; "he bears a charmed life," said he, "and only he who slays him with one stroke has any chance of killing him at all. No sword-edge can bite or wound him, he can only be slain by the first thrust of a spear, or blow of a weapon from a distance." "Then I will play a special feat on him," returned the boy; "surely it is to humble me you warn me thus." With that he took in his hand his hard-tempered iron ball, and with a strong and exact throw just as Foll was coming forth, full-armoured from the fort, he launched the ball, which pierced the warrior's forehead, so that he fell headlong on the ground, uttering his last cry of pain, and with that he died.

Within the fort his brothers heard that cry, and the second brother rushes out. "No doubt you think this is a great feat you have done, and one to boast of," he cried. "I think not the slaying of any single man a cause to boast at all," replied the boy; "but hasten now and fetch your weapons, for in the guise of an unweaponed messenger or chariot-boy come you hither." "Beware of this man," said Ivar; "Tuacall, or 'Cunning' is his name, for so swift and dexterous is he, that no man has ever been able to pierce him with any weapon at all."

"It is not fitting that you speak like this to me," said Cuchulain. "I will take the great spear of Conor, and with it I will pierce his shield and heart, before ever he comes near me."

And so he did, for hardly was the Cunning One come forth out of the fort, than Cuchulain threw the heavy spear; it entered his heart and went out behind him. As he fell dead, Cuchulain leaped on him, and cut off his head.

Then the third son of Nechtan came out, and scoffed at the lad. "Those were but simpletons and fools with whom thou hast fought hitherto," he said; "I challenge thee to come down to the ford, and out upon the middle of the stream, and we will see thy bravery there."

Cuchulain asks him what he means by this, and Ivar breaks in : " Do you not know that this is Fandall, son of Nechtan, and Fainle or Fandall, a ' Swallow,' is his name, because he travels over the water with the swiftness of a swallow, nor can the swimmers of the whole world attempt to cope with him. Beware of him and go not to the ford."

" Not fitting are such words to be spoken to me," replied the lad, " for do you not remember the river we have in Emain, called the Callan ? When the boy-corps break off their sports and plunge into the stream to swim, do you not know that I can take one of them on either shoulder or even on my palms, and carry them across the water without wetting so much as their ankles ? For another man, your words are good ; they are not good for me."

Then came Fainle forth, and he and the lad entered the stream together, and swam out and wrestled in deep water. But suddenly, by a swift turn, the youngster clasped his arms about him, laid him even with the top of the water, and with one stroke of Conor's sword cut off his head, carrying it shoreward in his hand, while the body floated down the current. Behind him he heard the cry of their mother, the wife of Nechtan, when she saw her three sons slain. Then Cuchulain sent her out of the fort, and he and his charioteer went up and harried it, and set it all in flames ; for an evil and a pirate fort had that fort been to Ulster, bringing many of their warriors to death, and spoiling all their lands. Then Cuchulain and Ivar turned to retrace their steps, carrying in their hands the heads of Nechtan's sons. They put their spoils and the three heads into the chariot, sticking the dripping heads upon the chariot-pole that

passed out behind, and set out in triumph towards Emain
and the palace of the King.

"You promised us a good run to-day," said Cuchulain to the charioteer, "and we need it now after the
contest we have made; away with us across Moy Bray,
and round the mountain of Slieve Fuad." Then Ivar
spurred the horses forward with his goad, and so fast did
they race onward that they outstripped the wind in
speed, and left the flying birds behind them. To while
away the time, Cuchulain sent stones speeding before
him from his sling; before the stone could reach the
ground, the chariot had caught it up and it fell again
into the chariot floor.

At the foot of Slieve Fuad a herd of antlered deer were
feeding beside a wood. Never before had Cuchulain
seen a herd of deer; he marvelled at their branching
antlers, and at the speed and lightness with which they
moved from place to place. "What is that great flock
of active cattle yonder?" enquired the boy. "Those
are not cattle, but a herd of wild deer that wander in the
dark recesses of the hills," replied the charioteer. "Which
would the men of Ulster think the greatest feat, to capture
one dead or to bring one home alive?" "Assuredly to
capture one alive," said Ivar. "Dead everyone could
bring one down, but seldom indeed can one be captured
alive." "Goad on the horses," said the lad; and this the
driver did, but the fat horses of the King, unused to such
a drive and rate of motion as they had had that day,
turned restive and plunged into the bog, where they
stuck fast. Eagerly Cuchulain sprang down, and leaving
the charioteer to struggle with the horses, he set off
after the flying deer, and by sheer running came up to
them, caught two of the largest stags by the horns, and

with thongs and ropes bound them behind the chariot between the poles.

Again, on their way to Emain, a flock of swans passed overhead, flying before them. " What birds are those ? " enquired the boy. " Are they tame birds or wild ? " " Those are wild swans," said Ivar, " that fly inland from the rocks and islands of the sea to feed." " Would the Ulstermen think better of me if I brought them in dead or if I captured them alive ? " again enquired the boy. " Assuredly to bring them down alive."

Then Cuchulain took his sling and with a well-aimed shot he brought down one or two of the swans. Again and again he aimed until several of the birds were lying on the path before them. " Ivar, go you and fetch the birds alive," said the boy.

"It is not easy for me to do that," he said. " The horses are become wild and I cannot leave them or leap out in front of them. If then I try to get out at the side, I shall be cut to pieces with the sharp rims of the chariot-wheels ; if I get out behind, the stags will gore me with their horns." " That is not a warrior's speech, but the speech of a coward," said the lad. " But come now, step out fearlessly upon the antler of the deer, for I will bend my eye on him, so that he will not stir or harm you, nor will the horses move when I have overlooked them." This then was done. Cuchulain held the reins, while Ivar got out and collected the fallen birds. With long cords the birds were fastened to the chariot, and thus they went on to Emain, with the wild stags running behind the chariot, and the flock of birds flying over it, and on the poles the bleeding heads of the three sons of Nechtan the Mighty.

On the walls of Emain a watchman was at the look-

out post. "A solitary warrior draws near to thee, O
Conor, and terribly he comes! Upon the chariot pole
are bleeding heads; white birds are flying round the car,
and wild unbroken stags are tethered fast behind.
Wildly and with fury he draws near, and unless some
means be taken to abate his rage, the young men of
Emain's fort will perish by his hand."

"Warriors will not stay his hand. I know that little
boy; it is my foster-son, who on this day has taken arms
and made his first champion-raid. But before women he
is ever courteous and modest; let then the women-folk
of Emain's fort, and our noble wives, go forth to meet
him, for that will tame his rage." So the champion's
wives and the women of Emain went out in a troop to
meet him, and when he saw them come, the fury of war
passed from Cuchulain, and he leaned his head upon the
chariot-rail, that they might not see the battle rage that
was upon his face. For in the presence of women
Cuchulain was ever calm and gentle-mannered.

Yet so warm and ardent was he from his warrior-raid,
that the champions of Ulster bathed him in three baths
of cold water before his heat and travel-stains were
passed away from him. And the water of the baths was
heated fiery-hot by his plunge into it. But when he
was washed, and arrayed in his hooded tunic and mantle
of bright blue, fastened with its silver brooch, the little
man's fury had all gone from him; he blushed a beautiful
ruddy hue all over, and with eyes sparkling, and his
golden hair combed back, he came to take his place
beside the King. And Conor was proud of the boy, and
drew him between his knees and stroked his hair; and
his place was ever beside the King after that.

Now a little boy that at the age of seven years—

continued Fiacha, who told the tale—could kill a man, yea, two or three men, whom all the champions of Ulster feared, and who could do such deeds, it were not wonderful if, in your war with Ulster, O Queen Meave, he should prove a formidable foe.

And Meave said thoughtfully, " It were not wonderful indeed."

Then the company broke up, preparing for the march upon the morrow. But that night Meave said to her spouse: " I think, O Ailill, that this young champion of Ulster is not of the make of mortal men, nor is he quite as other champions. And though our host is good and sufficient for ordinary war, to meet a foe like this, it seems to me that a great and mighty force is needed ; for I am of opinion that the war on which we are now come will not be a battle of a night or a day, but that it will be a campaign of many days and weeks and months against that lad. Therefore, at this time, let us return home again, and when a year or two is out, I shall have gathered such a host that the gods themselves could not withstand it." Thus Meave spoke boastfully, and Ailill was well content, for he liked not the war. So for that time, they all turned home again.

CHAPTER VII

Cuchulain's Adventures in Shadow-Land

WHILE Cuchulain was still a little lad, but strong and brave and full of spirit, it came into his mind that he would like to go out into the world to perfect himself in every kind of soldierly art, so that he might not be behind any warrior in feats of strength and skill. He went first to the Glen of Solitude in Munster, but he did not long remain there, but returned to Ulster, to invite his companions to go with him to visit the woman-warrior Scáth who dwelt in "Shadow-land." Where the land was, Cuchulain knew not, but he thought it was in Alba, or mayhap in the Eastern world.

Three of the chiefs of Ulster consented to go with him, Conall, whom men in after days called The Victorious, because of his many combats, and Laery the Triumphant, and Conor, Ulster's king. Conall was close friend to Cuchulain, and they had vowed to each other while yet they were but boys, that whichever of the two of them should first fall in battle or single combat, the other would avenge his death, whether he were at that time near at hand or far across the world in distant climes. And though Cuchulain was the younger, he it was who first fell, and Conall avenged his death in the Red Rout, as we shall hear. He was a great wanderer, and he was far away across the seas when Cuchulain fell, but for all that his promise held him, and his love for his friend, and amply and fully he avenged him on his foes.

Then these three friends set out together in Conall's boat the " Bird-like," which needed not to be guided or rowed, but which sped at its own will across the deep-green, strong-waved ocean, like the winging flight of a swift bird. It took its own way to strange lands, where none of those who travelled in the boat had ever been before, and they came at last to a dark gloomy shore where dwelt a fierce woman-warrior, Donnell the Soldierly, and her daughter, Big-fist.

Huge and ugly and gruesome were they both, with big grey eyes, and black faces and rough bright-red hair, and so cruel and vengeful were they that it was dangerous to quarrel with either of them. Yet they knew many feats of arms, so that the three warriors stayed with them a year and a day, learning all they knew. But Cuchulain was fain to go away from them, for the darkness and the gloom of the place and the ugly deeds of Big-fist troubled him, and he liked not at all to remain with her.

The year and the day being past, Cuchulain was walking by the brink of the sea revolving these things in his mind, when he saw close beside him, sitting on the shore, a man of enormous size, every inch of him from top to toe as black as coal. " What are you doing here ? " said the big black man to Cuchulain. " I have been here a year and a day learning feats of prowess and heroism from Donnell," said the little lad. " How so ? " said the big black man. " If you want to learn true knightly skill and feats of valour, it is not here that you will learn them." " Is that true ? " said Cuchulain. " It is true, indeed," said the big black man. " Is there any

woman-champion in the world who is better than the
woman-champion that is here?" said Cuchulain.
"There is indeed," said the big black man; "far better
than she is Scáth, daughter of Ages, King of Shadow-
land, who dwells in the Eastern world." "We have
heard of her before," said Cuchulain. "I am sure you
have," said the big black man; "but great and distant is
the region of Shadow-land, little man." "Will you tell
me all about it, and where it is, and how to find it?"
said Cuchulain, eagerly. "Never will I tell you a word
about it to the end of time," said the black man surlily.
"O hateful, withered spectre, now may knowledge and
help fail you yourself, when most you stand in need of
them," cried the boy, and with that the phantom disappeared.

Cuchulain did not sleep a wink that night thinking of
the great far-distant country of which the big black man
had told him; and at break of day on the morrow he
sprang from his bed and sought his companions, Conor
and Conall and Laery. "Will you come with me to seek
for Shadow-land?" he asked, when he had told them the
tale of the big black man. "We will not come," said
they, "for last night a vision appeared to each of us,
and we could not put it away from us. We saw before us
our own homes, and the kingly courts of Emain Macha
standing right before us in the way, and we heard the
voices of our wives weeping for our absence, and the call
of our clans and warriors for their chiefs; therefore to-day
we bid you farewell, for we return together to our homes.
But go you on to Shadow-land and perfect yourself
in feats with Scáth, daughter of Ages, and then return
to us." It seemed to Cuchulain that it was the big
black man who had raised this vision before the chiefs,

that they might separate themselves from him, so that he might find his death travelling to Shadow-land alone. So he bid the chiefs farewell with a heavy heart, and they set off for Erin in Conall's boat, the " Bird-like ; " and as soon as it was out of sight, speeding over the waves of the blue, surging ocean, Cuchulain set out alone along the unknown road. For he was determined to reach Shadow-land, or to die in the attempt. He went on for many days over great mountains and through deep impenetrable forests, and dark, lonely glens, until he came to a wide-spreading desert and a lightless land. Black and scorched and bare was that desert, and there was no path or road across it, and no human habitation was in sight. Cuchulain stood wondering and fearing to adventure forth alone across that terrible stony trackless waste, for he knew not whither to turn, or how to go. Just then he saw a great beast like a lion coming out of the forest on the border of the desert, and advancing towards him, watching him all the time. Now Cuchulain was but a little lad, and he had no weapons with him, and he was afraid of the mighty beast and tried to escape from him ; but whichever way he turned, the beast was there before him, and it seemed to Cuchulain that it was a friendly beast, for it made no attempt to injure him, but kept turning its side to Cuchulain, inviting him to mount. So Cuchulain plucked up his courage and took a leap and was on its back. He did not try to guide it, for of its own accord the lion made off across the plain, and for four days and nights they travelled thus through the dim, lightless land until Cuchulain thought they must have come to the uttermost bounds of men. But they saw a small loch and a boat on it, and boys rowing the boat backward and forward amongst the reeds of the shore, and the boys laughed at the sight of the hurtful beast doing service to a human being. Then Cuchulain jumped off the back of the lion and he bade it farewell and it departed from him.

The boys rowed him across the loch to a house where he got meat and drink, and a young man with a face bright like the sun conducted him on his way until he came to the Plain of Ill-luck, and there he left him. Difficult and toilsome was the journey across the Plain of Ill-luck; on one half of the plain the feet of the way-farer would stick fast in the miry clay, so that he could not move on, but thought he would sink into the earth at every step; and on the other half of the plain the grass would rise up beneath his feet and lift him up far above the ground upon its blades, so that he seemed to be walking in the air.

No road or comfortable way ran across that plain, and Cuchulain could not have made his way across, but that the young man with the face like the sun had given him a wheel to roll before him, and told him to follow wherever the wheel led. So he rolled the wheel, and bright shining rays darted out of the wheel and lighted up all the land. The heat that came out of the wheel dried up the clay, so that it became hard and firm to walk upon, and it burned up the grass, so that it made a clear path before Cuchulain all the way. And the noisome evil airs of the plain were sucked up by the heat and sunshine of the wheel, so that Cuchulain went on gladly and cheerfully until he came to the Perilous Glen. Then Cuchulain was afraid again, for he saw before him a narrow glen between high rocky mountain fastnesses, and only one road through it, and that as narrow as a hair. And on either side of the road and among the rocks were cruel savage monsters waiting to devour him. But the youth with the shining face had given him an apple, and he rolled the apple before him as he went along, and when the monsters saw the apple, they ceased watching Cuchulain and sprang after the apple. But the apple ran on and on, so that they could not come up with it, and as it ran the narrow path grew wider, so that Cuchulain could follow it with ease. By that means he passed the Perilous Glen, and he took the road that led across the terrible high mountains, until he came to the Bridge of the Leaps. And on the other side of the bridge was the isle where Scáth or Shadow, daughter of Ages, lived.

Now this is how the Bridge of the Leaps was made. It was low at the two ends, but high in the middle, and it passed over a deep and precipitous gorge, up which came foaming the waters of the wild tempestuous ocean. And fearful strange beasts and fishes were moving about in the waters below, which made a man's heart quail with fear to look upon, for it was certain that if he should fall, they would seize him in their jaws and devour him.

On the near side of the bridge were many youths playing hurley on the green, and Cuchulain saw amongst them champions from Ulster, Ferdia, son of Daman, and the sons of Naisi, and many others. They greeted him kindly and gladly, and they asked news of Ulster and of their friends and companions in Erin ; and Cuchulain was glad to see the faces of his friends, for he was weary and fatigued after his journey and after the terrors of the way across the Plain of Ill-luck and the Perilous Glen. Then Cuchulain asked Ferdia, for he was older than he, " How shall I get across the Bridge of the Leaps, to reach the fort of Scáth ? " " You cannot cross it," said he ; " for this is the manner of that bridge ; when anyone steps on one end of the bridge the other end leaps up, and flings the passenger off again upon his back. Not one of us has crossed the bridge as yet, for there are two feats that Scáth teaches last of all, the leap of the Bridge, and the thrust of the spear that is called the Body Spear, which moves along the water. When we have achieved valour, she will teach us the leap of the Bridge, but the thrust of the Body Spear she will not teach to any man of us at all, for she reserves that feat for the champion who excels in all other feats, and who is, out of all her pupils, the one whom she likes best.

" Tell me, O Ferdia, how Shadow herself crosses the bridge when she comes to teach you feats," said Cuchulain. " Only by two leaps can that bridge be crossed," they all reply ; " that is, one leap into the very centre of the bridge, and one upon the firm ground beyond ; but if the leap is missed, it is likely that the passer-by will fall into the gulf below, and woe to him if he should fall." Then Cuchulain looked at the bridge and he looked at the foaming gorge below, and at the open-mouthed monsters in the tossing waves, and he waited awhile until his strength was returned. But as evening fell he rose, and gathering all his forces together, he leaped upon the bridge. Three times he tried to cross it, and three times it flung him again upon the bank, so that he fell upon his back ; and the young men jeered at him, because he tried to cross the bridge without Scáth's help. Then Cuchulain grew mad with anger, and he leaped at one bound upon the very centre and ridge of the bridge. Here he rested a moment, and then he leaped again, and he gained the firm ground on the further side, and he strode straight up to the fort of

Shadow, and struck three thunderous knocks upon the door.

"Truly," said Scáth, "this must be someone who has achieved valour somewhere else," and she sent Uthach the Fearful, her daughter, to bring him in, and welcome him to the fort.

For a year and a day he remained with Scáth, and learned all that she could teach him, and he became the most renowned warrior of his time, or of any other time; and because Shadow loved his skill and his strength and comeliness, she taught him the feat of the Body Spear, which she had never taught to any before. And she gave the spear into his own keeping. When Ferdia saw the spear, he said, " O Scáth, teach me also this feat, for the day will come when I shall have need of it." But she would not, for she wished to make Cuchulain invincible, and that he should have one feat that was not known to any but himself. And she gave him the Helmet of Invisibility, which Manannan mac Lir, the ocean god, brought out of Fairy-land; and the mantle of Invisibility made of the precious fleeces from the land of the Immortals, even from the Kingdom of Clear Shining; and she gave him his glorious shield, with knobs of gold, and chased all round with carvings of animals, and the combats of fighting men, and the sea-wars of the gods. And he became companion and arms-bearer to Ferdia, because he was the younger and because they loved each other, and all the time he was with Scáth they went together into every danger, and every peril, and they took journeys together, and saw strange sights. And because the twain loved each other, they swore that never in life would either hurt or wound the other, or do combat or quarrel with the other, but that for ever and for ever they twain would aid and support each other in war and in combat, and in all the pleasant loving ways of peace. But Scáth knew that other days were coming, for she was a seer, and when Cuchulain bade her farewell, to return to Ireland, she spoke to him these words out of her prophet's shining ken : " Blessing and health go with thee ! Victorious Hero, Champion of the Kine of Bray ! Chariot Chief of the two-horsed chariot ! Beloved Hero of the gods ! Perils await thee ; alone before the foe I see thee stand, fighting against a multitude, fighting thy own companion and friend. Red from many conflicts are thy warrior weapons ; by thee men and champions will fall ; the warriors of Connaught and of Meave, the hosts of Ailill and of Fergus scatter before thy sword. The Hound of Ulster will be renowned. At his death will the glory of Ulster fail, the glory of Erin will depart from her. . . . Farewell, farewell, Cuchulain."

Then Cuchulain parted from her, and turned to go back to Erin, and a magic mist overtook him so that he knew not how he went, or by what road he came to the borders of the white-flecked, green-waved ocean, but he found Manannan's horses of the white sea-foam awaiting him near the shore upon the surface of the mighty main, and he caught their tossing white-tipped manes and they bore him out across the waves, and so he came to Ireland again. It was on the night of his return that he found and caught his two chariot horses, the Grey of Macha, and the Black Steed of the Glen, and this is how he caught them. He was passing along the borders of the Grey Lake that is near the Mountain of Slieve Fuad, pondering on the fate that was before him, and the work that he would do. Slowly he walked

along the reedy, marshy ground that lay along the lake,
till he saw a mist rise slowly from the mere and cover all
the plain.   Then, as he stood to watch, he saw the form
of a mighty steed, grey and weird and phantom-like,
rise slowly from the centre of the lake, and draw near
to the shore, until it stood with its back to him among the
rushes of the water's edge.   Softly Cuchulain crept
down behind the steed; but it seemed not to hear
him come, for it was looking out towards the centre of
the lake.   Then with a sudden leap, Cuchulain was on
its neck, his two arms clasped upon its mane.   When it
felt the rider on its back, the noble animal shuddered from
head to foot, and started back and tried to throw Cuchulain, but with all his might he clung and would not be
thrown.   Then began a struggle of champions between
those two heroes, the King of the Heroes of Erin and the
King of Erin's Steeds.   All night they wrestled, and the
prancing of the steed was heard at Emain Macha, so
that the warriors said it thundered, and that a great
storm of wind had arisen without.   But when it could by
no means throw Cuchulain from its back, the horse began
to career and course round the island, and that night they
fled with the swiftness of the wind three times round all
the provinces of Ireland.   With a bound the wild steed
leaped the mountains, and the sound of its coursing
over the plains was as the break of the tempestuous surf
upon the shore.   Once only did they halt in their career,
and that was in the wild and lonely glen in Donegal that
is called the Black Glen, where the ocean waves roll
inward to the land.   From out the waters arose another
steed, as black as night, and it whinneyed to the Grey
of Macha, so that the Grey of Macha stopped, and the
Black Steed of the Glen came up beside it, and trotted

by its side.   Then the fury of the Grey of Macha ceased, and Cuchulain could feel beneath his hand that the two horses were obedient to his will.   And he brought them home to Emain and harnessed them to his chariot, and all the men of Ulster marvelled at the splendour of those steeds, which were like night and day, the dark steed and the light, and one of them they called the Grey of Macha, because Macha was the goddess of war and combat, and the other they called the Black Steed of the Glen.

CHAPTER VIII

How Cuchulain Wooed his Wife

IT was on a day of the days of summer that Emer, daughter of Forgall the Wily, sat on a bench before her father's door, at his fort that is called Lusk to-day, but which in olden days men spoke of as the Gardens of the Sun-god Lugh, so sunny and so fair and fertile was that plain, with waving meadow-grass and buttercups, and the sweet may-blossom girdling the fields. Close all about the fort the gardens lay, with apple-trees shedding their pink and white upon the playing fields of brilliant green; and all the air was noisy with the buzz of bees, and with the happy piping of the thrush and soft low cooing of the doves. And Emer sat, a fair and noble maid, among her young companions, foster-sisters of her own, who came from all the farms and forts around to grow up with the daughters of the house, and learn from them high-bred and gentle ways, to fashion rich embroideries such as Irish women used to practise as an art, and weaving, and fine needlework, and all the ways of managing a house. And as they sat round Emer, a bright comely group of busy girls, they sang in undertones the crooning tender melodies of ancient Erin; or one would tell a tale of early wars, and warrior feasts or happenings of the gods, and one would tell a tale of lover's joys or of the sorrows of a blighted love, and they would sigh and laugh and dream that they too loved, were wooed, and lost their loves.

And Emer moved about among the girls, directing them; and of all maids in Erin, Emer was the best, for hers were the six gifts of womanhood, the gift of loveliness, the gift of song, the gift of sweet and pleasant speech, the gift of handiwork, the gifts of wisdom and of modesty. And in his distant home in Ulster, Cuchulain heard of her. For he was young and brave, and women loved him for his nobleness, and all men wished that he should take a wife. But for awhile he would not, for among the women whom he saw, not one of them came up to his desires. And when they urged him, wilfully he said: "Well, find for me a woman I could love, and I will marry her." Then sent the King his heralds out through every part of Ulster and the south to seek a wife whom Cuchulain would care to woo. But still he said the same, "This one, and this, has some bad temper or some want of grace, or she is vain or she is weak, not fitted as a mate to such as I. She must be brave, for she must suffer much; she must be gentle, lest I anger her; she must be fair and noble, not alone to give me pleasure as her spouse, but that all men may think of her with pride, saying, 'As Cuchulain is the first of Ulster's braves, the hero of her many fighting-fields, so is his wife the noblest and the first of Erin's women, a worthy mate for him.'"

So when the princely messengers returned, their search was vain; among the daughters of the chiefs and noble lords not one was found whom Cuchulain cared to woo. But one who loved him told him of a night he spent in Forgall's fort, and of the loveliness and noble spirit of Forgall's second girl Emer, the maiden of the waving hair, but just grown up to womanhood. He told him of her noble mien and stately step, the soft and liquid brightness of her eyes, the colour of her hair, that like to ruddy gold fresh from the burnishing, was rolled around her head. Her graceful form he praised, her skilfulness in song and handiwork, her courage with her father, a harsh and wily man, whom all within the house hated and feared but she. He told him also that for any man to win the maiden for his wife would be a troublesome and dangerous thing, for out of all the world, her father Forgall loved and prized but her, and he had made it known that none beneath a king or ruling prince should marry her, and any man who dared to win her love, but such as these, should meet a cruel death; and this he laid upon his sons and made them swear to him upon their swords, that any who should come to woo the girl should never leave the fort alive again.

All that they said but made Cuchulain yet the more desire to see the maid and talk with her. " This girl, so brave, so wise, so fair of face and form," he pondered with himself, " would be a fitting mate for any chief. I think she is the fitting mate for me."

So on the very day when Emer sat upon her playing-fields, Cuchulain in the early morn set forth in all his festal garb in his chariot with his prancing steeds, with Laeg before him as his charioteer, and took the shortest route towards the plain of Bray, where lie the Gardens of the Sun-god Lugh. The way they went from Emain lay between the Mountains of the Wood, and thence along the High-road of the Plain, where once the sea had passed; across the marsh that bore the name the Whisper of the Secret of the Gods. Then driving on towards the River Boyne they passed the Ridge of the

Great Sow, where not far off is seen the fairy haunt of
Angus, God of Beauty and of Youth; and so they
reached the ford of Washing of the Horses of the
Gods, and the fair, flowering plains of Lugh, called
Lusk to-day.

Now all the girls were busied with their work, when on
the high-road leading to the fort they heard a sound
like thunder from the north, that made them pause and
listen in surprise.

Nearer and nearer yet it came as though at furious
pace a band of warriors bore down towards the
house. "Let one of you see from the ramparts of the
fort," said Emer, "what is the sound that we hear
coming towards us." Fiall, her sister, Forgall's eldest
girl, ran to the top of the rath or earthen mound that
circled round the playing-fields, and looked out towards the north, shading her eyes against the brilliant
sun. "What do you see there?" asked they all, and
eagerly she cried: "I see a splendid chariot-chief coming
at furious pace along the road. Two steeds, like day
and night, of equal size and beauty, come thundering
beneath that chariot on the plain. Curling their manes
and long, and as they come, one would think fire darted
from their curbed jaws, so strain and bound they forward; high in the air the turf beneath their feet is thrown
around them, as though a flock of birds were following
as they go. On the right side the horse is grey, broad
in the haunches, active, swift and wild; with head
erect and breast expanded, madly he moves along the
plain, bounding and prancing as he goes. The other
horse jet-black, head firmly knit, feet broad-hoofed,
firm, and slender; in all this land never had chariot-
chief such steeds as these."

"Heed not the steeds," the girls replied, "tell us, for this concerns us most, who is the chariot-chief who rides within?"

"Worthy of the chariot in which he rides is he who sits within. Youthful he seems, as standing on the very borders of a noble manhood, and yet I think his face and form are older than his years. Gravely he looks, as though his mind revolved some serious thought, and yet a radiance as of the summer's day enfolds him round. About his shoulders a rich five-folded mantle hangs, caught by a brooch across the chest sparkling with precious gems, above his white and gold-embroidered shirt. His massive sword rests on his thigh, and yet I think he comes not here to fight. Before him stands his charioteer, the reins held firmly in his hand, urging the horses onward with a goad."

"What like is he, the charioteer?" demand the girls again.

"A ruddy man and freckled," answered Fiall; "his hair is very curly and bright-red, held by a bronze fillet across his brow, and caught at either side his head in little cups of gold, to keep the locks from falling on his face. A light cloak on his shoulders, made with open sleeves, flies back in the wind, as rapidly they course along the plain." But Emer heard not what the maiden said, for to her mind there came the memory of a wondrous youth whom Ulster loved and yet of whom all Erin stood in awe. Great warriors spoke of him in whispers and with shaking of the head. They told how when he was a little child, he fought with full-grown warriors and mastered them; of a huge hound that he had slain and many feats of courage he had done. Into her mind there came a memory, that she had heard of

prophets who foretold for him a strange and perilous
career; a life of danger, and an early death. Full many
a time she longed to see this youth, foredoomed to peril,
yet whose praise should ring from age to age through
Erin; and in her mind, when all alone she pondered on
these things, she still would end: "This were a worthy
mate! This were a man to win a woman's love!" And
half aloud she uttered the old words: "This were a man
to win a woman's love!"

Now hardly had the words sprung to her lips, when the
chariot stood before the door, close to the place where all
the girls were gathered. And when she saw him Emer
knew it was the man of whom she dreamed. He wished
a blessing to them, and her lovely face she lifted in reply.
"May God make smooth the path before thy feet," she
gently said. "And thou, mayest thou be safe from every
harm," was his reply. "Whence comest thou?" she
asked; for he had alighted from his seat and stood beside
her, gazing on her face. "From Conor's court we come,"
he answered then; "from Emain, kingliest of Ulster's
forts, and this the way we took. We drove between the
Mountains of the Wood, along the High-road of the Plain,
where once the sea had been; across the Marsh they call
the Secret of the Gods, and to the Boyne s ford named
of old the Washing of the Horses of the Gods. And now
at last, O maiden, we have come to the bright flowery
Garden-grounds of Lugh. This is the story of myself,
O maid; let me now hear of thee." Then Emer said:
"Daughter am I to Forgall, whom men call the Wily
Chief. Cunning his mind and strange his powers; for
he is stronger than any labouring man, more learned than
any Druid, more sharp and clever than any man of verse.
Men say that thou art skilled in feats of war, but it will be

more than all thy games to fight against Forgall himself; therefore be cautious what thou doest, for men cannot number the multitude of his warlike deeds nor the cunning and craft with which he works. He has given me as a bodyguard twenty valiant men, their captain Con, son of Forgall, and my brother; therefore I am well protected, and no man can come near me, but that Forgall knows of it. To-day he is gone from home on a warrior expedition, and those men are gone with him; else, had he been within, I trow he would have asked thee of thy business here."

"Why, O maiden, dost thou talk thus to me? Dost thou not reckon me among the strong men, who know not fear?" "If thy deeds were known to me," she said, "I then might reckon them; but hitherto I have not heard of all thy exploits." "Truly, I swear, O maiden," said Cuchulain, "that I will make my deeds to be recounted among the glories of the warrior-feats of heroes." "How do men reckon thee?" she said again. "What then is thy strength?" "This is my strength," he said. "When my might in fight is weakest, I can defend myself alone against twenty. I fear not by my own might to fight with forty. Under my protection a hundred are secure. From dread of me, strong warriors avoid my path, and come not against me in the battle-field. Hosts and multitudes and armed men fly before my name."

"Thou seemest to boast," said Emer, "and truly for a tender boy those feats are very good; but they rank not with the deeds of chariot-chiefs. Who then were they who brought thee up in these deeds of which thou boastest?"

"Truly, O maiden, King Conor is himself my foster-father, and not as a churl or common man was I brought up by him. Among chariot-chiefs and champions, among poets and learned men, among the lords and nobles of Ulster, have I been reared, and they have taught me courage and skill and manly gifts. In birth and bravery I am a match for any chariot-chief; I direct the counsels of Ulster, and at my own fort at Dun Dalgan they come to me for entertainment. Not as one of the common herd do I stand before thee here to-day, but as the favourite of the King and the darling of all the warriors of Ulster. Moreover, the god Lugh the Long-handed is my protector, for I am of the race of the great gods, and his especial foster-child. And now, O maiden, tell me of thyself; how in the sunny plains of Lugh hast thou been reared within thy father's fort?" "That I will tell thee," said the girl. "I was brought up in noble behaviour as every queen is reared; in stateliness of form, in wise, calm speech, in comeliness of manner, so that to me is imputed every noble grace among the hosts of the women of Erin."

"Good, indeed, are those virtues," said the youth; "and yet I see one excellence thou hast not noted in thy speech. Never before, until this day, among all women with whom I have at times conversed, have I found one but thee to speak the mystic ancient language of the bards, which we are talking now for secrecy one with the other. And all these things are good, but one is best of all, and that is, that I love thee, and I think thou lovest me. What hinders, then, that we should be betrothed?" But Emer would not hasten, but teasing him, she said, "Perhaps thou hast already found a wife?" "Not so," said he, "and by my right-hand's valour here I vow, none but thyself shall ever be my wife." "A pity it were, indeed, thou shouldst not have a wife," said Emer, playing with him still; "see, here is Fiall, my elder sister, a clever girl and excellent in needlework. Make her thy wife, for well is it known to thee, a younger sister in Ireland may not marry before an elder. Take her! I'll call her hither." Then Cuchulain was vexed because she seemed to play with him. "Verily and indeed," he said, "not Fiall, but thee, it is with whom I am in love; and if thou weddest me not, never will I, Cuchulain, wed at all."

Then Emer saw that Cuchulain loved her, but she was not satisfied, because he had not yet done the deeds of prime heroes, and she desired that he should prove himself by champion feats and deeds of valour before he won her as his bride.

So she bade him go away and prove himself for a year by deeds of prowess to be indeed a worthy mate and spouse for her, and then, if he would come again she would go with him as his one and only wife. But she bade him beware of her father, for she knew that he would try to kill him, in order that he might not come again. And this was true, for every way he sought to kill Cuchulain, or to have him killed by his enemies, but he did not prevail.

When Cuchulain had taken farewell of Emer and gained her promise, he returned to Emain Macha. And that night the maidens of the fort told Forgall that Cuchulain had been there and that they thought that he had come to woo Emer; but of this they were not sure, because he and Emer had talked together in the poet's mystic tongue, that was not known to them. For Emer and Cuchulain talked on this wise, that no one might repeat what they had said to Forgall.

And for a whole year Cuchulain was away, and Forgall guarded the fort so well that he could not come near

Emer to speak with her ; but at last, when the year was out, he would wait no longer, and he wrote a message to Emer on a piece of stick, telling her to be ready. And he came in his war-chariot, with scythes upon its wheels, and he brought a band of hardy men with him, who entered the outer rampart of the fort and carried off Emer, striking down men on every side. And Forgall followed them to the earthen out-works, but he fell over the rath, and was taken up lifeless. And Cuchulain placed Emer and her foster-sister in his chariot, carrying with them their garments and ornaments of gold and silver, and they drove northward to Cuchulain's fort at Dun Dalgan, which is Dundalk to-day.

And they were pursued to the Boyne, and there Cuchulain placed Emer in a house of safety, and he turned and drove off his enemies who followed him, pursuing them along the banks and destroying them, so that the place, which had before been called the White Field, was called the Turf of Blood from that day. Then he and Emer reached their home in safety, nor were they henceforth parted until death.

CHAPTER IX

Meave demands the Brown Bull of Cooley
and is refused

FOR many years Meave had been making preparations for her war with Ulster. To the East and South and West she had sent her messengers, stirring up the chiefs and calling them to aid her in her attack on Conor's land. From every quarter she asked for supplies of men and food, and if these were refused, she sent her fighting-bands into the district to waste and destroy it, and to carry off the cattle and produce by force. All the princes of Ireland stood in awe of Meave, so ruthless and proud was she, and so quick in her descent upon the lands of those who would not do her will. For had they not regarded her request, all Ireland would have been set in flames; for she would plunder and destroy without pity or remorse. So in their own defence, the princes of the provinces promised her fighting-men and provender whenever she should call upon them, and month by month she gathered round her fort at Cruachan herds of cattle and swine and sheep, ready for the war.

Now Meave was looking about for a cause of contest between herself and Ulster; for she knew that Cuchulain was yet young, and she desired to begin the war before he came to his full strength; moreover, she had heard that upon Ulster at that time there lay a heavy sickness, which had prostrated its fighting-men and warriors, its princes and captains, and that even Conor, the King, himself lay ill.

No common sickness was that which lay upon the Province, but it came of the wrath and vengeance of the gods. For in the days gone by the goddess Macha, one of the three fierce goddesses of war and battles, had visited Ulster as a mortal maid, to bring aid and comfort to one of the nobles of Ulster who was in sore distress. And the King and people had reviled her, and brought shame and scoffing upon her, because they saw that she was not as one of themselves; for they liked not that a woman greater than themselves should take up her abode amongst them. They made game of her in the public assembly, crowding round her, and scoffing at her courage and her splendid form and at her swiftness of running beyond any of the men. For they knew not that she was one of the great gods, and they were jealous of her, because they felt that she was nobler than they. Then Macha cursed the men of Ulster, and told them that in a time of danger and sore need, when all the chiefs and warriors of Ireland should gather round its borders, plundering and destroying, she would cast upon their warriors weakness and feebleness of body and of mind, so that they could not go forth in defence of the Province, and the land should be a prey to their enemies. Only upon Cuchulain she laid not her curse, for he was young, and it fell not upon women and little children, but upon full-grown warriors only, because it was the men of Ulster who had insulted her. Then she went away from them, and in dread of her they called the palace of the King

Emain Macha, or the " Brooch-pin of Macha," to this day.[1]

When then Macha saw Meave gathering her hosts together to war against Ulster, she brought upon them this sickness, as she had prophesied. And Meave, hearing of this, hastened her preparations for the war, for she was determined that, come what might, she would march into Ulster at that time and smite it in its weakness, so that once and for ever Ulster would be subdued to Connaught by her hand. And her pride waxed greater at the thought.

There were in Ireland at that time two famous bulls, unlike to any kine that ever have been in Ireland from that time until now. For these bulls were cattle of the gods, and they had come to abide among men for this purpose only, to incite and bring about a war between Connaught and Ulster. For Macha watched o'er men, and she awaited the day when her revenge upon Ulster should fall. Now these cattle were born, one in the Province of Connaught among the cattle of Meave, and the other in Ulster among the cattle of Daire of Cooley, in Cuchulain's country. Meave knew not that these were immortal beasts, for that was in the secrets of the gods, but she knew well that among her cattle was one bull of extraordinary size, and fierceness, and strength, so that no other member of her herds dared to come near it; moreover, fifty men were required to keep it. And of all her stock, there was not one that Meave counted worth a metal ring beside this bull. She named him the Finn-bennach or " White-horned," and she believed that not in Ireland nor in the whole world beside, was

---

[1] The raths or earthworks of Emain Macha are still to be discerned two miles west of Armagh, at a place now called Navan Fort.

Macha curses the Men of Ulster

the equal and the fellow of this bull. One day, before the war began, while Meave was meditating in her mind what challenge she should send to Ulster, she caused all her cattle to be arrayed before her.

From pastures and meadow-lands, from hills and vales, she called in all her stock, her sheep and swine, her cattle and her steeds. Ailill also, her husband, caused his flocks and herds to be brought in, and reckoned alongside of hers. For Meave had boasted to her spouse that in all possessions of kine and live stock, as also in household goods and utensils, in jewels and ornaments, in garments and in stuffs, her share was greater far than his, so that, in fact, she was the better of the two, the real ruler and prince of Connaught.

Ailill liked not this boasting of his wife ; so when their flocks were driven in, their vessels and vats and mugs collected, their clasped ornaments and rings, as well arm-rings as thumb-rings, brooches and collars of carven metal-work, with their apparel and stuffs, it pleased the King to find that the share of Meave and of himself was exactly equal and alike. Among Meave's horses was a special mare, and she thought there was no mare in Ireland to equal it, but Ailill had one just its match. Among the sheep Meave owned one mighty ram, and among the swine one eminent boar, but Ailill proved that amongst his flocks and herds he had the same. Then Meave said: "Among the cattle, however, certain it is, that there is no bull to be named in the same breath with the White-horned." "Ay, no, indeed," said the herds-man, "the White-horned surpasseth all beasts; but, a week ago, he left the company of thy cattle, O Queen, and went over to the cattle of the King. 'Tis my opinion that he heard the keepers say that it was strange that so

F

powerful a bull should be under the dominion of a woman; for no sooner were the words out of their mouths, than he broke loose from his stall, and, head in air and bellowing loudly, he passed over to the herds of Ailill. Nought could stay him or bring him back; and all that stood in his path were trampled and gored to death."

Now when Meave heard that the White-horned was no longer in her keeping, not one of her possessions had any value in her eyes; for, because she had not that especial bull, it was in her esteem as though she owned not so much as a penny's worth of stock.

When Mac Roth, her herald, who stood at her right hand, saw the Queen's vexation, he said, " I know, O Queen, where a better bull than the White-horned is to be found, even with Daire of Cooley, in Cuchulain's country, and the Dun or " Brown Bull " of Cooley is its name; a match it is to the White-horned; nay, I think that it is yet more powerful than he."

" Whence came these bulls ? " said Meave; " and what is their strength and their history ? Tell me, Mac Roth, yet further of this bull."

Then Mac Roth said: " This is the description of the Dun. Brown he is, and dark as night, terrific in strength and size. Upon his back, at evening-tide, full fifty little boys can play their games. He moves about with fifty heifers at his side, and if his keepers trouble him, he tramples them into the earth in his rage. Throughout the land his bellowings can be heard, and on his horns are gold and silver tips. Before the cows he marches as a king, with bull-like front, and with the resistless pace of the long billow rolling on the shore. Like to the fury of a dragon, or like a lion's fierceness is his rage.

Only the Finn-bennach, the White-horned bull, is his mate and match; his pair in strength, in splendour, and in pride."

And Meave said: " What and whence are these kine, and wherefore did they come to Ireland ? "

Mac Roth replied : " These are the cattle of the gods ; out of the Fairy Palaces they came to Erin, and into the Fairy Palaces they will return again. For the disturbance and downfall of Erin are they come, to awaken wars and tumults among her people. Before they became cattle, they have lived many lives in many forms, but in whatever form they come to earth destruction and warfare haunt their steps. At the first they were two swineherds of the gods, dwelling in the underworld, and they kept the herds of the fairy gods of Munster and of Connaught. But a mighty war was fought between them, so that all Erin was disturbed and troubled by that war ; and each of them tore the other in pieces, so that they died. But they were born again as two ravens, dwelling upon earth, and for three hundred years they lived as birds, but in the end they pecked each other till they died.

" Then they became two monsters of the sea, and after that two warriors and two demon-men. But in each of all these forms they met together in terrific contest, so that the world of men and even the dwellings of the gentle gods were stirred and agitated by their wrath. For when men hear the sighing of the wind, or the wild turmoil of the billows on the shore, then, indeed, it is the bulls in fight wherever they may be, or in whatever form. And now that they are come to earth again, no doubt some mighty contest is at hand ; for surely they are come to stir up strife and deadly warfare between man and man, and Connaught and Ulster will be concerned in this."

"That likes us well," said Meave, "and for this contest we will well prepare. So, since the fellow of the White-horned dwells in Cooley, take thou with thee a company, Mac Roth, and go and beg this excellent bull from Daire, that henceforth my cattle may compare with Ailill's kine, or that they may surpass them. Give all conditions he demands and promise what thou wilt, so only Daire give up the bull. And if he give it not up willingly, then will we come and seize the bull by force."

For to herself she said : "The taking of this bull will be a thing not easy to accomplish ; if Daire, as is likely, refuse it to me, war will arise between Connaught and Ulster, and this, seeing that the warriors of Ulster are now lying in their pains, we much could wish. For our hosts are gathered and our provisions ready, while on Ulster's side there are but women and little children and Cuchulain ready and fit to meet us ; quickly in that case we shall march into Ulster's borders and raid the country up to Emain's palace gates, carrying off the spoils ; the Brown Bull also we will bring with us, and henceforth not Ailill, nor the King of Ulster, nor all Ireland besides, will hold up their heads against ourselves or boast themselves our equal."

So Mac Roth with nine of his company travelled to the house of Daire in Cooley, and welcome was made for them, and fresh rushes strewn upon the floor and viands of the best were set before them, as became the chief of Ireland's heralds. But before they sat down to meat, Daire inquired of them : "What is the cause of your journey here to-day?" And Mac Roth replied : "A quarrel that has arisen between Ailill and Meave, the King and Queen of Connaught, about the possession of the White-horned, for Meave is sorrowful and vexed because the King hath a better bull than she. She craves therefore, that a loan of the Dun or Brown Bull of Cooley be made to her, that she may say that she hath the finer kine. And if thou thyself wilt bring the bull to Cruachan, good payment shall be given thee : that is, due payment for the loan of the bull, and fifty heifers into the bargain, besides a stretch of country of the best in Connaught, and Meave's close friendship along with this."

This pleased Daire so well, that he threw himself upon his couch, and he laughed loud and long, so that the seams of the couch burst asunder under him. " By our good faith," he said, " the offer is a good one, and whatever the men of Ulster may say to my lending away their precious bull, lend it I will with all my heart."

Then supper was served, and the messengers of Meave ate and drank, and Daire plied them with strong wines, so that they began to talk at random to each other. " A good house is this to which we have come, and a wealthy man is Daire," said one to his fellow. " Wealthy he is indeed," said the other. " Would you say that he was the best man in all Ulster, and the richest ? " pursued the first who had spoken. " Surely not," replied the other, " for Conor the King, at least, is better in every way than he." " Well, lucky it is, I say," pursued the first, " that without bloodshed or any difficulty raised, he yields the bull to us nine messengers ; for had he refused it, I trow that the warriors of all Ireland's Provinces could not have carried it off from Ulster." " Say not so," cried another, " for in truth, little matter to us had it been if Daire had refused it, for had we not got the bull by fair means, we would have carried it off by foul."

Now just at that moment in came the steward, with fresh viands to set before the guests, but when he overheard their conversation, and the slighting way in which his master was spoken of by the heralds of Connaught, he set down the meat without a word and without inviting them to partake, and out he went at once and told his master what the heralds had said.   Then Daire was very angry, and he exclaimed, " By the gods, I declare, that never will I lend the bull ; and that now, unless by foul means they carry him off from me, he never shall be theirs."

The next morning, the messengers arose, having slept off their carouse, and they went to Daire's house, and courteously said : " Show us now, noble Sir, the way to the place where the Brown Bull is, that we may proceed with him on our journey back to Cruachan."

" Not so, indeed," said Daire, " for were it my habit to deal treacherously with those that come in embassage, not one of you would have seen the light of the sun to-day."   " Why, how now, what is this ? " they asked, surprised, for they had forgotten what they had said over their cups the night before.   " 'Tis plain enough, I think," said Daire ;   " your people said last night that if I gave the bull not up of mine own will, yet Meave and Ailill would make me give it up by force. Let Meave and Ailill come and take it if they can.   All Ulster will prepare to hold the bull."

" Come, come," said Mac Roth, " heed not what foolish men said after food and drink ; Ailill and Meave had no ill intent in sending us to ask the bull of you.   It were not right to hold them responsible for the loose words of their messengers." " Nevertheless, Mac Roth, and however this may be, at this time you do not get my bull."

So Mac Roth and the nine messengers returned to Rath Crogan,[1] and Meave inquired for the bull. And when she heard their tale, she said, " I thought as much, Mac Roth : it was not intended that you should have the bull. The bull, which is not to be got by fair means, must be got by foul ; and by fair or foul, he shall be got by us."

---

[1] Cruachan (now Rath Crogan) is in Co. Roscommon ; tumuli mark the site of the ancient kingly fort.

CHAPTER X

The Plucking out of the Four-pronged Pole

THEN Meave gathered her hosts together and set out from Cruachan, each party under its own leader, marching in order of rank, with Fergus mac Roy guiding the entire army, and Meave bringing up the rear, in order that she might keep all her troops under her own eye. Meave's way of travelling when she went into battle was in a chariot, with her bodyguard of chosen warriors around her, who, in any time of danger, interlocked their shields to form a rampart and protection on every side as she moved along.

Gaily her troops marched in their many-coloured garb, their short kilts falling to the knee, their long cloaks over that. And the colour of the kilts of each troop was different, so that each man knew his own comrades by the pattern of his kilt. In their hands they carried shields and spears upon long shafts, while others had five-pronged spears, or mighty swords, or javelins.

It was in the beginning of winter that they set out, and already snow lay heavy on the ground; on the very first night it fell so thickly, that it reached to the chariot-wheels and almost to their very shoulders, nor could they find any track or way.

Meave called Fergus, and said to him: " Go on before the hosts, O Fergus, and find us out the shortest road into Ulster, for in such weather as this, it is not well that we lose time by wandering out of the right way." So with a few companions Fergus went on ahead ; but as he drove along, the memory of old friends and of his home and country came upon him, and an overwhelming affection for Ulster took hold on him, and in his mind there arose shame and bitter self-reproach that he, the former King of Ulster, should be leading Ulster's foes against her. For he liked Meave and he liked her not ; her kindness to himself and the exiles of Ulster had prevailed with him to aid her in her war upon the province ; but her wiles and cunning and manlike ways he cared not for, and in his heart he had no wish to see the province subdued to her. So to the North and the South he misled the host, making them walk all day by difficult paths far out of their way, while in the meantime he sent swift messengers to Conor and the Ulster chiefs, but especially to his own foster-son Cuchulain, whom he loved, to call their men at arms together, because Meave and a host of warriors from all the provinces of Ireland were on their borders. At night, after a long day's march, the army found itself back in the very spot from which it had set out, not far beyond the banks of the River Shannon. Then Meave called Fergus, and angrily she spoke to him : " A good guide to an army art thou, O Fergus, bringing it back at night to the very place from which in the morning it set out. A good enemy of Ulster this. A good friend to Connaught and its queen ! " " Seek out some other leader for your troops, O Meave," said Fergus, " for never will I lead them against the province of Ulster and against my own people and my foster-son ! But this I tell you, beware and look out well for your troops to-night and every night from this ; for it may be that Cuchulain will stand between you and

Ulster, and the standing of Cuchulain will be as the crouching of the Hounds of War upon your path; therefore beware and guard yourselves well before him!"

Now that very night Cuchulain got the message of Fergus, for he was with his father, Sualtach, not far from this place. Together in their chariot they drove to the borders of the country where the army was encamped to seek for the trail of the hosts; but they found it not easy to discover the trail, because of the snow and because of the wandering path that Fergus had taken the troops. They unyoked the chariots, and turned the horses out to graze at a certain pillar-stone beside a ford; and on one side of the pillar-stone the horses of Sualtach cropped the grass down to the very ground, and on the other the horses of Cuchulain did the same. Then Cuchulain said: " To-night, O father, I have a shrewd suspicion that the host is near; depart thou therefore to warn Ulster, and to bid them arise and come by secret ways to meet the men of Erin."

Now in his heart was Sualtach glad and pleased to be gone, because he was not a man who loved to stand in the gap of danger, nor to risk his life before an enemy stronger than himself; but yet he was loth to leave his son alone. So he said, " And thou, beloved, what wilt thou do?"

" I will stand between the men of Ireland and the province of Ulster," said the boy, " so that no harm or hurt befall the province until Ulster be ready for battle; here on the borders do I take my stand, and I will so harry and trouble the hosts of Meave that they will wish the expedition had never been undertaken."

So Cuchulain hastened his father, and Sualtach bade him farewell, and slipped away to Emain Macha. But

when he found the warriors were asleep, his old lethargy
came over Sualtach, and he forgot the message of Cuchulain, and under Emain's ramparts he took up his abode.
" Here will I wait in safety," he thought ; " and when
the King and chiefs awake, I, with the first of them,
will march to war with Meave. I will not be behind,
but all alone I have not the heart to fight."

No sooner had Sualtach gone his way than Cuchulain
entered a forest close at hand and out of an oak sapling
cut a four-pronged pole, which with one sweep of his swift
sword he cleared of all its twigs and leaves and small
branches. With the finger-tips of his right hand he
hurled it out behind his chariot, going at full pace, so
that it sank into the ground in the middle of the stream,
and stood up just above the water. Upon the pole he
flung a ring or twisted collar of young birch, and on the
ring he carved his name and a message in secret runes.
Just at that moment two young men of the host of
Meave, gone out before the troops to scout, came near
and watched him. No time had they to turn and flee,
for with one leap Cuchulain was upon them, and both
their heads struck off. These and the two heads of their
charioteers were soon impaled on the four points of the
forked pole ; but the chariots he turned back, driving
them towards the host of Meave. When the warriors
saw the chariots return with headless men, they thought
the army of Ulster must be close before them, waiting
their coming at the ford. Therefore a great company
of them marched forward to the stream, ready and armed
for battle, but nothing did they see but a tall pole that
stood upright in the swirling waters of the stream, bearing
a rude carved collar on its top, and on the point of every
branching prong a bleeding new-slain head.

"Go now," said Ailill to his man, "fetch me the collar here." But all in vain he tried to read the words engraven on the ring. "What, Fergus, are the words inscribed upon this ring?" said he. "Who could have written them? A strange thing, verily, it seems to me, that two brave scouts could have been slain like this, well-nigh within the sight of all our men. A marvel, I confess, this thing to me."

"Not that it is at which I marvel," Fergus said; "I marvel rather that with one sweep of the sword this tree was felled and cleaned of all its twigs. See, it is written on the ring that with one hand this pole was thrown, and fixed firmly in its bed; it is written here, moreover, that the men of Erin are forbidden to pass this ford, until in exactly the same manner it is plucked up again."

"One man only in the army can do that, namely, you yourself, O Fergus!" answered Meave. "Now help us in this strait and pluck the pole out of the river's bed for us."

"Bring me a chariot, then, and I will see what I can do."

A chariot was brought and Fergus mounted into it. With all his force he dashed down into the water, and with his finger-tips in passing by he tried to draw the pole out of its place. But all in vain; the pole stood fast, and though he tugged and strained, so that the chariot flew into little bits and fragments, he could not stir or move the pole an inch. One chariot after another he essayed, and all of them went into splinters, but not one whit the looser was the pole. At last Meave said: "Give over, Fergus; enough of my people's chariots are broken with this game. Get your own chariot and pull out the pole. Right well I guess your purpose; for you have in mind to hamper and delay the progress of our host till Ulster be aroused and come to meet us ; but that your guidance led us all astray, we might be even now in Ulster's border-lands."

Then Fergus's own mighty chariot was brought, all made of iron, studded o'er with nails, heavy and massive in its make. Upright he stood in it, and with a powerful, superhuman pull he wrenched with one hand's finger-tips the pole from out its bed, and handed it to Ailill.

Attentively and long the King considered it, and then he asked, " Whom thinkest thou, O Fergus, it might be who threw this pole into the river-bed and slaughtered our two scouts ? Was it Conall the victorious, or Celtchar, or even Conor himself ? Surely it was some brave, well-seasoned man, some warrior of old renown, who did a deed like this ! " " I think," said Fergus, " that not one of these three heroes would have come alone from Ulster, unattended by their bodyguard and troops." " Whom, then, thinkest thou was here ? " persisted Ailill ; " who could have done this deed ? " " I think," said Fergus, " that it was Cuchulain, Ulster's Hound."

CHAPTER XI

The Deer of Ill-Luck

WHEN Meave heard that already the Hound of Ulster stood upon her path, the words spoken by the fairy Feidelm and the Druid came back into her mind, and she resolved that not a moment would she linger by the way, but now at once, before the men of Ulster were risen from their weakness, she would push on direct to Emain Macha. " If one man alone and single-handed be formidable to us," she said to Ailill, " still more formidable will he be with the gathered hosts of Ulster at his back, fighting for their country and their fatherland."

So that very night she gave command that the army should move on, taking the direct way into Ulster ; and when the men complained there was no road, she bid her soldiers take their swords and hew for the chariots a path straight through the forests. Haughtily she cried, " Though mountains and high hills stood in my way, yet should they be hewn down before me and smoothed to level lands. So by new paths mayhap we shall slip by Cuchulain unperceived, and fall on Ulster sleeping; thus shall we take Cuchulain in the rear."

But whichever way the army turned, from that night forward Cuchulain was on the path before it, and though the warriors could not catch sight of him, at every point he cut off twos and threes, whenever scouts were sent before the host. At length they could not get the scouts to go, and whole bands went out together, but even so but few returned alive. And strange things happened, which alarmed the men, and Meave herself at last grew sore afraid. One evening, thinking that all was safe, Meave and her women walked to take the air, she carrying on her shoulders her pet bird and squirrel. They talked together of the wonders that Cuchulain wrought, and how that very day he had fallen alone upon a troop of men who cut a path through woods some miles away beyond the camp to eastward, and how but one of them escaped to tell the tale. Just as they spoke, a short sharp sound was heard, as of a sling-stone passing near their heads, and at Meave's feet the squirrel dropped, struck through the heart. Startled, she turned to see whose hand had killed her pet, but as she turned, down from the other shoulder dropped the bird, slain also by a stone. "Cuchulain must be near," the women cried; "no other hand but his so surely and so straight can sling a stone," and hastily they turned and sought the shelter of the camp again. Meave sat down beside the King to tell him what had happened. "It could not be Cuchulain," said the King; "he was far off on the other side of the host to-day." Even as the words passed from his lips, close to them whizzed a hand-sling stone, carrying off the coronet or golden 'mind' that bound Meave's hair, but hurting not so much as a lock upon her head. "A bad stroke that," laughed out the fool that gambolled round the King, joking to make him merry; "had I been he who shot that stone, the head I would have taken off and left the 'mind' behind."

Hardly were the words out of his foolish mouth, than a second stone, coming from the same direction as the first, in the full middle of his forehead struck the fool, and carried off his head, while at Meave's feet dropped down his pointed cap. Then Ailill started up and said, " That man will be the death of all our host, before we ever step on Ulster's soil. If any man henceforth makes mock at Cuchulain, 'tis I myself will make two halves of him. Let the whole host press on by day and night towards the coasts of Ulster, or not one of us will live to see the gates of Emain Macha."

So day and night the camp moved on, but not thus could they outstrip Cuchulain ; march as they would, he still was there before them. Yet, though they chased and sought him day and night, they caught no sight of him ; only he cut off their men.

One day a charioteer of Orlam, Ailill's son, was sent into a wood to cut down poles to mend the chariots broken by the way. It happened that Cuchulain was in this wood, and he took the charioteer to be a man of Ulster come out before their host to scout for them.

" The youth is foolhardy who comes so near the army of Queen Meave," Cuchulain thought ; " I will e'en go and warn him of his danger."

So he went forwards, and said, " And what, my lad, art thou doing here ? " Not knowing who it was who spoke to him, the lad replied, " I am come out to polish chariot-poles, because our chariots have been sorely damaged in our chase of that famous wild deer, Cuchulain ; and indeed, good warrior, I am making all the haste I can, for fear this same Cuchulain may pounce down on me. Certainly he would make short work of me ; therefore, O Youth, if thou hast time, lend me a hand and help me with my task." " Willingly," said Cuchulain, " will I help thee. Take thou thy choice ; shall I cut down the holly-poles ? or shall I smooth them for thee ? " " To trim them is the slowest work ; therefore while I hew down the trees do thou smooth off the branches and the twigs."

Cuchulain set to work to trim the holly-poles, and quickly were they done. Simply by drawing them between his fingers and his toes, he finished them to perfect smoothness, and threw them down without a twig or bit of bark or any rough excrescence on the ground. Closely and with surprise the young man watched this feat. At last he said : " I am inclined to think that thou art accustomed to some higher work than cutting chariot-poles. Who art thou then at all ? "

" I am that notable Cuchulain of whom just now thou spakest," the hero said. " Art thou indeed ? then am I but a dead man," the youth cried, trembling as he spoke ; " no one escapes Cuchulain's hands alive."

" Fear nothing," replied Cuchulain, " for I never slay a man unarmed or charioteer. Whose man art thou, and where is thy master to be found ? " " A servant I of Orlam, son of Meave, who awaits my coming near at hand," replied the charioteer. " Take him this message then," Cuchulain said. " Tell him the Hound of Ulster is at hand, and bid him guard his head, for if we meet, his head will surely fall."

Then the charioteer, right glad to get away, sought out his master with all haste ; but before he could reach him, Cuchulain had outstripped him, and struck off the head of Orlam, holding it aloft and shaking it before the men of Erin.

From that time forward Cuchulain took up his position nearer to the host, cutting off and destroying

G

them, and at evening he would brandish and shake his weapons before the army, so that men died of pure fear of him.

"Our army will be destroyed before ever we reach Emain Macha," said Meave at length. "If I could but see this hero who troubles our armies, and speak to him myself, I would offer him terms; for if we could persuade him to forsake Ulster, and come over to our side, it would go hard with us, if all Ulster would not be subdued before us, and ourselves return from this expedition the greatest monarch in Ireland." Calling Mac Roth, her herald, she said to him, "Prepare your chariot, Mac Roth, and seek out for us this Deer of Ill-luck who is pursuing our army and bringing misfortune upon us. Offer him terms to forsake the service of Conor and to enter our own service. Give him whatever terms he asks, and bid him come himself to-morrow to confer with me, but not to cross the glen. Well should I like to see this mighty man, but I would not have him come too near."

"I care not to go on this embassy," quoth Mac Roth; "besides, I know not where to find Cuchulain." "Fergus will know," said Meave, for she believed that Fergus was in league with his foster-son, and she forgave him not that he loved Ulster still, in spite of all that she had done for him; so she said, "Fergus will surely know."

"I know not," said Fergus, "but this I know, that after any feat of war or combat with an enemy it is not by sleep or lazy loitering Cuchulain rests himself, but by exercising in the open air and sun, letting the cool breezes blow upon his wearied body. Likely it is, that somewhere 'twixt the mountains and the sea he will be found."

Mac Roth set off. Now all the land was covered with a mantle of fresh snow, and, true enough, Cuchulain warmed himself by practising javelin feats out on the mountain-side, in the full air and sun.

His charioteer looked forth and saw a man approach. "A warrior comes, O little Cu," he said. "What sort of warrior is he who comes?" Cuchulain asked, but did not cease to fling his javelins in the air. "A massive, goodly, dark-faced man, clad in an ample mantle of dark brown, that fastens at his throat with a delicate, richly ornamented pin of bronze. Beneath the mantle a strong coat of skins, and sandals bound with leather thongs are on his feet. A sharp-edged sword he carries in one hand, and in the other holds a hazel-switch, to keep in order two great noble hounds that play around his steps."

"These are the trappings of a herald," said Cuchulain; "no doubt he comes from Meave and Ailill to propose terms to us."

Mac Roth came to the place where Laeg was awaiting him. "Who is your master, man?" said he. "My master is the young man over there; I am his charioteer," replied Laeg. Mac Roth turned half round and saw Cuchulain. "And who may you serve, my young man?" quoth he. "I serve King Conor," said the hero. "Cannot you tell me something more precise than that?" inquired Mac Roth again. "That much will serve your turn," replied the youth. "Can you then tell me where I could find this renowned Cuchulain, who is so frightening the men of Erin now?" pursued Mac Roth. "What do you want to say to him that cannot be said as well to me?" "I come in embassage from Ailill and from Meave, with power to propose terms of truce, and with an invitation from the Queen that Cuchulain should meet and confer with her." "What terms do you propose?" he asked again. "With bounteous offers I am come from Meave, promise of wealth in cattle and in flocks, and welcome of an honoured guest to Cruachan and a place near Meave's own side; all this and more, if he will quit the petty chieftain Conor, and will enter her service, and if, moreover, he will hold his hand from smiting down our hosts; for, in good sooth, the nightly thunder-feats he plays upon the warriors please not the host at all."

Anger came upon Cuchulain to hear King Conor styled a petty chief by this contemptuous messenger of Meave. "Go back to those who sent you," he replied, "for if in truth Cuchulain heard your terms, he would reject and fling them back with scorn. To-morrow I engage that the hero will confer with Meave herself, but only if she come under the escort and the charge of Fergus."

Mac Roth returned with haste, and in the camp he sought out Connaught's Queen. Eagerly she asked, "Well, did you find the champion, Mac Roth?" "All that I found was a terrible, angry, surly fellow airing himself between the mountains and the sea; but whether it were the formidable hero of whom men speak or no, indeed, I know not."

"Did he accept our terms?" pursued the Queen. "The man I saw rejected them outright, flinging them back at us with angry scorn. Only he promised that to-morrow, in the glen, Cuchulain would be found to talk of terms, but that you needs must go in company with Fergus."

"To-morrow I myself will offer terms," said Meave, "and he will not refuse." So on the morrow Meave and

Fergus sought the glen, the Queen keeping carefully to the far side of the valley, with the wooded dell between themselves and the place where she believed Cuchulain would be found. Eagerly she scanned the glen on every side, expecting on the opposite ridge to see a mighty, ugly warrior, fully armed, who waited for her coming. " Why comes he not, Fergus ? " she said at last. But Fergus answered not, for he was standing all engrossed in watching a young stripling, lithe and radiant, who on the other side the glen was practising sling-feats, shooting at the passing birds that flew above his head, and bringing them down alive.

" Cuchulain is there before you," Fergus said. " I see no one at all save one young lad, who seems expert in feats," replied the Queen ; " I cannot see a warrior near or far."

" That young lad it is who has done damage to your hosts, however," was the reply. " Is that boy, the young boy yonder, the famous hero of whom all men speak ? " Meave cried astonished. " Small need, methinks, to be afraid of him, myself will speak to him and offer him my terms." Then in a high and haughty voice, as when a Queen speaks to an underling, Meave called across the valley to Cuchulain. She set before him honourable terms if he would leave the service of King Conor and enter hers. Promptly, without an instant's thought, he set them all aside. Then as he seemed about to turn away to practise feats again, in despair the Queen called out, " Are there no terms whatever that you will accept ? it is not pleasant to our people, nor likes it them at all, to be cut off and slaughtered night by night and harassed by your precious thunder-feats."

" I tell you not my terms," replied the youth ; " it is for you to find them out yourself."

As Meave and Fergus drove back to the camp, the Queen asked Fergus if he knew the terms Cuchulain would accept.

" I do not know," said Fergus, " but just now there came into my mind a conversation that I had when Cuchulain was yet a child and in my house as foster-son. We spoke together of a champion who had accepted conditions of his country's foes, and I remember that Cuchulain thought not well of him for doing so. He coloured up and said, ' If I were offered conditions by my country's enemies, these are the sort of terms I would accept. I would demand of them each day one of their foremost warriors to meet me at the ford in single combat ; and for the space of time while I am hewing down that man, I would permit them to march onwards with their host, and short would be that space of time, I ween ! But when the man was dead, until the sunrise on the morrow's morn, I would not have them move. Thus I would keep them well in sight, and would pluck off their warriors one by one. Also,' he said, and laughed, ' I would require my enemies to keep me well supplied with food and raiment while I fought with them ; so would there be much trouble saved, and with their food I would grow strong to fight against themselves. These are the terms that I would ask, O foster-father Fergus, of my foes.' Those were his words, O Queen, when he was but a child ; I trow he will not be contented now with less."

Then Meave said thoughtfully : " It seems not worse that one man should be slain each day than that a hundred men should fall at night, even were that one man a champion of our host. I think it better to accept his terms. Go back to him, O Fergus, and if he is agreed, say we accept and will abide by those conditions. So we may find at length a little peace."

CHAPTER XII

Etarcomal's Well-deserved Fate

SO Fergus turned his horses to go back where he had
left Cuchulain. He thought to go alone, attended
only by his charioteer, but as he drove along, the
sound of wheels behind him made him turn, and close
to him he saw a youth who, sitting in his chariot, seemed
to follow hard behind, as though to catch him up.
Fergus recognized the rider as a rich young chief, brave
but foolhardy, who was known among the host as one
who thought too highly of himself, considering he had
little experience of war.

"Whither away, Etarcomal?" said Fergus, for that
was the youth's name. "I wish to go with you,"
replied the lad; "I hear that you are on your way
to seek this wonderful Cuchulain, of whom all men
talk. I feel inclined myself to have a look at
him."

"I give you sound advice," said Fergus, "and best it
were for you to heed my words. Turn round your
chariot, and go home again."

"Why so?" Etarcomal asked. "Because I know full
well that if you, with your light-minded insolence, come
into contact with this great Hound of War, in all his
fierceness and his terrible strength, trouble will befall.
You will provoke him with your childishness, and ill will
come, before I can prevent it. Go home again, I will

not have you come." "If we fell out, could you not rescue me ?" Etarcomal said. "No doubt I should endeavour to succour you ; but if you seek a quarrel, or with your foolish words provoke Cuchulain, I make no promises ; you must defend yourself, and take your chance."

"Truly I seek no quarrel with this valiant mighty chief ; I will but look upon his powerful form and note his face, and then return with you." "So be it, then," said Fergus, "let us on."

Afar off, Laeg espied them as they came. He and his master sat beneath the trees close on the borders of a little wood, playing a game of chess ; but none the less he kept a sharp lookout, watching where lay the distant camp of Meave. A single chariot approaches from the camp, and furiously it drives across the plain : "I think he comes to seek us, Cucuc," said the man. "What sort is the rider in that chariot ?" questioned Cu. "I know him well, and short the time since he was here before. Like to the side of a massive mountain, standing sheer from out the plain, the chariot in which that warrior rides. Mighty as the leafy branching crown of a kingly tree which grows before a chieftain's door, the bushy, loose, dark-ruddy locks upon that warrior's head. Around him is a mantle of a noble purple hue, with fringes of bright gold, clasped with a pin of gleaming gold and set with sparkling stones. In his left hand he bears his bossy shield and in his right a polished spear, with rings of metal bound from point to haft. Upon his thigh a sword so long and great, I took it for the rudder of a boat, or for a rainbow arched across the skies. Far-travelled and a man of might, meseems, the guest who cometh here." "Welcome to me the coming of this hero and old friend," Cuchulain cried, " my master Fergus, who approaches us."

" I see behind a second smaller chariot, which seems to accompany the massive chariot of Fergus. Spritely and full of life are the two prancing chariot-steeds, and young and bright the man who sits within."

" 'Tis likely that some one of Erin's youthful chiefs has ventured out to have a look at me, under the guardianship of Fergus. I hear they all are talking of me in the camp. Perhaps he wants to have a bout with me, good Laeg, but better were it that he stayed at home."

Up dashed the steeds of Fergus' chariot, and in an instant he had sprung to earth and stood beside Cuchulain. " Welcome, O Fergus, old familiar friend. Welcome, my foster-master and my guardian," Cuchulain cried, and warmly he embraced him. " Upon this lonely watch that I am forced to keep all solitary and unaided day by day against the men of Erin, most welcome the dear face of an old friend."

" Then thou art glad indeed ? " Fergus exclaimed, surprised.

" Certainly and indeed, I am right glad ! Not much have I to offer in this wild desert place, but all I have is fully at your service. When o'er the plain a flock of wild-duck wings its way, one of them you shall have, with, in good times, the full half of another ; if fish come up the estuary, a whole one shall be yours, with all that appertains to it ; a handful of fresh cress straight from the brook, a spray of marshwort or of green sorrel shall be yours ; 'tis all I have to give. When you are thirsty, from the running stream that trickles through the sand, you'll get a drink ; and if, some fall of day, a hero calls you to come down and wage a single combat at the ford, you shall take rest and sleep, while I will fight your enemy or keep watch."

" Truly I well believe it," Fergus said. " Too well I know what straits for food and drink have fallen on thee in this raid, and well I know thy hospitable mind. But at this time we seek not food and drink, nor can we stay for combats or for rest ; I come at Ailill's and at Meave's command, to tell thee what we think are thy conditions, and that we will hold and keep to them."

" I too will keep the compact brought by Fergus' hand, and to the letter I will carry it out," the hero said ; " only abide awhile with me, and let us waste a little time in talk of olden days."

" I dare not stay to talk at this time, O beloved foster-son," Fergus replied ; " the men of Erin doubt me, and will think that I am proving traitor to their cause, and betraying them to thee ; for well they know I love thee, though, alas ! at this time I am fighting with my country's foes and thine. One thing I ask of thee for old affection's sake, because thou art my pupil and my friend, that if at any moment in this war, thou and myself art found opposing each the other face to face, thou then wilt turn and flee before me, that upon my pupil and my foster-son I be not forced to redden my sword in fight. Promise me this."

" Though I be indeed thy pupil and thy foster-son," replied the youth, " yet loth am I to promise this ; never have I turned my back on any friend or foe, and to flee even before thee, O Fergus, likes me not. Ask me not this, but any other thing gladly and joyfully I grant to thee." " No need for thee to feel like this," Fergus replied ; " no shame to thee is what I contemplate, but only that our ancient love and friendship be not marred

Do in this thing but what I ask, and I in my turn, in the final battle of the Raid, when thou art wounded sore and drenched with blood, will turn and flee from thee. And surely if the men of Erin see Fergus in flight, they too will fly, and all the host of Meave will scatter and disperse, like clouds before the sun."

"On these terms willingly I give my word; for so will Ulster profit by my flight. Now fare thee well, good Fergus. Bid the host of Meave to send their strongest and their best to combat with me, one by one, and I will give a good account to Ulster of them, or will die." Then a right loving leave they took each of the other, and Fergus set out to return to the camp.

But the lad Etarcomal sat on still, looking at Cuchulain, and for the first time the hero noticed him.

"Who are you, and what are you staring at, fellow?" he asked. "I look at you," he said. "You can see me easily enough, I am not very big. But if you knew it, little animals can be dangerous sometimes, and so can I. But now that you have had a good look at me, tell me what you think of me."

"I do not think much of you," Etarcomal said. "You seem to me a very nice, wonderfully pretty youth and clever at playing sports and feats; but that anyone should think of you as a good warrior or a brave man, or should call you the 'Hero of Valour' or the 'Hammer of Destruction,' that I cannot understand. I do not know, indeed, why anyone should be afraid of you. I am not afraid of you at all."

"I am aware," said Cuchulain, "that you came hither under the protection of my master Fergus, and that he is surety for your safe return; but by the gods whom I adore, I swear that if it were not for the honour of Fergus, only your broken bones and disjointed members should have been sent back to Meave after those insolent words."

"No need to threaten me," said Etarcomal; "I was here when you made an agreement with Fergus to fight every day one of the men of Ireland. By that wonderful agreement that he made with you, none other of the men of Erin shall come to-morrow to meet you but only I myself. To-day I do not touch you, but let you live a little longer."

"However early you may choose to come to the ford," said Cuchulain, "you will find me there before you. I promise you I will not run away."

Etarcomal turned his chariot to drive back to the camp. But hardly had he started when he exclaimed, "Do you know, fellow, I have promised to fight the famous Cuchulain to-morrow at the dawn? Now, do you think it best to wait till then, or to go back and fight him now? I do not know that I can wait."

"I should say," replied the charioteer, "that if you mean to fight Cuchulain at all, 'twere better to get it over while he is close at hand." "Turn the chariot, and drive it left-handwise towards Cuchulain, for by that sign we challenge him. I swear by all my gods, I never will go back until I take the head of this wild youth, and stick it up on high before the host."

Laeg saw the chariot returning over the plain. "The last chariot-rider who went from us is coming back again, Cucuc!" said he. "What does he want?" said Cu. "He is challenging us by driving with the left side of the chariot towards us," answered Laeg.

"I do not want to fight the boy," Cuchulain said. "Shamed should I be were I to slay a lad who came hither under the guardianship of Fergus. Get me my sword out of its sheath, however, Laeg; I'll give him a good fright and send him home."

Etarcomal came up. "What do you want now, fellow?" cried Cuchulain, vexed. "I am come back to fight you," said the lad. "I will not fight you, now or any time," Cuchulain said. "By all the rules of war you are obliged to fight, for I have challenged you."

Then Cuchulain took his sword, and with one stroke he sliced away the sod beneath Etarcomal's feet, laying him flat upon the ground, his face turned upwards. "Now go," Cuchulain said, "I wash my hands of you. Had you not come under the care of my good master Fergus, I would have cut you into little bits a while ago. Beware, for I have given you a warning." Slowly Etarcomal rose from the ground. "I will not budge a step until I have your head," he said doggedly, though in his heart he began to be afraid. Then Cuchulain played on him another sword-feat; with one clean stroke he shore off all his hair, from back to front, from ear to ear, till not a hair remained; but not a single drop of blood he drew or even scratched his skin. "Now off with you," he said a second time, "you look absurd enough, I promise you. The men of Erin and the chiefs will laugh when you go back, and cool your pride a bit."

"I will not stir until I have your head; either you gain the victory over me, and win renown, or I take off your head from you, and get the glory and the praise of it," he sullenly replied.

"Well, let it be as you desire, then, and I am he who takes your head from you, and I shall win the glory and renown of which you make so much." And at that word, with one stroke of his weapon Cuchulain smote the boy,

and cut him right in twain, so that he fell divided to the
ground. Terrified, the charioteer turned round the
horse's head and fled back towards the camp. Close to
the tents he came on Fergus, who leisurely and thoughtfully drove home. He saw the empty chariot passing
him. "Where is your master, fellow?" Fergus cried.
"Has he not come with you?" "Even now he has been
cut in twain by that fierce, powerful hero, at the ford,"
the man cried, looking scared; and, waiting not for any
answer, he tore on to the camp.

"O come, my wild young fosterling," thought Fergus
to himself, "this is too bad indeed, to slay a lad who came
under my protection. Turn back the chariot," said he
aloud, "we go back to Cuchulain at the ford."

No sooner had they come where Cuchulain stood
brooding above the body of Etarcomal, and wiping down
his bloody sword, than Fergus called aloud, "What came
to you, you hasty sprite, you hot-headed young fury;
could you not keep your hands from slaying even a lad
who came merely to look at you and under my protection? This act of yours I do not understand at all. It
is not like the deed or custom of my foster-son."

"Be not so angry, O my friend and master," gently
Cuchulain replied; "all that I could I did to send him
safely home. Ask his own charioteer all that has taken
place. He would not take a warning, and in the end
I must have stood and had my head chopped off without
defence, or, as I did, taken his head from him. Would it
have pleased you better had I let the lad take off my
head from me?"

"Indeed, I should not have been pleased at all; the
lad was insolent and foolhardy, and right well deserved
his ignominious death. Tie his feet to the chariot-tail,

my charioteer, and I will take him home." So to his own chariot Fergus tied the boy, and dragged him back to camp. Meave saw them come, and heard the people shouting as they passed, the bleeding body draggled in the dust.

"Why, how is this?" she cried. "Is this, O Fergus of the mighty deeds, the fashion in which you bring back the tender whelp who went out from us but some hours ago, brilliant in life and gaiety and youth? the whelp we sent out safely, as we thought, in Fergus' guardianship? Of wondrous value is the guardianship of Fergus; and safe is he who trusts himself to it!"

"It is not well, O Queen, that whelps so brazen and untried as this should face the Hound of War; let them remain henceforth in safety in their kennels, gnawing their bones. The lad Etarcomal was bold and insolent; full well he reaped the fate he brought upon himself!"

Sadly, but with all honour, they buried Etarcomal, heaping his grave, and rearing a stone above it with his name engraven thereupon in ogam lines. That night Cuchulain did not molest the men of Erin because they were occupied with funeral rites; but provisions and apparel were sent to him, according to the treaty made between them.

CHAPTER XIII

The Fight with Spits of Holly-Wood

THENCEFORWARD day by day some warrior of the camp of Meave and Ailill went forth to fight Cuchulain, and day by day they fell before him. But at first, because he was young, the prime warriors of Connaught despised him, and refused to fight with him, and Meave offered them great gifts and made large promises to persuade them to contend with him. Among the chiefs was a rough burly man and a good fighter, whose name was Nacrantal, whom Meave used all her arts to force to challenge Cuchulain. And in the end, when she had promised him large gifts of land and even Finnabar, her daughter, to be his wife, he was induced to go. But even so he went not out as though to fight an equal. No arms or armour would he take, but for his sole protection nine spits of holly-wood, sharp at the points and hardened in the fire.

With these small weapons in his hand, one morning early he set forth to seek Cuchulain. He found the hero busied in pursuing wild-fowl that were flying overhead; for from the birds of the air and fish of the streams, and from the berries of the hedge and cresses of the brook, long had he been obliged to get his daily meal. And even now, although at times Meave kept her word and sent provision over to her foe, yet often she forgot or failed to keep her promise, so angry was she when from day

H   113 to day her strong men were cut down before his sword.

He spied Nacrantal advancing thus unarmed, and, all as though he had not seen him come, he went on with the stalking of the birds.

Closer the warrior drew and with good aim he flung his spits of wood to pierce Cuchulain. But still the youth, not stopping for a moment in his task, leaped lightly over each spit as it fell, so that they struck the ground quite harmlessly, not one of them so much as touching him. The nine spits thrown, Nacrantal turned away and sought the camp. " Not much I think of this renowned Cuchulain of whom men talk so big ; hardly had he perceived me coming up, than off he ran as fast as he could go ! "

" We thought as much," said Meave ; " right well we knew that if a warrior brave and fully trained were sent against him, soon would this beardless braggart take to his heels."

When Fergus heard these boasts of Meave, he grew ashamed ; for strange, indeed, it seemed to him to hear it said that his young foster-son would flee from any single man, however bold or stout that man might be. Straightway he called for one of the princes of Ulster who was in Meave's camp, and sent him to Cuchulain. This was the message that he bore. " Fergus would have Cuchulain understand, that though when standing before warriors he once had done great deeds, better it were that he should hide himself in some secret place where none could find him or hear of him more, than that he should run away from any single man, whoever that man might be. Say to Cuchulain that not greater is the shame that falls upon himself,

than Ulster's shame and ignominy and disgrace, because
he stands to watch the border-land in Ulster's stead."

"Who said I ran away?" Cuchulain said, surprised,
when the message was delivered to him. "Who dared
to brag and tell such tales of me?"

"Nacrantal told this story in the camp, and all the
warriors boast among themselves that at the very sight
of a trained warrior you were afraid and quickly put to
flight."

"Did you and Fergus heed a boast like that?"
replied the youth. "Do you and Fergus not yet understand that I, Cuchulain, fight no men unarmed, or
messengers, or charioteers, but only men-at-arms, fully
equipped? That man came out against me all unarmed;
no weapons in his hand but bits of wood, with which he
played some childish games, throwing them in the air.
Let but Nacrantal come to-morrow morn and fight me
like a warrior at the ford, with all his weapons, manlike, in his hand; he then shall take his answer back
from me. And tell him, that if he comes before the day
dawn, or long after it, he will find Cuchulain waiting there
for him."

Long and tedious seemed that night to Nacrantal, for
eagerly he watched the coming of the hour when he
should meet Cuchulain at the ford, and make an end of
him. Early he rose, and bade his charioteer to bring his
heavy weapons in a cart, while he went forwards to the
meeting-place. There at the ford he saw Cuchulain
stand, awaiting his coming, as he had promised.

"Are you Cuchulain?" said Nacrantal, for now he
stood much closer to him and observed his youthfulness.

"What if I were?" said he. "If you are Cuchulain,
indeed, I am come here to tell you that I will not fight

with any beardless boy; not in the least inclined am I
to carry back to camp the head of a little playful lamb!"

"I am not the man you seek at all," Cuchulain cried;
"go round the hill and you will find him there."

Now while Nacrantal made his way to the other side
of the hill, Cuchulain came to Laeg, his charioteer.
"Smear me a false beard with blackberry juice," he
said. "No warrior of fame will fight with me, because
I have no beard." Laeg took the juice of blackberries,
and sheep's wool, and with it made a long two-pointed
beard, such as prime warriors wore, and twined the ends
and caught them in his belt, dyeing it black with juice.
Then on the hero came anger and his battle-fury, such
as came on him when a combat lay before him with a
good warrior, or when he alone should fight a host.

A subtle change came over all his face. The radiant
youthfulness passed away, and all the boyishness
Nacrantal had seen a while ago, and in its place a stern
ferocious look, as of a prime warrior waiting for his foe.
His stature seemed to grow, his form to enlarge, and
terrible in its strength and fierceness was his aspect as
he donned his fighting-gear. He grasped his weapons
in his hand, and with great strides he hastened round
the hill.

So great his wrath and eagerness for combat, that as
he passed a standing pillar-stone no smaller than himself, in flinging his mantle round him as he went he caught
the stone up in his mantle's folds and carried it along
with him, but never was he conscious of its weight, or
even knew he carried it.

Now in this guise Nacrantal knew him not. "Where is
Cuchulain?" inquired he of the men who came with him.
"The lad said that we should find him round the hill."

" Cuchulain stands before you yonder," said the Ulstermen who had come out to watch the fight.

" It was not thus that he appeared before me yesterday," Nacrantal said. " Cuchulain seemed a stripling, and his beard not grown, but this prime warrior hath a mighty beard."

" Nevertheless, I counsel you, defend yourself from this prime warrior," Fergus replied; " that will be much the same to you as though you did contend with Cuchulain himself."

Then Nacrantal made a furious onset at Cuchulain with his sword, but it struck on the pillar-stone that he carried beneath his cloak, and broke off short, close to his hand. Before he could recover from the thrust, Cuchulain sprang upon him, and lifting his sword on high with both hands, he brought it down on his adversary's head, and there on his own shield he fell dead, smitten with one blow. " Alas!" said Nacrantal as he fell, " they said true who said that you were the best warrior in all Ireland."

From that time forward, it was not easy for Meave to get her men of war to enter into combat with Cuchulain; for each one of them said, " Not I; I will not go, why should my clan furnish a man to go out to certain death?" So Meave was forced to promise great rewards and possessions to her warriors before she could induce them to take arms against Cuchulain.

CHAPTER XIV

The Combat with Ferdia

NOW among the hosts of Meave was Ferdia, son of Daman, Cuchulain's companion and friend when together they learned warlike feats in Shadow-land.

All the while that Cuchulain fought with the chiefs of Connaught, Ferdia remained aloof, keeping within his tent, far from the tent of Ailill and of Meave, whose ways and cunning plans he liked not. For though against the men of Ulster in general he would have aided them, he would not take part in single combat against his friend and fellow-pupil. For he thought on his love for his old comrade, and the days of youth that they had spent together, and the conflicts and dangers that side by side they twain had faced; and day by day he sent his messengers to watch the fighting and to bring him word, for he feared lest harm should come to Cuchulain, fighting alone and single-handed against all the mighty men of Meave. Each evening came his watchers back, bringing him tidings, and greatly he rejoiced because he heard of the prowess of Cuchulain and of destruction inflicted on the hosts of Meave.

But one day, when the fighting had been going on for weeks, and many of her best men and fighting warriors had been plucked off, Meave thought of Ferdia; and at the council-meeting of that night, when the chief men

118

and counsellors met to settle who should go on the
morrow to fight Cuchulain, she said, " Who should go,
if not Ferdia, son of Daman, the warrior whose valour
and feats are as the valour and feats of Cuchulain himself?
For in the one school were they trained, and equal they
are in every way, in courage and the knowledge of
weapons and in skill in feats of strength.   Well matched
these two would be, if they were to fight together."
And all the men of war said, " It is a good thought;
Ferdia shall go."

So messengers were sent to Ferdia to bring him to
Meave, for she said she would see him herself, to persuade him with her own mouth to go against his comrade.   But when the heralds came to the tent of Ferdia,
he knew well enough for what purpose they had come,
and he refused to see them, neither would he go with
them to Meave.

When Meave heard that, she sent again, but her
messengers this time were not men of war and heralds,
but satirists, to abuse him and to warn him that he
should die a shameful death, and that disgrace should
fall upon him before all the host, if he obeyed not the
Queen's commands.   And they gave their message to
Ferdia, and told him that his warrior fame would pass
away from him, and that he would be spoken of by his
comrades with ignominy and disgrace if he did not come.

When Ferdia heard that they would spread evil tales
about him, and disgrace him before the host of his own
fellow-warriors, he said, " If I must die, it were better
to die in fair and open fight, even with a friend, than
to die disgraced, skulking as a coward before my fellow-
men and comrades."

So he went with the messengers, and when he came to

the Queen's tent, all who were in the tent, both great
lords and nobles, rose up to receive Ferdia, and he was
conducted with honour and reverence to the presence
of the Queen.   Then the Queen greeted him and rose up
and placed him at her right hand, and spoke kindly to
him.   And a great feast was made, and that night Ferdia
was entertained with right great dignity, and food and
pleasant liquors were served out of the best, so that he
became merry and disposed to do all that Meave demanded.   Then, when he was forgetful of all but the
company in which he was, Meave set before his mind the
princely gifts that she would bestow upon him if he
would free her from her enemy Cuchulain, the destroyer
of her host.   These were the great rewards she offered
him ; a noble chariot with steeds such as befitted a king,
and a train of twelve men-at-arms, fully equipped, to
accompany him, as princes and great chiefs are accompanied, wherever he moved.   Moreover, she promised
him lands broad and fertile on the plains of Connaught,
free of tribute or rent for ever, and that he should be her
own son-in-law and next the throne, for she said that
she would give him her daughter Finnabar to wife.
Now Finnabar sat next to Ferdia at his left hand, and
she was fair to look upon, with ruddy cheeks and hair of
gold, and the garments of a princess flowing round her ;
and Ferdia was dazzled with her beauty, and with the
lavish offers made by Meave, until he was ready to
promise anything in life she wished.   And when, the
banquet over, young Finnabar arose and filled a cup
brim full with mead, and kissed the cup and handed it to
him, he knew not what to say.   For still the memory of
his youth in Shadow-land, Cuchulain's love to him and
his love to Cuchulain came over him again, and more than

half he loathed what he had done. So looking now behind and now before, and loitering in his mind, he said aloud, "Rather, O Meave, than do the thing you ask, and ply my warrior-hand upon my friend, I would pick out six champions of your host, the best and bravest among all your men, and fight with them. With each alone or all together willingly would I contend."

Then from her queenly robe Meave plucked her brooch, more precious to her than any gift, for all the kings and queens of Connaught had worn that splendid brooch, the sign and symbol of their sovereignty; she stooped, and with her own royal hands, she placed the glittering jewelled pin in Ferdia's mantle.

"See, warrior," she said, "I have bestowed on you the princely dignity, so that you now will rank beside the King; and as for those six chosen champions you have named, I give them to you as your sureties that these our promises will be fulfilled; go now and fight Cuchulain." At that Ferdia looked up, and caught the glance of Finnabar most sweetly smiling down into his face, and close beside her the queen bending over him, and Erin's chiefs and warriors standing round; and all his mind was lifted up within his breast, and he forgot Cuchulain and their ancient love, and said: "Though in this fight I fall, O Queen, I go to meet the Hound."

Fergus was standing at the king's right hand, and when he overheard those words that Ferdia spoke, fear for his foster-son rose in his heart. For well he knew the might of Ferdia's arms, and that he was of all the chiefs of Meave the bravest and the best, and well he knew that all the feats that Scáth had taught to Cuchulain, save only the "Gae Bolga" or Body Spear, she taught to Ferdia likewise. Ferdia besides was older than Cuchulain, and riper in experience of war, well-built and powerful. So when he heard those words, Fergus went out in haste, and though the night was late he sprang into his chariot, and set forth to find Cuchulain.

"I am rejoiced at thy coming, my good friend Fergus," said Cuchulain, as the chariot drew up beside him; "too seldom is it that on this Raid of Cooley we twain meet face to face."

"Gladly I accept thy welcome, O foster-son and pupil," Fergus said. "I come to tell thee who it is that on the morrow has bound himself to meet thee at the ford, and urge thee to beware of him."

"I am attentive," Cuchulain answered. "Who is the man who comes?"

"'Tis thine own friend, thy comrade and fellow-pupil, the great and valiant champion of the west, Ferdia, son of Daman, called of all men the 'Horn-Skin,' so tough and strong for fight is he, so hard to pierce or wound with sword or spear. Beware of him, it may be even the Gae Bolga will not avail to harm the flesh of Ferdia."

"Upon my word and truly," cried Cuchulain, "this is ill news you bring; never should I have thought my friend would challenge me."

"We thought as much," Fergus replied; "we all avowed thou wouldst not relish the coming of Ferdia; for of all warriors that have hitherto come to the combat at the ford, he is most formidable and best prepared. Be wary, therefore, rest well this night, and try and prove thine arms; come to the combat fresh and amply armed."

"Utterly dost thou mistake my meaning, Fergus, my friend; not from any fear of him, but from the greatness of my love for him, I hold his challenge strange and unwelcome. For this cause only I regret his coming."

"Yet and in truth," Fergus replied, "no shame to thee or any man to be afraid of Ferdia, for in his arms is strength as of a hundred men; swords wound him not, spears pierce him not, and tried and mettlesome his heart and arms."

"Now this, O Fergus, deem I strange indeed, that thou of all men shouldst warn me to be careful before any single warrior in Ireland; well it is that it was thee, O Fergus, and not another man, who brought me such a warning. From the beginning of winter till the coming of spring have I stood here alone, fighting each day a hardy warrior, and never have I turned back before the best fighting man whom Meave has sent against me, nor shall I turn back before Ferdia, O Fergus. For as the rush bows down before the torrent in the midst of the stream, so will Ferdia bow down under my sword, if once he shows himself here in combat with the Hound of Ulster."

That night there was no cheerfulness nor gaiety nor quiet pleasure in the tent of Ferdia, as there was wont to be on other nights; for he had made known what Meave had said to him and the command laid upon him to go on the morrow to combat with Cuchulain; and though Ferdia was merry and triumphant on his return, because of the gifts of the queen and the affection of Finnabar, and all the flattery that had been skilfully put upon him, it was not so with the men that were of his own household, for they understood that wherever those two champions of battle, those two slayers of a hundred should meet together, one of the two must fall, or both must fall: and well they knew that if one only should fall there, it would not be Cuchulain who would give way, for it was not easy to combat with Cuchulain on the Raid of the Kine of Cooley.

As for Ferdia, through the first part of the night, he slept heavily, being overcome with the liquor he had taken, and the fatigues of the day ; but towards the middle of the night, he awoke from his slumber, and remembered the combat on the morrow, and anxiety and heavy care began to weigh him down ; fear of Cuchulain on the one hand, and sorrow that he had promised to do combat with his friend, and fear of losing Finnabar and Meave's great promises on the other ; and he tossed about, and could sleep no longer.   So he arose and called his charioteer, and said, " Yoke me my horses, and come with me ; I shall sleep better at the ford."   But his charioteer began to dissuade him, " It would be better for you not to go," said he, " trouble will come of this meeting.   It is not a small thing for any warrior in the world to do combat against the Bulwark of Ulster, even against Cuchulain."   " Be silent, my servant," he said ; " though the ravens of carnage croak over the ford, ready to tear my flesh, it is not the part of a valiant man to turn back from his challenge ; away with us to the ford before the break of dawn."   So the horses were harnessed and the chariot yoked, and they dashed onwards to the ford.   " Take the cushions and skins out of the chariot, good my lad," said Ferdia, " and spread them under me upon the bank that I may take deep repose and refreshing sleep upon them ; little sleep I got this night, on account of the anxiety of the combat that is before me on the morn."   So the servant unharnessed the horses, and spread the skins and chariot-cushions under Ferdia, and yet he could not sleep.

" Look out, lad, and see that Cuchulain is not coming,"
he said. " He is not, I am sure," said the lad. " But
look again for certain," said the warrior. " Cuchulain
is not such a little speck that we should not see him if
he were there," replied the lad. " You are right, O boy ;
Cuchulain has heard that a prime warrior is coming to
meet him to-day, and he has thought well to keep away
on that account."

" I should not say bad things about Cuchulain in his
absence," said the lad. " Do you not remember how,
when you were fighting in Eastern lands, your sword was
wrenched from you, and you would have perished by
the hands of your enemies, but that Cuchulain rushed
forward to recover it, and he slew a hundred warriors
on his path before he got your sword and brought it back
to you ? Do you remember where we were that night ? "
" I have forgotten," Ferdia said. " We were in the
house of Scáth's steward," said the boy; "and do you
not remember how the ugly churl of a cook hit you in the
back with a three-pronged meat-spit, and sent you out
over the door like a shot ? And do you not recollect,
how Cuchulain came into the house and gave the rascal
a blow with his sword, and chopped him in two to
avenge you ? If it were only on that account, you should
not say that you are a better warrior than Cuchulain."
" Why did you not remind me of all these things before
we came here ? " said Ferdia; " I doubt whether I
should have come if I had remembered all this at first.
Pull up the cushions under my head, or I shall never get
to sleep. Will you be sure to keep a sharp look-out ? "
" I will watch so well, that unless men drop out of the
clouds to fight with you, no one shall escape me," said
the boy; "and I will sing you to sleep with a lullaby."

Then as Ferdia sank into repose and refreshing slumber, he began to croon this ancient song which Grainne sang over Dermot, when he was hiding from Finn in the forests of the west.

" Sleep a little, a little little, thou need'st feel no fear or dread,
Youth to whom my love is given, I am watching near thy head.

Sleep a little, with my blessing, Dermot of the lightsome eye,
I will guard thee as thou dreamest, none shall harm while I am by.

Sleep, O little lamb, whose home-land was the country of the lakes,
In whose womb the torrents rumble, from whose sides the river breaks.

Sleep as slept the ancient Poet, Dedach, minstrel of the South,
When he snatched from Conall Cernach, Eithne of the laughing mouth.

Sleep as slept the comely Finncha 'neath the falls of Assaroe,
Who, when stately Slaine sought him, laid the Hard-head Failbe low.

Sleep in joy, as slept fair Aine, Gailan's daughter of the West,
Where, amid the flaming torches, she and Duvac found their rest.

Sleep as Dega, who in triumph, 'ere the sun sank o'er the land,
Stole the maiden he had craved for, plucked her from fierce Decell's hand.

Fold of Valour, sleep a little, Glory of the Western World,
I am wondering at thy beauty, marvelling how thy locks are curled.

Like the parting of two children, bred together in one home,
Like the breaking of two spirits, if I did not see you come.

Swirl the leaves before the tempest, moans the night-wind o'er the lea,
Down its stoney bed the streamlet hurries onward to the sea.

In the swaying boughs the linnet twitters in the darkling light,
On the upland wastes of heather wings the grouse its heavy flight.

In the marshland by the river sulks the otter in its den,
And the piping of the peewect sounds across the distant fen.

On the stormy mere the wild-duck pushes outward from the brake,
With her downy brood around her seeks the centre of the lake.

In the east the restless roe-deer bellows to its frightened hind,
On thy track the wolf-hounds gather, sniffing up against the wind.

Yet, O Dermot, sleep a little, this one night our fear hath fled,
Lad to whom my love is given, see, I watch beside thy bed."

CHAPTER XV

The Fall of Ferdia

ON that night before the conflict, Cuchulain also was preparing himself for what lay before him on the morrow. No sooner had Fergus left him, than Laeg his charioteer came to him, and said, "How, my master, will you spend this night?" "I had not thought," said Cuchulain, "of spending it in any other way than other nights. What would you have me do?"

"I am thinking," said the charioteer, "that Ferdia will not come alone to the ford to-morrow, but that in such a fight as this, the chief warriors and nobles of Ireland will be present to see the combat. And sure am I that Ferdia will come to the combat washed and bathed, with his hair fresh cut and plaited, in all the magnificence of a battle-champion; but you are fatigued and worn after these combats, unwashed and uncombed, for it has not been possible to adorn yourself in these times of strife and lonely living. Glad should I be, therefore, if you would return to your wife, to Emer of the beautiful hair, where she is awaiting you at Slieve Fuad, and there adorn yourself, so that you may not appear dishevelled and distressed before the men of Erin." So that night Cuchulain went home to Emer, and gentle and loving was she to him after their separation from each other; and very early in the

128

morning he returned refreshed and comforted to the place where he had been encamped. " Harness our horses for us now, O Laeg, and yoke our war-chariot, for an early-rising champion was Ferdia in the old time. If he is waiting for us at the ford, maybe he is thinking the morning long."

So the chariot was yoked and Cuchulain sprang into it, and with the speed of a swallow, or of a wild deer flying before the hounds, he set forth to the place of conflict. And round the head of the High Rock and Bulwark of Ulster, even Cuchulain, there gathered the Fairy People of the Glens and the Wild Wizard Folk of the air and mists, and the demon sprites of war and battle, shouting and screaming before the impending conflict; they hovered over him and around him, as it was their wont to do when he went to mortal combat, and the air was filled with their noises and hoarse wailings, rejoicing in the slaughter.

Soon, indeed, the charioteer of Ferdia heard the uproar, and he arose and began to awaken his master, chanting a song in praise of Cuchulain, and calling on Ferdia to arise and meet him. Then Ferdia sprang up.

" How looks Cuchulain this morning ? " he cried. " Surely weak and faint he comes to the ford, after a whole winter passed in combating the men of Erin."

" Not with signs of weakness or of faintness advances the warrior towards us," the charioteer replied, " but with clangour of arms and clatter of wheels and the trampling of horses equal to a king's, this warrior draweth nigh. The clanking of the missile-shields I hear, and the hiss of spears, the roll of the chariot with the beautiful silver yoke. Heroic the champion who urges on the steeds, a noble hawk of battle, a martial hero, a Hound of Combat. A year agone I knew that he would come, the stay of Emain, Ulster's watchful Hound. Over Bray Rossa I perceive him come, skirting the hamlet of the Ancient Tree, along the broad highway; the Hound, the Hound of Ulster in his might."

"O come, fellow, have done with this belauding of our enemy; methinks a bribe has passed from him to you, to bid you sing his praises. He has slept sound, no doubt, for he is late. I tire of waiting here to kill him. Let us get ready now at once to meet him."

Then Cuchulain drew up on the borders of the ford. And on his way he had appealed to his charioteer, instructing him that should he grow weak in the fight, or seem to be giving way before Ferdia, he was to taunt him with cowardice, and fling reproaches and bad names at him, so that his anger would arise and he would fight more valiantly than before; but if he were doing well, his charioteer was to stand upon the brink and praise him, to keep his spirits up. And Laeg laughed and said, " Is it on this wise that I must taunt thee ? ' Arise, Cuchulain, a yearling babe would fight better than thou ; that man Ferdia overthrows thee as easily as a cat waves her tail ; like foam dancing on the water, he blows thee along ; he pulls thee about as a mother might play with her little boy ! ' How will that do ? "

"That will do very well," said Cuchulain, laughing also; " surely I shall fight better after that." And with that they came to the ford, and Cuchulain drew up upon the north side, and Ferdia on the south side of the stream.

"What has brought thee hither, O Cua ? " said Ferdia. Now Cua means " squint-eyed," and Ferdia called him by this scoffing name, because he wished to appear bold and unconcerned, though in his heart he feared and was ashamed; yet he liked not to show his fear. "Welcome thy coming, O squint-eyed one."

But Cuchulain answered seriously, "Up to to-day, O Ferdia, no greeting would have been more welcome than greeting of thine, for I should have esteemed it the welcome of a friend. To-day, however, I do not count it such. And indeed, Ferdia, more fitting would it have been that I should offer welcome to thee, than that thou shouldst offer it to me, seeing that it is thou who hast intruded into my province and not I into thine. It was for me to challenge thee to fight, and not for thee to challenge me."

"What induced thee to come to this combat at all, O Cuchulain," replied Ferdia, "as though thou wert mine equal? Dost thou not remember, that in the old days when we were with Scáth, thou wast in attendance on me as my pupil, and thy place it was to tie up my javelins for me, and to make my couch?"

"That indeed is true," Cuchulain answered gravely; "for I was in those years thy junior in age and standing, in feats and in renown. I did then but my duty. But to-day it is no longer so; there is not now in the world any champion to whom I am not equal, or whom I would refuse to fight. O Ferdia, my friend, it was not well for thee that thou didst listen to the enticements of Ailill and of Meave, urging thee to come out and fight with me. When we were with Scáth it was side by side that we went to every battle and every battle-field, to conflicts and to feats of war. Together we wandered through strange unknown lands, together we encountered dangers and difficulty; in all things we stood side by side, aiding and supporting one another.

"We were heart's companions.
  Comrades in assemblies,
Brothers, who together
  Slept the dreamless sleep.
In all paths of peril,
  In all days of danger,
Each of us, as brothers,
  Would his brother keep."

"O Cuchulain of the beautiful feats," Ferdia replied, " though together we have learned the secrets of knowledge, and though I have listened now to thy recital of our bonds of fellowship, it is from me that thy first wounds shall come; think not upon our old comradeship, O Hound, for it shall not profit thee; O Hound, it shall not profit thee. We lose our time in this wise; let us choose our weapons and begin. What arms shall we use to-day, O Cuchulain ? "

" It is thine to choose our arms to-day, for it was thou who first didst reach the ford."

" Dost thou remember," said Ferdia, " the missile weapons we used to practise with Scáth ? "   " Full well I remember them," said Cuchulain.

" If thou dost remember them, let us have recourse to them now," said Ferdia.

So they took in their hands their two great protecting shields, engraved with emblematic devices, to cover their bodies, and their eight small sharp-edged shields to throw horizontally, and their eight light javelins, and their eight dirks with ivory handles, and their eight little darts for the fight. Backward and forward flew the weapons between them like bees on the wing on a sunny day. From the dim light of early dawn until midday they continued to throw those weapons, yet although their aim was so good that not one of them missed its mark, so skilful also was the defence, that not a drop of blood was drawn on either side ; all the missiles being caught full on their protecting shields.

" Let us drop these feats now, O Cuchulain," said his adversary, " for it is not by them that our contest will be decided."

" Let us drop them, indeed, if the time be come." Then they ceased from casting, and threw their weapons into the hands of their charioteers.

" What weapons shall we resort to next, O Cuchulain ? " said Ferdia.

" With thee is the choice of weapons to-day," said Cuchulain again.

" Let us then take our straight, polished, hardened spears," said Ferdia, " with their flaxen strings to cast them with." So they took their great protecting shields in their hands, and their well-trimmed spears, and they continued to shoot and harass each other from the full middle of the day till eventide. And although the defence was not less careful than before, yet was the casting so good, that each of them drew blood and inflicted wounds upon the other that afternoon.

" Let us now stop casting for the present, O Cuchulain," said his adversary. " Let us stop, indeed, for the evening has come."

They ceased, and threw their weapons into their charioteers' hands, and they ran towards each other, and each put his hands round his comrade's neck, and they gave three loving kisses of old-time friendship to each other before they separated for the night. That night their horses were stabled in the same paddock, and their charioteers lay beside the same fire ; and for the two combatants their charioteers spread beds of green rushes, with pillows such as are needed for wounded men. And the wise physicians and men of healing came to heal and tend them, and they applied salves made from plants, such as wise men know, to their hurts and gashes, and soothing herbs to their wounds; and of every herb and soothing salve that was applied to the wounds of Cuchulain, he sent an equal portion over the ford to Ferdia, so that no man among the host of Meave should be able to say, if Ferdia fell by him, that it was because Cuchulain had better means of healing than he. Also of every kind of food and of pleasant delicious drink that the men of Erin sent to Ferdia, he would send a fair half over the ford northward to Cuchulain, because Cuchulain had few to attend to his wants, whereas all the people of Meave's host were ready to help Ferdia.

So for that night they rested, but early the next morning they arose and came forward to the ford of combat. " What weapons shall we use to-day, O Ferdia ? " said Cuchulain. " Thine is the choice to-day," said Ferdia, " because I chose yesterday."

" Let us then take our broad-bladed heavy spears to-day, for more grave will be the fight between us from the thrusting of our massive spears, than from the shooting of our light casting weapons yesterday, and let our chariots be yoked and our horses harnessed, that we may fight to-day from our chariots." " Let us do so," said the other.

Then the two warriors took their great protecting shields in their hands, and their broad-bladed spears, and they continued to thrust at, to wound and pierce each other from the dim light of early morning till the close of day.

Great and gaping cuts and wounds were upon both of them before the evening-tide. Even their horses were exhausted, and the heroes themselves were fatigued and worn out and dispirited. At length Cuchulain said, " O Ferdia, let us now cease from this, for even our very horses are fatigued, and our charioteers are exhausted. We are not like the Fomors, the giants of the sea, who must be for ever combating against each other ; let the clamour of battle now cease between us, and let us be friends once more."

And Ferdia said, " Let us be at peace, indeed, if the time has come."

Then they ceased fighting, and threw their arms into the hands of their charioteers, and they ran to each other, and each of them put his arms about the neck of the other, and gave him three loving kisses of old friendship.

Their horses were again in the same paddock that night, and their charioteers slept by the same fire ; and beds of green rushes were made for the warriors, with pillows to ease their wounds ; for their injuries that night were so terrible, that the men of healing and the physicians could do nothing for them except to try to stanch the blood that flowed from them with charms and incantations.

And of all the charms and healing salves that were applied to sooth Cuchulain, he bade them take the same to Ferdia, and of every sort of dainty food and of pleasant satisfying drink that Ferdia received, he sent a good half to Cuchulain.

That night they rested as well as they could for their wounds, but early in the morning they arose and repaired to the ford of combat. Cuchulain saw an evil look and a dark lowering brow upon the face of Ferdia that day. " Ill dost thou look to-day, O Ferdia," said Cuchulain. " Thy hair seems to have become darkened, or is it clots of blood I see ? Thine eye is dimmed, and thy own bright face and form have gone from thee. A deep disgrace it is in thee to have come out to fight with thy fellow-pupil; not Finnabar's beauty, nor the praises of Meave or Ailill, nor all the wealth of the world, would have brought me out to fight with thee, my comrade and my friend. Turn now back from this fight to-day, for a fight to death it must be between us, and I have not the heart to fight against thee ; my strength fails me when I think of the evil that will befall thee; turn back, turn back, O friend, for false are the promises of Finnabar and Meave."

" O Cuchulain, gentle Hound, O valiant man, O true champion, bid me not return till the fight be done. Ill would it become me to return to Ailill and to Meave until my task be done. It is not thou who dost work me ill, O Cu of gentle ways ; take the victory and fame that are thine by right, for thou art not in fault. Meave it is who is my undoing; but for all that I shrink not from the contest. My honour, at least, will be avenged ; no fear of death afflicts me. There is a fate that brings each one of us to the place of our final rest in death, a fate none may resist. Reproach me not, O gentle friend and comrade, but let us fight the combat out to-day, as becomes two valiant men and warriors."

" If it must be so, what weapons shall we use ? "

" Let us to-day take to our heavy smiting swords; for sooner shall we attain the end of our conflict by hewing with our swords, than by the thrusting of our spears yesterday." " Let it be so," said Cuchulain. So all that day they hewed and hacked each other with their long, two-edged, heavy swords, and at evening they were wounded and torn from head to foot, so that it was hard to see a whole place on either of them.

"Let us cease now, O Cuchulain," said Ferdia. "Let us cease, indeed, if the time be come," he said.

They threw their arms into the hands of their charioteers, and, though pleasant and cheerful had been the first meeting of those two, it was in sadness and misery that they parted that night.

That evening their horses were not placed in the same paddock, nor did their charioteers sleep beside the same fire, but the charioteer of Cuchulain slept with his master on the north of the ford, and the charioteer of Ferdia slept on the south side of the ford.

Next morning Ferdia went forth alone to the ford of battle, for he knew that on that day the combat would be decided; that then and in that place one of them or both of them would fall.

On that day both heroes put on their full fighting array, their kilts of striped silk next their skin, and a thick apron of brown leather above that to protect the lower part of the body. And they put on their crested battle-helmets, with jewels of rubies and carbuncles and crystals blazing in the front, gems that had been brought from the East to Ireland. And they took their huge shields which covered the whole body, with great bosses in the centre of each shield, and their swords in their right hands, and thus they came forward to the battle. And as they went they displayed the many noble, quick-changing feats that Scáth had taught them, and it was difficult to tell which of them exceeded the other in the performance of those skilful weapon-feats.

Thus they came to the ford. And Cuchulain said:

" What weapons shall we choose this day, O Ferdia ? "
" Thine is the choice to-day," said he. Then Cuchulain
said, " Let us then practise the Feat of the Ford."

" We will do so," said Ferdia; but though he said that,
sorrowful was he in saying it, for he knew that no warrior
ever escaped alive from Cuchulain when they practised
the Feat of the Ford.

Terrible and mighty were the deeds that were done
that day by those two heroes, the Champions of the West,
the pillars of valour of the Gael. Quietly they used
their weapons in the early morning, parrying and casting
with skill and warily, and neither did great harm to the
other ; but about midday, their anger grew hot, and
they drew nearer to each other, and Cuchulain sprang
upon his adversary, and made as though he would cut
off his head over the rim of his shield. But Ferdia gave
the shield a stroke upward with his left knee, and cast
Cuchulain from him like a little child, and he fell down
on the brink of the ford. Now Cuchulain's charioteer,
who was watching the combat from the bank, saw this,
and he began to reproach Cuchulain as his master had
bade him do, if he should give way in the fight.

" Ah, indeed," said Laeg, " this warrior can cast the
Hound of Ulster from him as a woman tosses up her
child ; he flings thee up like the foam on a stream ; he
smites thee as the woodman's axe fells an oak ; he darts
on thee as a hungry hawk pounces on little birds. Henceforth thou hast no claim to be called brave or valorous
as long as thy life shall last, thou little fairy phantom ! "

When Cuchulain heard these scoffing words, up he
sprang with the swiftness of the wind, with the fierceness of a dragon, and with the strength of a lion, and his
countenance was changed, and he became mighty and

terrible in appearance, towering like a Giant or like a
Fomor of the sea above Ferdia. A fearsome fight they
made together, gripping and striking each other from
middle day to fall of eve ; and their charioteers and the
men of Erin who stood by shivered as they watched the
conflict. So close was the fight they made that their
heads met above and their feet below, and their arms
around the middle of their mighty shields. So close
was the fight they made, that their shields were loosened
at their centres, and the bosses that were on them
started out. So close was the fight they made, that their
spears and swords were bent and shivered in their hands.
The fairy people of the glens and the wild demon folk
of the winds, and the sprites of the valleys of the air,
screamed from the rims of their shields and from the
points of their spears and from the hafts of their swords.
So closely were they locked together in that deadly
strife, that the river was cast out of its bed, and it was
dried up beneath them, so that a king or a queen might
have made a couch in the middle of its course without a
drop of water falling on them, though drops of blood
might have fallen on them from the bodies of the two
champions contending in the hollow of the stream.
Such was the terror of the fight they made, that the
horses of the Gaels broke away from their paddocks,
bursting their bonds and rushing madly in their
fright into the woods, and the women and young
people and camp followers fled away southwards out of
the camp.

Just at that time Ferdia caught Cuchulain in an un-
guarded moment, and he smote him with a stroke of his
straight-edged sword, and buried it in his body, so that
his blood streamed down to his girdle, and all the bottom

of the ford became crimsoned with his blood. So rapid were the strokes of Ferdia, blow after blow, and cut after cut, that Cuchulain could abide it no longer. And he turned to Laeg, and asked him to give him the Gae Bolga. Now, when the Gae Bolga was laid upon the water, it would move forward of itself to seek its enemy, and no one could stand before its deadly dart. So when Ferdia heard Cu ask for the Gae Bolga, he made a downward stroke of his shield to protect his body. But when Cuchulain saw that, he flung his spear above the shield and it entered the hero's chest ; and as he fell, the Gae Bolga struck him and entered his body from below. " It is all over now, I fall by that," said Ferdia. " But alas that I fall by thy hand. It is not right that I should die by thee, O Hound."

But Cuchulain ran towards him, and clasped him in his two arms, and carried him in his fighting array across the ford to the Northern side of the stream and laid him down there. And over Cuchulain himself there came a weakness and faintness when he saw Ferdia lying dying at his feet, and he heeded not the warnings of his charioteer telling him that the men of Erin were gathering across the ford to do battle with him and to avenge the death of their champion. For Cuchulain said, " What availeth me to arise, now that my friend is fallen by my hand ? For when we were with Scáth, Mother of great gifts, we vowed to each other that for ever and for ever we should do no ill to each other. And now alas ! by my hand hast thou fallen, my comrade, through the treachery of the men of Erin, who sent thee to thy fate. And oh ! Ferdia, ruddy, well-built son of Daman, until the world's end will thy like not be found among the men of Erin ; would that I had died instead of thee, for

Ferdia falls by the Hand of Cuchulain

then I should not now be alive to mourn thy death. Brief and sorrowful will be my life after thee.

> " Dear was to me thy comely form,
>   Dear was thy youthful body warm,
>   Dear was thy clear-blue dancing eye,
>   Dear thy wise speech when I was by.

" Let me see, now, O Laeg, the brooch that was given to Ferdia by Meave ; the brooch for which he lost his life, and did combat with his friend." Then Laeg loosened the brooch from the mantle of Ferdia, and Cuchulain took it in his hand and looked upon it, and tears such as strong warriors weep poured from his eyes, and he lamented over Ferdia, and over the brooch for which he had given his life.

" And now," said Cuchulain, " we will leave the ford, O Laeg ; but every other fight that I have made till now when I came to fight and combat with Ferdia, has been but play and sport to me compared with this combat that we have made together, Ferdia and I." And as he moved away he sang this lay :—

> " Play was each, pleasure each,
>   Till Ferdia faced the beach ;
> One had been our student life,
>   One in strife of school our place,
>   One our gentle teacher's grace,
>   Loved o'er all and each.

> " Play was each, pleasure each,
>   Till Ferdia faced the beach ;
> One had been our wonted ways,
>   One the praise for feat of fields,
> Scáthach gave two victor shields
>   Equal prize to each.

Cuchulain

" Play was each, pleasure each,
    Till Ferdia faced the beach ;
Dear that pillar of pure gold
    Who fell cold beside the ford
Hosts of heroes felt his sword
    First in battle-breach.

" Play was each, pleasure each,
    Till Ferdia faced the beach ;
Lion fiery, fierce, and bright,
    Wave whose might no thing withstands,
Sweeping, with the shrinking sands,
    Horror o'er the beach.

" Play was each, pleasure each,
    Till Ferdia faced the beach ;
Loved Ferdia, dear to me ;
    I shall dree his death for aye
Yesterday a Mountain he,—
    But a shade to-day." [1]

[1] From Dr George Sigerson's *Bards of the Gael and Gall.* The translation is in the metre and style of the original.

CHAPTER XVI

Ulster, Awake !

AFTER the combat with Ferdia weariness and great weakness fell upon Cuchulain. From the beginning of winter to early spring he had watched and safe-guarded the frontier of Ulster, alone and single-handed, and all that time he had never slept a whole night through. Saving only a brief snatch at midday, he often did not sleep at all, and even what he had was taken sitting, with his spear ready in his hand, and his head resting upon the shaft, as it stood between his knees.

The host of Meave was encamped on the plain of Murthemne, in Cuchulain's district, but the Brown Bull and the cattle they had sent away northward for safety into the hill passes of eastern Ulster.

Beside the grave of Lerga, overlooking the camp of the men of Erin, Cuchulain lay beside a fire that Laeg had kindled. Now, as the shades of evening fell, the hero looked abroad, slowly and with pain raising himself upon his elbow, and on every hand he saw the glint and gleam of the weapons of the men of Erin, caught by the light of the setting sun. Before him lay the great expanse of tents, and the multitude of the host, and he would have rushed upon them then and there, but all his body was riddled with wounds, and his strength was utterly gone from him. In his anger and despair he brandished

143

his sword and waved his shield and uttered forth his hero's shout. So horrible was that shout that the goblins and sprites and daft people of the air and of the glens answered it, and many of the men of Erin died of pure terror at the sound. Then across the camp of the enemy Laeg descried a figure, as of a tall and stately champion advancing calmly towards them. Straight through the tents of Erin he passed on, but no man seemed to see ; no head was turned as he went by, nor did the sentries bar his way, yet in his hand he carried a drawn sword.

Astonishment and awe fell upon Laeg as, from his seat beside his master, he beheld the warrior draw near.

" It seems to me, O little Hound," he said, " as though a visitant from fairyland drew near. Like one in high authority is this young man, and like the sun at junction of the day and night the gentle radiance of his lofty brow ; methinks that in its midday glow no mortal eyes could bear the shining of its wondrous light. The armour of Manannan clothes him round, and none can pierce or wound him through its joints ; the sword of Manannan is in his hand, from which no enemy returns alive, while on his head the jewelled helmet of Manannan gleams."

" 'Tis true, indeed," replied the wounded man, " Lugh the Long-handed, mightiest of the gods, is come to succour me. Bright as the sun rising at early dawn out of the glowing east the hero's face, giver of light and warmth to human-kind ; with his long arms stretching across the sky he floods the world with light. In his right hand he bears the sword of day, though now in shades of night his face is veiled. No human eye, save his whose inward mind has pierced the realms of fairy mysteries, can see the god, when in Manannan's helmet of invisibility he comes to earth. To comfort and to solace me he comes, for well he knows my plight. My comrades of the fairy-folk have pity on my pain and my despair."

The warrior stood close beside Cuchulain's bed and gazed upon his wounds, and noble pity stood within his eyes. "A manly fight, I see, you made, my son, and worthy are those wounds."

"I think not much about the wounds, O Lugh, but this is troubling me ; behold, below, yon host of mighty men who threaten Ulster's land, and here I lie, as weary as a child, and cannot rise to wreak my wrath on them. Were but my strength returned and my wounds healed, I would not long be lying here in grief, idle and cast away. But if, O Father Lugh, for this one night you would keep watch and ward for me the while I sleep, then could I for a space take peaceful rest."

"I come for that," said Lugh, "from fairy land. Sleep then, O Ulster's Hound, and by the grave of Lerga deeply rest ; no harm shall come to Ulster while you sleep, for I will watch and battle with the host." Then in deep peace and slumber Cuchulain took his rest, and for three days and nights he stirred not once, but slept a dreamless, torpid sleep. And fairy-folk brought magic herbs to put into his wounds, to soothe and heal him while he slept, and all the while Lugh sat at his right hand, guarding his rest, save when some feat of slaughter was to do upon the men of Erin.

But Sualtach, father of Cuchulain, heard of the distressed condition of his son, and well he knew that unless the warriors of Ulster woke from their magic sleep, and gathered to his help, the hero must give way before his foes. Now Sualtach was no battle-champion or warrior

K

of renown, but just a passable good fighting-man; he had no thought or wish to stand by his son when he fought single-handed with the choicest of Meave's host; nor had he gone to help him even when he heard that between life and death he lay, covered with gaping wounds. Yet still the news stirred some increase of courage in him, and though he would not fight in an uneven war, he now resolved to arm himself and ride to Emain's gates and call the sleeping Ulstermen to rise and hurry down to aid Cuchulain, before it was too late. He caught the Grey of Macha, Cuchulain's horse, and mounted him, and, spear and shield in hand, he rode straight up within the gates of Emain Macha. Silent and still as death was all the kingly fort. No sentinel looked forth to guard the door, no warrior strode round the deserted walls, and all within was silent as the grave, save for the weeping women and the little children's play, and lowing of the untended cows wandering between the outer and the inner raths. Within, in Emain's halls, each warrior sat apart sunk deep in sleep, his head upon his hands, his arms clasping his knees, or stretched in slumber full-length upon the floor; and round them lay their weapons, idle and rusting from long want of use, dropped from their nerveless hands. Mighty they looked, well-built and good men all, but no more strength had they than little babes but newly come to birth. Even when the women shook them, thy looked up but for one moment with lack-lustre eyes, and straightway sank to sleep again. Young children played about and over them, as though they had been statues made of stone, and yet they heeded not. Beside them, at their feet, lay crouched their noble hounds, loose from the leash, stretched out asleep, each one his muzzle lying on his paws. From time to time, the war-dogs turned and growled, as though they dreamed bad dreams; the warriors moaned as if they were in pain, but no one moved or rose.

Within the inner fort King Conor lay, surrounded by his chiefs, sunk deep in coward slumber each upon his couch; for Macha's hand lay heavy on them all, and her revenge was come.

But in the playing-fields outside, the Boy-corps still kept up their sports, and played at mimic warfare as of yore, though all their chiefs and teachers were asleep; and still their laughter, shrill and bright, rang through the silent halls, as one boy caught the hurley ball a good swing with his club, or threw his fellow in their feats of strength. The little son of Conor, Follaman, had made himself their leader, and willingly they mustered under him.

Then up rode Sualtach upon the Grey, and three times over he gave forth his cry. The first shout went up from the playing-fields, the second from the rampart wall, the third he gave standing aloft upon the summit of the mound where lay imprisoned the hostages of Ulster chained in their hut beside the kingly fort.

"Your men are being slain," he cried, "your cattle driven away, your women fall as captives to the men of Erin. In wild Murthemne's plain Cuchulain all alone still held the foemen back until the fight with Ferdia robbed him of his strength. Wounded in every joint Cuchulain lies, his gaping sores stuffed in with sops and bits of grass, his clothes held on with spikes of hazel twigs. On Emain Macha press the enemy, all eastern Ulster is in their hands; Ailill and Meave have harried all your coasts. Ulster, Arise, arise!"

Three times he gave the shout, ringing and clear upon the silent air, but still no watchman's voice gave forth reply.

Now in the kingly fort a rule of courtesy forbad that any man should speak before the King, save only his three Druids, who were his counsellors. After a while, as for the third time the voice of Sualtach came floating through the hall, one of the Druids stirred and said, " Who is the fellow brawling in the court ? Fitting it were to take his head from him." " Fitting it were, indeed," replied the King, " and yet I think the thing he says is true." And all the warriors muttered in their sleep, " Fitting it were, indeed."

When Sualtach found that no man answered him, in violent anger he turned back again. In his fierce wrath he dragged the bridle-rein, so that the Grey of Macha reared, and stumbled on a sleeping man, and swerved aside, flinging Sualtach forward on its neck. His head struck on the sharp edge of his missile-shield, so that it sheared it off, and the shield fell from his hand, his head within it, at the horse's feet, the body hanging yet upon its back. At that the Grey turned round, and made its way into the inner court and onward to the hall, the lifeless body still upon its neck, dragging the head along upon the shield, whose strap had caught into its feet. And all the way they went, passing the outer and the inner courts into the very presence of the King, the voice of Sualtach from the dissevered head still called aloud, as though he were alive, " Your men are being slain, your cattle driven away ; your women fall as captives to the men of Erin. In wild Murthemne's plain Cuchulain all alone still holds the foemen back. Ulster, Arise, arise ! "

"Too noisy is that head," King Conor said, moving again and stirring in his sleep; "put it upon the pillar of the house that it may go to rest." Then one of the warriors, hearing his King's voice, bestirred himself, and lifted up the head and set it on a pillar; but again, and even louder than before, the head cried out: "Your men are being slain, your cattle driven away, your women fall as captives. Ulster, Arise, arise!" So noisy was the head, that one warrior and then another rose upon his elbow and looked up at it, and bade it hold its peace, but when they spoke the head but called out louder than before. Then, looking round, they saw the mighty horse standing, gaunt and stock-still, within the very centre of the hall, the headless rider sitting on its back. And when they saw the horse bearing the headless rider in their midst, and heard the head still calling from the pillar top, as though it were alive, a shout of laughter, as of olden days, went up from one and all, and the King bestirred himself at the un-wonted sound. Then all the chiefs, seeing the King arise, shook themselves lightly and began to stand or sit up where they slept. They stooped to pick their weapons from the ground, to try the edges of their swords, to rub the rust that dulled their scabbards and the fine points of their spears. For memory and the love of life and war began to stir in them, and wonder at their own long idleness. And at the last the King stood up and cried, "True is the message that the head has brought. Ulster lies bound before her enemies, while we rust here in sleep. By all the gods my nation loves, I swear, unless the stars of heaven shall fall upon our heads, or the strong solid earth give way beneath our feet, I and my chiefs will restore each captive woman to her child and home, each cow to her own meadow, and each stolen piece of land to its own lords, so that in shame with heavy loss the foes of Ulster shall return to their own country."

Then a great shout went up from the men of Ulster, and their warrior spirit began to revive in them. And to each in turn the King applied, bidding him go forth and summon his clan and followers to meet him that day week upon the Hill of Slane in Meath, for he himself would call a muster there.

Gladly and eagerly the chiefs issued forth, for they heard the sounds of stirring men and the welcome bark of the hounds without.

As for the King himself, his mind was so confused with the magic sleep in which he had lain, that he remembered not the dead from the living, but stood, calling on the dead to come to his aid, as though they had been yet alive.

Throughout all the land he sent heralds to call together his men-at-arms; and with one heart and mind the men of Ulster responded to his call. Troop on troop they flocked to Emain, from North and West and East, each mighty leader surrounded by his host clad in the kilt and colours of his clan. As for the clans that were south of Emain, they tarried not to assemble at the kingly fort, but made their way, each by his own route, straight forward to the Hill of Slane.

For after their long rest and weakness their hands itched to be upon their swords again.

CHAPTER XVII

The End of the Boy-Corps

HARDLY had the King arisen from his sleep, than he remembered the Boy-corps. "Go," said he to one of his heralds, "and see how the Boy-corps fares. Tell the youths that we depart hence within a while to battle on the Hill of Slane in Meath, but that before we set forth on our march, we fain would see them once again at play. Bid Follaman and bid them all prepare." So the herald went out to warn the Boy-corps, but the playing-field was silent and deserted, nor was there any sign of Follaman or of the boys. "What is become of the corps?" he asked, alarmed, for among the boys were the sons of the bravest chiefs of Ulster and the King's own son besides. But none could give him a reply. In one corner of the playing-field he espied a little lad, the youngest of the corps, who sat alone, crying by himself. The herald asked him what it was that ailed him, and where were all the others, his companions. "The boys are gone to help Cuchulain, their comrade, who is sorely wounded," said the child; "they heard the words of Sualtach, calling on the Ulstermen to rise and come to Cuchulain's help against the men of Erin. But all the champions were asleep and heard not; only they, the Boy-corps, heard. And Follaman their leader said, 'Cuchulain, our comrade, is in sore distress, and none are ready to go to his aid; therefore we ourselves will go.' And all the Boy-corps said that they would follow him, and protect the coasts of Ulster while Cuchulain was asleep, and do combat for him with the enemy. But me they left behind," the child continued, weeping, " because they said I was too young to go; but I would have handled my little sword as well as any of them. I heard Follaman say that he would never return to Emain unless he brought with him Ailill's head, with its coronet of gold, to lay at Conor's feet."

When the herald heard this tale, he went hurriedly to the palace and told the King what the child had said. A great cry arose in the palace when it was known that the boys had gone to do battle with grown warriors of Erin; for each chief and each champion had a son, or two or three sons, among the corps, and the King himself had Follaman, his youngest and his darling. Then the King sent out word that before one hour should be past, he and his troops would take the road to Slane; if so perchance they might arrive in time to save the Boy-corps from its fate. For all his strength and vigour returned to Conor when he heard of the peril which beset the Boy-corps, and bitterly did he rue the inaction in which he and his warriors had lain, when the children had gone forth to fight.

Now at the end of his three days' sleep, Cuchulain had awakened from his trance; he passed his hand across his face, and opened his eyes and saw Lugh sitting beside him. From head to foot he blushed a rosy red, for he felt shame that a champion like himself should be found sleeping before his foes. " Warrior, how long have I been sleeping here ? " said he. " Three days and three nights," said Lugh, " and no shame to thee that

thou shouldst sleep, for even yet thou art not fit to rise."
" That indeed is true," replied Cuchulain, for he tried to
sit up on his couch, and fell back again. " Though my
wounds are closed and healing, my strength has not
returned; and all this time the hosts of Erin have been
unmolested."

" Nay, nay, indeed," cried Lugh, " no step forward
have they made; my hand hath held them back. Moreover," but here his voice grew grave and stern, " the
Boy-corps from Emain were here last night." " The
Boy-corps from Emain," Cuchulain cried; " what did
they here ?   No games or child's play have we here suited
to their age, but grim and deadly deeds of war. I trust
no hurt or damage came to them." " Alas, alas,"
said Lugh, " they came at night; I knew not they
were here. Straight to the tent of Ailill and of Meave
marched on the boys, clad in their mimic armour, with
all their pennons flying in the wind. Follaman, Conor's
son, was at their head, a brave and dauntless lad ; and on
them all, although they were but growing boys, men say
was seen the dignity of heroes, and the fearlessness of
seasoned wariors. Follaman demanded combat with
Ailill himself, he being a King's son, and thus, he said,
unfit to fight with common men.

" With jeers and taunts they drove the brave lads back
out of the camp and downward to the ford ; but there at
last the Boy-corps took its stand. ' Here wait we,' cried
the lads, ' here stand we to the death; the honour of
Cuchulain and of Ulster is in our hands. Come out and
fight !' Alas, alas," said Lugh again, " this morning
when I walked beside the ford, to guard the banks from
any man of Meave's, all up and down the strand fair
bodies lay, mangled and cut and hewn by cruel hands,

and on the stream bright hair was tossing from fair
severed heads. Follaman lay prone on the farther side,
his cold hand grasping still a warrior's hair, his arms
locked tightly in that warrior's arms, dragged down
together and o'erwhelmed beneath the wave. And all
around a bloody fight had been. Many a good warrior
had gone down before those hero boys ; many a strong
arm by them was stilled in death. Brave lads ! the
pride of Ulster and of Ulster's chiefs ! "

"The Boy-corps dead ! " Cuchulain cried, " dead to
retrieve my honour and the darkened fame of Ulster's
chiefs ! Ill is the deed that thou hast done me, O my
Father Lugh ; had I been roused from sleep the Boy-corps
had not perished thus. Follaman, Conor's son, would
not have fallen, and this shame would not have been
added to Ulster's other shames. Alas, and thrice alas !
And now, my Father Lugh, hark to my prayer ; stay
but one night beside me, and together we will avenge the
fall of the Boy-corps. Before the arm of Lugh the Long-
handed and the might of Ulster's Hound, no foe could
stand ; let us then do a glorious deed, that Ulster's honour
be by us avenged."

"Nay, not so," said Lugh, " for thine own strength is
not come back to thee, and I must back to fairy-land
again. My work is done, the gods await me there. The
wrong will be avenged, as is most meet, by Ulster's
champions, the fathers of the boys. See, even now
over the Hill of Slane their pennons wave."

Most true it was ; Cuchulain looked and saw, right in
the north and passing out beyond him to the west,
the gathering of a mighty host. Far as the eye could
reach they came with swinging gait, battalion on battalion, up the hill ; their tents on every side they pitched,

and martial strains and trampling of men's feet resounded through the plain. Beneath their heavy tread the very earth seemed quivering as they moved; the trees of the forest crashed their branches, and their tops swung together in the violence of the wind they made in passing up the glen. In the dim mist of early morn their spear-points glittered like sparks of fire, caught by the first beams of the rising sun; the thunder of their chariots, the clatter of their arms and horses' hoofs, so terrified the wild things of the woodlands, that they fled panting before them to the open plain.

"Carry me where I can mark the clans as they come up, O Laeg," Cuchulain said. Laeg lifted up the wounded hero in his arms, and laid him on the north side of a rising mound whence he could see the path by which the armies came. He marked the Druids marching on in front, scanning the sky for portents and muttering their spells. Then came the bards, pouring forth rhapsodies, and singing battle-chants, and near them were the bright-faced men of healing, carrying salves and medicines in their bags, to succour wounded men.

Right well Cuchulain recognized them all, the corps of Laery, named Triumphant, marching in impetuous style; the clan of Conall the Victorious, his early friend, all young and hardy men; the clan of Conor's son, he whom men called "The Stutterer," because he stammered in his speech. These latter were so eager for the fray, that, fearing to spring forth before the time, they knelt upon the ground, their chins resting on the rims of their enormous shields. All day they came, from morn to fall of night, till the whole hill and wide surrounding plain were covered with their tents. But in the midst

Cuchulain saw his own corps swinging up the hill, brilliant in their flying plaids, all mighty men and strong. They only, among all the host, marched mournfully and sadly to their camp; no sound of music, no martial warrior-chant, rose from their lips, for they as orphans marched without a father, or as a body left without a head. Now when Cuchulain marked his own corps coming up, no words of Laeg could stay him, nor could his bands and shackles tie him down. Violently and with tremendous force he sought to rise, to greet his own battalion. So vigorous were the efforts that he made, that even Meave and Fergus heard. "Surely it is Cuchulain trying to arise and join his own battalion!" Fergus said; " well is it for us that he is lying ill! Happy the men who have the aid of Cuchulain's corps, and woe to those whom they oppose! Were but their chief amongst them at this time, no other clan had need to be called out against the men of Erin."

"I fear them not," said Meave; "we have good men and brave to answer them."

"I swear by Ulster's gods," Fergus replied, "that when once Ulster is aroused, no host on earth can answer them."

"Send satirists and men of evil nature from us to Cuchulain," said Meave to her attendants, "and let them jeer him in his weakness, saying to him that Conor will be routed, Ulster put to shame, and Fergus slain while he is lying on his couch in idleness. Let him not think that it is we who send, but his own people jeering at his wounds. Tell him his own corps call on Ulster's Hound, but, like a pet-dog in a lady's lap, he lies down to be fondled and caressed. Send women mourners to weep over him false noisy tears, and tear their hair, and keen, as though he even now were dead. Thus will he fall into despair and do himself some harm, and so our victory will be assured. Away, and spare him not."

So keening women and hired mourning men went to the mound whereon Cuchulain lay, exhausted with his effort to arise; for Laeg had bound the hero fast with cords, so that he might not struggle to get up. For much he feared that he might inflict some injury on himself in trying to rejoin his corps. But Cuchulain thought not on his wounds at all, for all his mind was bent in following Laeg's account of what was passing in the camp; and when the messengers of Meave came close, and began to weep and wail, and hurl at him abuse and scornful words, he neither saw nor heard them, so that at length they ceased, disheartened and ashamed.

Eagerly Cuchulain addressed himself to Laeg. "Tell me, O Laeg, how stands our host together, and what do they now?"

"So close stand now the serried ranks, that though Conall's charioteer and mine tried side by side to force our way across the clustered spearpoints of the host, no smallest object from our chariots dropped among the men could find its way between them to the ground. I see King Conor's chosen men-at-arms coming toward the hill, where Conor's tent is pitched, higher and far more spacious than the rest. I see Meave's warriors withstanding them; they make a hollow circle, hoping, I think, to take the King alive. But, as though they hardly saw the opposing band, the King and his brave followers stride on. I see them now entering the hollow mass of fighting men; alas, they will be caught and fall. But no! I see, I see them soon emerge again, unharmed and safe. Right through the enemy they have forced their way, to join the main contingent of the troops. The clans of Ulster rise on every side as Conor gains his tent upon the utmost summit of the hill, and in a mighty shout, rending the clouds of heaven, the men of Ulster now acclaim their King."

" There is the stuff for a great battle among those hosts," Cuchulain cried; " bloody the deeds that will be wrought at sunrise on the morrow's morn. Let nothing pass you; tell me all you see."

" So far as I can mark, you shall know all," replied the charioteer; " but shades of evening fall apace on us, and hard it is to distinguish friend from foe. The warriors all betake them to their rest. Watchfires are lighted, and around their blaze they sit in peace and eat their evening meal. Far in the west, I see a little herd emerge upon the plain, a great Bull at its head, and all around a troop of cows and heifers, fifty or more, their heads held well in air. A band of youths are trying to restrain them and turn them back into the camp of Meave; but still they advance, careering o'er the plain, as though to join the hosts of Ulster's King. The youths of Ulster are battling with those other youths, trying to gain possession of the Bull." " And so indeed they may," Cuchulain said, " the Dun of Cooley is that Bull you see, for whom this war is fought. How are the youths of Ulster bearing themselves in this fray ? " " They fight like men," said Laeg, " but now I see the Bull has broken from them all. Away he goes, toward the west, making as though for Connaught." " He feels in him the call of war," replied the wounded man; " he seeks the White-horned, left in Cruachan.   No man, nor any band of men can stay the Dun, when once the time is come for his great onset on the Connaught Bull.   Fearful will be the war between those twain.   All Ireland will hear their furious charge, and tremble at their fall."

CHAPTER XVIII

The " Rising-Out " of Ulster

BEFORE the dawn of the ensuing day, Sencha the Druid seated himself upon the summit of the Hill of Slane, beside the tent of Conor, to watch for the first ray of light arising in the east. The Druids had foretold that if the men of Ulster went into battle before the break of day, they must fall before their enemies, but if they waited till the early dawn flooded the hills and vales of Ireland, then it was they who would come off victorious.

So eager were the warriors for the fight, that it was hard to hold them till the night was past. On every side, long ere the dawn had broken, they pushed aside their tent-doors and came forth. Nay, many of the host there were, who would not wait their turn to issue from the doors; but all unclothed, their weapons in their hands, they rushed out from their tents, forcing their way through every side at once.

King Conor gave command, " Bid them to halt until the word be given." And all the host stood silent where they were, gazing toward the summit of the hill whereon the bearded Druid stood erect.

At length in the dim east the sun arose, its first rays shooting up along the sky. Then to his full height Sencha arose and raised his arms on high, his snowy garments waving in the wind.

"The moment of good-luck is come"

" The moment of good-luck is come," he cried. " Let Ulster's heroes meet their enemies ! Let Macha's king arise ! "

Then with their weapons brandished in their hands, and with a horrid whoop of war, the men of Ulster rushed into the fight. The men of Erin arose on every side, and furiously and fiercely was the battle joined. From dawn to noon the conflict raged, now here, now there, across the plain of Meath. At length Meave said, " Call Fergus to me. I would send him to the fight "; for Fergus had remained behind, among Meave's body-guard, for loth he was to lift his hand against the men of his own province. " It is the part of a true hero, O Fergus," said Meave, deriding him, " to remain behind within the tents when a conflict to the death is going forward. Many good things, our hospitality and love, you took from our hand when Ulster exiled you. We fed and clothed your troops, we offered you a home. For many years you lingered in our land, wanting neither for wealth or honour while you were with us ; now when the moment of our peril comes, when in your cause we come to fight with Ulster, to restore yourself and all the exiles to their homes, 'tis Fergus lags behind. The common men and chiefs may die, you say, so I remain in peace among the tents. Now I myself, Queen Meave, descend into the fray ; in my own person I will lead my troops, like any valiant captain of my host. I go to seek out Conor, who supplanted Fergus on the throne ; will Fergus stay behind ? "

When Fergus heard of Conor he exclaimed, " My hand I will not lift against the chiefs of Ulster, who are all my friends ; but against Conor will I lift my hand, the wily, bad, supplanting king who stands where I should stand.

L

By all my gods I swear, had I but my own sword, the mighty ' Hard One ' whose blade is like a beam, or like a rainbow stretched across the sky, I now would ply it upon Conor's shield. Fetch me my sword ! " Then Ailill commanded that the sword of Fergus, called the Calad-cholg, or the ' Hard-sword,' brought by Mac Leda out of fairy-land, should be given to him, for he had hidden it, until the time should come. So Fergus' sword was brought, and Ailill put it into Fergus' hand ; and with a shout of welcome, Fergus grasped his sword, huge-handled, double-bladed, terrible ; so that no hand but Fergus' hand could hold it in its grasp. " Welcome, Calad-cholg ; welcome, O Leda's sword ! Woe to the fosterling of war who feels thy edge to-day ! On whom now shall we try thy might ? "

" Upon the host that rings us round, O Fergus," said the Queen ; " none shall turn back in peace before thy sword, none may it spare, save only some dear friend of other days."

Then into the battle-field, standing erect within her chariot, with all her champions round her as she rode, went queenly Meave, her golden circlet on her head, her weapons in her hand. On either side, holding aloft their swords, rode Ailill and Fergus, each with his own bodyguard. Terrific was their onset and before their chosen men, rushing like winds of March into the fray, Ulster gave way and fled. Three times they led their men into the very centre of the host, scattering it right and left, till Conor cried : " Who is this foe, who, three times to the North has scattered all mine host ? " " Fergus it is and Meave," they all reply ; " furiously they cut their way across the clans, who fly before them as they come." Now by the rules of Ulster's warfare, the king might never expose his person in battle, but only, from some post of vantage, watch the onset of his men. But now King Conor said, " Hold you this hill, I will myself go down and rally to their duty the flying hosts of Ulster." And when they found the king determined to go down, with one mouth his bodyguard replied, " Unless the earth should burst beneath our feet, or the blue sky fall on us from above, we steadfastly will hold this post for you, O King."

Then round the king a body of his bravest warriors locked their shields, and made a rampart; thus the king went down into the battle with his followers around him, he himself holding his mighty horned shield, the Ochain, in the midst. For they knew that if the king should fall, the men of Ulster would, as one man, take to flight.

Fergus was seeking everywhere throughout the host for the king of Ulster, and when he saw the linked shields of Ulster's greatest champions he knew that the king was in their midst. He made a mighty onslaught on the rampart of shields, and broke through it, scattering the chiefs to right and left. Then he approached the king, and with his ' Hard-Sword ' smote three mighty blows on Conor's shield. And the shield screamed aloud and roared, as was its wont when Conor was in peril or distress; and when the warriors of his host heard the screaming of the shield, all their weapons echoed in reply, and the shields that hung on the walls of Emain Macha fell down flat upon the ground. Far off, where he lay, Cuchulain heard the sound. " Surely," he cried, " I hear the shield of Conor roar; some deadly peril must beset the king, and I lie here alive and help him not ! Set free my bonds, or, on my word, I will break loose from them!" Then with a mighty effort, putting forth all his strength, Cuchulain wrenched his bonds, breaking and scattering them; and when he saw that nothing would avail to hinder him, Laeg cut the cords, and with one cry, the hero sprang upon his feet. "My weapons and my war-chariot," he cried, and Laeg brought out his chariot, sorely broken as it was after the fight with Ferdia at the ford. In it he fixed the iron spikes and points and nails that strengthened it in time of war, and made men fear to approach too near; into its wheels, on either side, the sweeping scythes were fastened that mowed the enemy like grass as it swept through the host. The Grey of Macha and the Black Steed of the Glen neighed loudly, and came whinnying to Laeg's call, and slowly Cuchulain's old strength returned to him again. He sprang into the seat, and with a noise like thunder dashed onward to the place whence came the tumult of King Conor's shield. Standing erect, it was as though a light streamed from his hair, rising up toward the heavens; while on either hand the sods flew from the chariot-wheels, making the air dark about him as he came. His own corps perceived him coming through the host, and loud their shout of welcome rose, and all the men of Ulster sent forth a cry of exultation and of joy. Even the enemy held his hand awhile, and Fergus himself fell back before the king.

"Away with you, my Master Fergus," Cuchulain cried, "turn about, and begone; dare not to strike King Conor's shield." But Fergus answered not, until a third time Cuchulain cried. And then he said, "Who is this, of Ulster's host, who dares to address me in strong warrior words?"

"'Tis even I, thy foster-son, Cuchulain, son of Sualtach,

loved of the great god Lugh ! Dost thou not remember,
Fergus, how thou didst promise that what time I should
be wounded in the fight thou wouldst turn and make as
though to flee before me, so that the host of Erin should
follow after thee ?   The time is come, turn now and flee,
or else stand fast and try thy strength with mine."

" I promised that, indeed," said he, " and truly I will
now fulfil my words.   Not fit or strong enough art thou
at this time to contend with me.   Stand back awhile,
and I will make as though I fled before thy onset."

Then Fergus turned, and fell back three full warrior-
paces before Cuchulain, as if he fled before him, trailing
his mighty sword behind him on the ground.   And
when the host of Meave saw Fergus turn, they thought
that all was lost, and with one consent they turned about
and fled.

Breaking their ranks, in wild disorder they streamed
westward o'er the plain, each man making for his home.
On every side they cast away their arms, so that the
ground was strewn with shields and spears, and vainly
Meave and Ailill called on them to turn.   Seeing the
rout, the men of Ulster followed hard, pressing upon their
rear, and cutting off a multitude of men.   From noon
till twilight's fall they fled, nor halted till they reached
the Shannon's ford, to pass across it and regain their
homes.   And, haughtily and undauntedly, Cuchulain
pursued the host, making a red rout of the flying men,
so that the way was strewn with dying and with dead.

Close at his side, urging on his withered steeds, rode
aged Iliach, Ulster's valiant chief.   Old and beyond the
fighting-age was he, yet, when the muster of the corps
was made, he would not stay behind.   " Bring me my
chariot and my steeds," said he.   Now many years had

passed since last the old man went into the field.   Rusted
and broken was his chariot, his weapons bent and worn ;
as to his ancient chariot-steeds, they were but lean and
wasted beasts, long since turned out to grass.   No
cushions had the chariot, nor any seat at all ; just as it
was the steeds were harnessed to the metal frame, and
in his hand he took his blunt and rusty spears.   All
round him on the chariot-floor were piled up flags and
rocks and stones ; with these, when his old worn-out
weapons broke in twain, he plied and mightily discomfited
the enemy.

Yet, as he stood erect, his white hair streaming on the
wind, so strange and formidable was his look, so flashing
was his eye, that all the men of Erin shrank before him
as he passed.   At length his vigour ebbed, his strength
gave out, the handle of his sword dropped useless from
his hand.   He called upon his charioteer.   " My work
is done," he said, " take thou my head from me upon my
chariot's rim ; I would not fall into the enemy's hand.
My honour and the honour of my country is avenged.
I die content."   Then with his own old sword, upon the
side-edge of the chariot his charioteer hewed off his
head.   Cuchulain turned and saw what had been done.
" Bear thou the head to Emain," said he, " and let his
body be buried with all honour near his home.   Iliach
died as a hero should.   So die all Ulster's heroes, avenging
Ulster's honour on her foes."

CHAPTER XIX

The Humbling of Queen Meave

TOWARDS the fall of day, Cuchulain reached the ford of the Shannon at the place that is now called Athlone. He saw the army of Meave flying, broken and disbanded, across the river, and weariness and dislike of the rout overtook him, so that he turned aside into a wood close by to rest awhile, for of his chariot there remained but a few bent ribs, and the wheels were loosened from the pole. "I will watch the flying host," he thought, "until the Ulster-men come up, and together we will smite them and cut off their rear." As he pushed his way into the wood, he saw before him, in the dimness of the fading light, Queen Meave herself, fallen, forsaken and exhausted, on the ground. So close was she that he could have smitten her from behind, and taken off her head, had he so willed. But it was not the wont of Cuchulain to smite from behind, or ever to hurt a woman. But he stood over her, and sternly spoke.

"What dost thou here, O Meave, O captain of the host of Erin? Behold thy army flies, broken and discom-fited, across the stream, seeking its native province, and the army of the men of Ulster presses hard upon their rear. No leader have they to guide their flying bands; why liest thou here alone?"

Then the haughty queen replied sadly, and with all her

spirit gone : " Queen as I am, and captain of mine host, yet have I but a woman's strength ; my forces are exhausted, and my power is gone ; fain must I lie and rest. Help me, O generous foe, I claim a boon from thee ! "

" What boon is this that thou dost crave of me, O Meave, mine enemy ? "

" I ask of thee to take myself and all my host under the strong protection of thy arm ; keep thou the ford for them ; ward off the men of Ulster who press on us from behind ; let Connaught's bands return in peace and safety to their homes. Guard me besides till to my help Ailill and Fergus come, and safe to Cruachan escort me back again. Full many and many a time have I, in folly, bragged about my strength and all the power of my enormous host ; now all is come to nought, and I am spent and ill. To thee, my foe, I turn ; protect me now."

" Never shall it be said," Cuchulain replied, " that I was heedless of a woman's appeal. Lie there in peace. I will protect the host."

So while the twilight deepened into night, Cuchulain stood up, dauntless and alone, between the men of Erin and their foes. Safely they crossed the stream, while his own followers Cuchulain held at bay, hindering and staying them from cutting off the rear. Chafing and vexed they stood, yet at Cuchulain's command they restrained themselves, nor was one man of Erin's host cut off till all in safety reached the further side.

Late in the evening came Fergus up, looking for Meave to conduct her back to Cruachan. Strange was the sight he saw. In peace and quiet, Meave was taking rest beneath the forest trees ; her troops all passed across the ford, save for late stragglers who came safely through the Ulster troops, no one destroying them. There on

the brink Cuchulain stood, leaning upon his sword the
' Little Hard,' his face lined deep with toil and thought.
He seemed to guard the enemy's troops from his own men.
Amazed, and uttering not a sound, Fergus stood still
awhile to watch.   Then in a mighty laugh that reached
the firmament he burst forth : " Verily and indeed," he
cried, " strange is the ending of this day.   A woman's
lead we followed in this war, fighting against the bands
of our own kith and kin, to gratify a woman's jealousy.
To-day our host is cleared and swept away ; it flies
without a path, without a lead, caring for nought but
safely to reach home.   Our queen lies at her ease, and
our worst enemy is he who guards and shields our troops.
Surely and in truth, 'tis wise and champion-like to follow
·where a woman leads the way."

Cuchulain heard that scornful laugh, and looking up,
saw Fergus standing contemplating him and them.

" High time thou camest, my foster-father Fergus, to
guard and help thy queen.   I leave her now to thee ; my
task is done.   Yet that it never may be said that
cowardice or weakness made Cuchulain spare the flying
troops of Ulster's foes, one blow I strike in Ulster's
honour here."   Then turning quickly, his ' Little Hard '
he swung aloft, and on the summit of a hillock near
at hand he brought it down, shearing its top clean
off.   " Between Connaught and Ulster let that hill
stand evermore, a witness to our strength and to our
gentleness ! "

Then once again into his ruined chariot he sprang,
and fast as his two steeds would bear him on, he hurried
back to Ulster and the king, returning glad and full of
victory among his troops to Emain and to Emer once
again.   And from that time Connaught withheld its

hand, nor did Meave venture ever again to dispute or war with Ulster.

Now the Brown Bull had passed over the Shannon westward, accompanied by his fifty heifers. With head in air and bellowing loudly he surveyed the great trackless land that lay before him. The Whitehorned heard his bellowing and came to meet him, and when they saw each other, straightway with terrific force they rushed together.

A paroxysm of exceeding fury came upon them, and up and down they moved, their nostrils distended and with lowered horns, pushing and driving and goring, until the ground was red with blood and the sods torn up and flung on high. Had any ventured near them, he would without doubt have been crushed to death beneath their hoofs; and when night came, no one in all the country dared to sleep, for terror at the bellowing and noise they made. But at length the Whitehorned gave way before the Brown Bull, and by him was chased and gored until no spark of life was left in him, and portions of his flesh were caught upon the Brown Bull's horns. Then, as he was, all red with blood and fearful to behold, the Brown Bull took his path back to his native home, scattering the people right and left before him, or trampling them into the earth beneath his hoofs. And, at the last, exhausted with his flight, the spirit fled from him, and with a mighty roar and fearful bellowings, the great Brown Bull of Cooley's raid fell dead.

CHAPTER XX

The Fairy Swan-Maidens

ONCE a year, in the autumn days, a great gathering was made of the men of Ulster, and from all parts men and women would come to share in the sports and marketing, and to meet their friends, and make merry. The place was joyous and full of gaiety with musicians making music on harps and fiddles, and singers singing, and jugglers plying their feats, and horse-racing in open spaces. The warriors, too, were to be seen exhibiting their trophies of war, and telling tales of their combats and victories, and all were dressed in their best, and feasting and eating was to be found in every part of the assembly.

One day during an autumn feast, in the calm and quiet evening, Cuchulain and Emer his wife and a band of the brave men of Ulster who accompanied Cuchulain, and of the gently bred women who were Emer's companions, were amusing themselves strolling and sitting beside a lake, apart from the people who were making merry, when they saw coming from a distance a flock of white, very beautiful swans, which settled down upon the lake, and began to swim out two and two. "How I wish," Emer said, "that I could have two of those birds, one on each of my shoulders." "All of us are longing for those birds," cried her companions, and one woman said, "If only my husband were here"; and another woman said, " If only my husband were here, he would fetch me the birds."

And Emer looked at Cuchulain, and said, " I think if anyone should have the birds, it is I who ought to have them first."

But Cuchulain seemed to take no notice of what they were saying. And Emer was afraid to ask him, so she went to Laeg, his charioteer, and said, " Come thou and tell Cuchulain that the women are asking for the birds." So Laeg spoke to Cuchulain : " The women wish that you should go and hunt the swans for them to-day."

But Cuchulain looked angry. " Can the women of Ulster find no better occupation for me," he said, " than to set me catching birds for their amusement ? Let them set their own husbands to this business, for it is not a fitting sport for me." " This is their fête-day," said the charioteer, " and they would like a gift from you."

" Bring me my chariot, then," Cuchulain said ; " a fine heroic deed it is to be taking birds for women, and worthy of a champion's valour."

Angrily he went to the water's edge, and pursued the swans in his chariot, bringing down a number of them with his sword and with stones, so that they fell, flapping their wings against the water. And he picked them up, and threw them down before the women, and returned to Emer, but to her he gave not any birds at all.

" Are you angry ? " he said to her. " Certainly I am not," said she ; " you gave the birds to the women, and this was the same as though I myself had given them ; right glad I am that you did this to please the women." Then Cuchulain's brow cleared, and he said, " Whenever birds come again on our plain, the two most beautiful of all I will bring down for you."

Hardly were the words out of his mouth, than slowly sailing out of the far distance and bearing down towards them, they saw two noble swans, larger and more splendid than any of those that had been on the lake before. The birds were chanting a gentle, mystic song, that soothed all who listened to it to sleep; and they were linked together with a golden chain. White and soft was their plumage, and they seemed to have human reason, for they moved together, with one mind, towards Cuchulain and his wife.

" There are your birds, O Emer," said Cuchulain, and he rose up to pursue them and fetch them down for her. But Emer was afraid. " Go not against those birds," she said, " you shall get birds for me another day ; there is some magic power in those birds, and you may come to harm."

" I am not afraid of birds," Cuchulain said, and laughed ; " place a stone in my sling, O Laeg."

So he took the sling and made a very careful aim, but for the first time in his life he missed his aim, and the stone went past the birds. " On my word," said Cuchulain, " this is a strange thing; from the day on which I first assumed arms till now, never have I missed a mark. Give me another stone."

Then he aimed again, more carefully than before, but again the stone went past them, and they sailed along unheeding. Then Cuchulain was angry, and he seized his spear, and flung it at the birds. And the aim was so good that it seemed as though the spear went through the swans, but for all that they flew away unhurt, save that the wing of one of them was broken. But when Cuchulain saw that the swans were taking flight, he flung off his mantle and ran after them, Laeg following hard behind. The swans flew slowly round the bend of the lake, and disappeared beneath the water; and when Cuchulain came after them round the point of land, he saw them no more, and though he gazed far out upon the water, and up to the passing clouds of heaven, he could not tell whither the birds were gone.

He looked about him, but he did not recognise the place in which he was, although he was on the Plain of Murthemne, in his own country.

"Where are the birds gone, and where are we, O Laeg?" said Cuchulain, for he was sore perplexed. And a strange weariness overtook him, and he leaned his back against a pillar stone that was hard by, and drowsiness fell upon him. But Laeg seemed to be asleep, for he gave no answer.

Then in a vision Cuchulain saw two graceful women approach him, clad in fairy mantles of green and purple, and they had little switches of osier in their hands, and they began to strike him gently with the rods, first one and then the other, as though they played a game with him, and it seemed to Cuchulain that all his strength departed from him while they touched him with their rods.

Then he said, but his voice sounded to himself but far away and strange, "Who are ye, fair ladies, and what do ye want with me?" "We are come," said the first, "out of Moy Mell, the Land of all Delight, the radiant Honey-Plain beyond the waves, to seek thy friendship. Liban am I, wife of Labra the Swift, the Wielder of the Sword, the monarch of that land. I come to bid thee welcome, if thou wilt succour him against his foes; for Senach the Spectral has challenged him to battle, and alone he is not strong enough to meet him and his gruesome phantom host. Come therefore to his help. Never until this day has monarch out of Fairy-land called for the help of any mortal man, but on the Plain of all Delights thy fame and thy renown are known; Cuchulain of the hundred feats is known."

"We come," said the second lady, "upon another quest. With Labra, called the Swift, the Wielder of the Sword, dwells beauteous Fand, betrothed to old Man-annan of the Waves. Above the splendour of all women of this earthly world shines out the noble loveliness of Fand, Manannan's chosen wife. Like the pure crystal clearness of a tear is the fairness of her face, and for that reason is she named Fand, that is, 'a tear.' Now tales of thy renown have come to Fand, the praise of young Cuchulain, Champion of Murthemne's plain, and sore she longeth with her own eyes to look on thee, and see thy warlike, comely form. Therefore we come, that if thou wilt, we may conduct thee to the Honey-plain, the Land of all Delights. We are the swans that swam upon the lake, and see, with thy rough spear, how thou hast torn and hurt my hand."

"I am in no fit state to-day to contend with men or demon hosts," Cuchulain said; "let Laeg go with you, and let him come again and tell me of your land. I am not strong or well to-day, and over and above all this, never would I, with any man or host do battle on the asking of a woman."

"Come thou, then, Laeg," she said; "I will take care of thee, and bring thee safely back. But it is woe and alas that thy master will not come."

"Indeed," said Laeg, "never in all my life until to-day have I been put under a woman's guard. This kind of woman's rule, I vow, pleaseth me not at all."

"Nevertheless, O master Laeg," she said, "it is only under my guidance that thou canst reach Moy Mell. Haste then, and come, for Labra waits for us." Still Laeg protested, and would not have gone, but that Cuchulain urged him; and at the last forward they went, Laeg and the women, walking together a long while, till they perceived an island in the lake, and on the near side lay a skiff of bronze, burnished and very light, waiting, it seemed, to carry them across. It had no oar or sail or men to guide or ferry it along, but as they touched it with their feet, swiftly it moved outward from the bank, and with straight aim across the lake it bore them to the door of the palace that was in the island.

About the palace-gate they beheld a troop of warriors, coming out to meet them. "Where is Labra the Swift-handed?" demanded Liban. "He returns from gathering his troops and armies for the conflict on the morrow," they replied; and even as they spoke, the rattle of a chariot was heard approaching. "He comes, make way," they cried; "Labra Swift-handed, Wielder of the Sword, returns from the battle-field."

Then drew near a dark, stern warrior, whose horses out-stripped the March wind in their swiftness. In his right hand he held his upright long-shafted spear, and at his side hung a terrible two-handled sword, double-bladed, strong. Rugged and full of care was that warrior's face, and gloom sat on his brow. And Liban said, "The spirit of Labra is depressed to-day; I will go out and greet him." She went forward to bid him welcome, and when he saw her, his face cleared, and he exclaimed, "Has the Hound of Ulster come?" "The Hound of Ulster cometh not to-day," she said, "but Laeg is here, and surely he himself will come to-morrow.

Fear nothing, Labra, Wielder of the massive sword, King of the Honey-plain, the hosts shall be hewn down before thee, and women shall weep their dead, when once Cuchulain comes.

Then Labra called Laeg and said, " Welcome, O Laeg ; for the sake of him from whom thou comest, for the sake of the lady with whom thou comest, thrice welcome to this land. But now return to thine own home, O Laeg, and set my message before thy master, before the Victorious Hound, and bid him come and help me, for the Plain of Honey is changed to a plain of slaughter and red war, and hosts are gathering to destroy us ; seest thou yonder how they come ? "

Then Laeg looked, and far off on the plain he saw armies coming up like hosts of demon men, obscure and silently ; in bands and troops they ranged themselves across the plain. Afar and farther yet he saw them crowding on, while over them their dusky pennons flew, and their great spears pointed aloft. Yet though so great a host was assembling, never a sound was heard ; but like an army of the dead they moved, noiseless and swift ; only upon the air there came a sound, low and soft and still, like wailing of the wind in forest trees, and then Laeg knew that they were playing the Dord Fiansa upon the points of their great spears.

" To-morrow will the battle be joined," said Labra, " and though our warriors are good, we cannot stand before this host. Pray therefore thy most valiant lord without loss of time to come and succour us."

And Laeg said, " Surely he will come," and with that he set out to return again.

Now when Laeg left his master at the pillar-stone, Cuchulain lay for a long while in a trance ; and there

M

Fergus and the men of Ulster found him, and they were perplexed to guess what had happened to him or whither Laeg had gone. At length Cuchulain sat partly up, but all his strength was gone from him And he said, "Carry me to the Speckled House of the Red Branch Champions of Ulster, and lay me there among the weapons." For the Champions of Ulster were called 'Champions of the Red Branch,' and they had three halls set apart for them in the palace of the King at Emain Macha. In the speckled house they hung their weapons and stored their trophies; it was called the Speckled House because of the bright spots of light made by the flickering of the sun as it danced on the weapons round the wall.

So they carried Cuchulain to the Speckled House and laid him there upon a bed with his own weapons hung above his head; and Fergus and Conall the Victorious, and the other warriors who were his friends took turns to watch him as he lay. For a whole year he lay thus in trance and no word did he speak all that time. For a year with mortal men is but a day in fairy-land.

At the end of the year Laeg returned, and he found his master thus asleep and speechless, but he knew not that he had been away more than a single day. Greatly was Laeg disturbed at the condition of his master, for he knew that Labra awaited his coming on the morrow. Then, as he pondered how he should awaken him, there came amongst them, silently and unannounced, a noble youth of princely mien, who stood at the foot of the bed and looked down on Cuchulain as he lay. They knew not how he had come in, for the doors were shut, and no man had seen him enter. Fergus and Conall the Victorious sprang to their feet and laid their hands on their swords to protect Cuchulain. But the stranger said, " I am Angus, god of youth, come out of fairy-land to heal Cuchulain ; if the man who lies there sick were but in health, he would be a protection to me against all Ulster. Although he now lies ill, he still is my protector, and so much the more than if he were in health, for sure am I that none would hurt me, while he is unfit to take my part."

" None here will hurt or injure you," said all ; " welcome art thou for the sake of him for whom thou hast come."

Then the stranger stood up and sang to Cuchulain a mystic strain, which none of those who stood by could understand ; but in truth, he was calling Cuchulain to Fairy-land, the Plain of all Delight, for Fand it was who sent him to invite Cuchulain thither. And as he sang, lo ! Cuchulain sat upright in his bed, and his vision went from him, and he felt his natural strength returning to him again. But when they looked, Angus was gone, and they knew not whither or how he went.

But Fergus and Conall greeted Cuchulain lovingly and said, " Tell us now what happened unto thee." And Cuchulain told them all that had come to him, and of the fairy women with their wands of osier who had met him, and how his strength departed when they touched him with the wands.

Then Cuchulain called Laeg, and said, " Go to Emer of the beautiful hair, who is sorrowing for me in my own home, in Dun Dalgan, and say to her that the fairy women have taken my strength from me, and that I am not able to come to her ; but tell her that it goeth better with me from hour to hour, and that I would have her come to me to comfort me."

And Laeg took that message to Emer, and he found her weeping in Dun Dalgan. And she said, " It is strange to me, O Laeg, that though for a whole year your master has been lying ill, not one of you has sought to heal or succour him. Well known is it that you possess the power to go away to fairy-land, where all herbs of healing are to be found, yet never have you sought a fairy herb to cure your master. Surely some warrior or wise man of Ulster might have done some heroic deed to bring him back from the sore sickness in which he lies ! Had Fergus or Conall been sick or wounded, or had they lost their sleep, or had King Conor been bound down in enchanted slumber as now Cuchulain is, short would have been the time till Cuchulain would have done some mighty deed or have sought some magic means of healing them. Certain it is he would have gone into the fairy mounds, or through the solid earth itself ; the great wide world he would have searched from end to end, until he found some plant of healing that would have saved and wakened them. But as for me, for a whole year have I not found one night of sweet repose, since he, the Hound of Ulster, lay bound down with magic chains. Sore is my heart and sick ; bright music nor the voice of pleasant friendship strikes my ear ; blood presses on my heart since Cuchulain lay in fairy toils."

Then to the Speckled House she went in haste, and stayed not until she entered the hall where Cuchulain lay, weak and prostrate upon his bed.

She seated herself at the side of the bed and touched Cuchulain's hand, and kissed him, and she called on him to come back from fairy-land. " Awake, awake, O champion of Ulster, shake off this fairy sickness ; not fit is it that a chariot-warrior should lie upon his bed. Lo ! Ulster calls upon her Hound of Battle. Lo ! friends and comrades call. Lo ! I, thy wife, am at thy side. Awake ! awake ! O Hound ! "

At that, Cuchulain stood up and opened wide his eyes, and he saw Emer of the beautiful hair seated at his side. Then he passed his hand across his face, and his heaviness and weariness passed away from him, and he arose and embraced his friends and is own and only wife ; and he felt his strength returning to him, and his old vigour coming to him again.

And he said to Emer, " For one day, O wife, spare me yet ; for there is a deed of battle-valour that I must perform to-day, and after that I will come home to you. Go before me to Dun Dalgan, and prepare a feast and call my comrades and my friends together. I will but go and come again." Then Emer set out for Dun Dalgan to prepare the feast, but for a whole year she waited for Cuchulain, watching day by day, and yet he came not.

CHAPTER XXI

How Cuchulain went to Fairy-Land

WHEN Cuchulain left Emer, he went forward to the fairy-rath where he had seen Liban, and he found her waiting for him to take him to Labra's Isle.

It seemed to him that the way they took was long, for they passed over the Plain of Speech, and beyond the Tree of Triumphs, and over the festal plain of Emain, and the festal plain of Fidga, until they came to the place where the bronze skiff awaited them, to take them to the Isle of all Delights. A noble and right hospitable welcome was prepared for Cuchulain in that Isle, but he would not rest for that, but bade Labra conduct him without delay to the Plain of Combat. So Labra bade him mount his chariot and together they passed on to the Plain of Combat, where the armies of the phantom hosts were assembled for the fight upon the morrow. On one side were the hosts of Labra, very few, but picked and chosen men in splendid garb, with arms of the best in their hands ; but on the side of Senach the Spectral, as far as eye could reach on every side, rose lines of black and gloomy tents, with black pennons flying from their poles. Gaunt heroes clothed in black moved about amongst the tents, and all the horses that they rode were red as blood with fiery manes. And over the whole there hung a mist, heavy and lowering, so that Cuchulain

182

could not see how far the host extended for the gloom of that heavy mist.

And sounds rose on the air, like the muttering of a demon host, quarrelling and wrangling, so that a man might well shiver before such a sound. But when he saw the demon host, the spirit of Cuchulain revived within him, and he felt his old force and courage and his strength returning to him, and all his weakness passed away.

And he said to Labra, " I would fain drive round the host and number them." In ever-widening circles he began to drive round the tents. But, as he drove, on every side they sprang up before him innumerable as the blades of grass on a meadow-field, or as the stars on a brilliant summer's night, or like the grains of sand upon the ocean's shore. Black and gloomy they stood on every hand, and grim and gaunt the warriors who moved about amongst them, and terrible their blood-red steeds. It seemed to Cuchulain that the smell of blood was already in the air, and all the plain was dark and dim with mist, so that he could not count or number them, or see the end of them at all.

But the spirit of Cuchulain faltered not, and he returned to Labra, and said to him, " Leave me now alone with this great army and take away with you the champions you have brought. This battle I will fight alone."

So Labra and his men departed and Cuchulain remained alone facing the phantom host. Then two ravens, the birds of knowledge and destiny, with whom are the secrets of the druids, came between Cuchulain and the host, and all that night they made a dismal croaking, so that the demon men grew sore afraid.

" One would think," they said, " that the Madman
of Emain Macha were close at hand, from the croaking
of those ravens; " for it was thus they spoke among
themselves of Cuchulain, because he changed his aspect
in time of combat, and a wild and strange appearance
came upon him. And they chased away the ravens,
and left no place of rest for them in all that land.

All that night Cuchulain stood with his hand upon his
spear, watching the demon host. Very early in the
morning, he saw one of their chief leaders going forth
out of his tent, to bathe his hands at the spring; and
his tunic fell back and left his shoulder bare. At once,
with a cast of his spear, Cuchulain transfixed him
through his shoulder to the earth.

When the demon host saw their captain fall, they arose,
and in swarms and close battalions they came down
upon Cuchulain. Then his war-fury came upon him,
and wildly and terribly he attacked them, scattering
them to right and left; and so furious was he and so
deadly were his blows, that they feared to come nigh
him. It filled them with awe to see one single man
fighting with a host; but as the shining of the sun
drives the mist before it on a dewy morn of early spring,
so did the radiance of the face of Cuchulain disperse and
drive away the army of the demons, for they could not
stand before the splendour and the shining of his
countenance. Then Senach the Spectral attacked him,
and furious was the contest fought between them, but
in the end Cuchulain prevailed and slew him; and all
the host, when they saw that, turned and fled.

At length Cuchulain returned, his sword dripping with
blood; and the heat of his body after the fight was such
that water had to be thrown over him, before he could

be touched ; and the men of Labra feared that his wrath would turn against themselves. They brought him into the house and bathed him and changed his raiment, and slowly his own appearance came back upon him ; and after that, they led him to Fand, who awaited his return with her fifty maidens round her. Very beautiful was the house in which Fand and Labra awaited Cuchulain. Couches of copper with pillars of fine gold were ranged around the hall, and soft pillows and cushions of coloured silk were piled on each of them ; the flashing of the jewels from the golden pillars giving light to all who were in the house. Noble youths in glossy garments of smooth silk offered drink in golden goblets, and as they drank, the harpers and musicians gave forth sweet music, and the story-tellers recited their tales. Laughter and merriment were heard throughout the house, while from the eaves the fairy-birds warbled in harmony with the music of the harps. Fifty youths of stately mien, and fifty maidens with twisted hair bedecked with golden coronals waited on Fand, on Labra and his spouse. Near the house to westward, where the sun went down, stood dappled steeds, pawing the ground and ready for their riders. On the east of the house stood three bright apple-trees, dropping ruddy fruit, and in front of the door a tree that gave forth sweetest harmony, such as would sooth wounded men to sleep, or bring health to women in their sickness. Above the well another tree, with silver leaves that reddened in the sunlight, dropped fragrant food, pleasant to all who tasted it. Ever on the gentle breeze the tops of the tree swayed together, and ever they swung wide ; and as they met food fell down sufficient for thrice three hundred men. A vat stood in the hall, full to the top of mead and sparkling ale, and all the porch, above its silver posts, was thatched with wings of birds, in stripes of brown and red.

Now Fand sat on a daïs, waiting for Cuchulain. And when he came before her, clothed as a king, his noble manly form bathed and refreshed, his golden hair gathered above his brow round an apple of bright gold, and all his face aflame with the vigour of the fight, she thought that she had never looked upon a man so brilliant as he.

And he, when he looked on her, knew that never in his life had he seen woman half so fair as Fand. " Art thou he, Cuchulain of Murthemne, the Hound of Ulster ? " she asked, and even as she spoke the whole band of youths and maidens rose to their feet, and sang a chant of welcome to Cuchulain.

Then Fand placed Cuchulain at her right hand, and happy and gladsome were they together, and for a while Cuchulain forgot Ulster, and his place at Conor's hand, and all the cares and troubles of the other life ; nay, he forgot Emer his own wife and the feast she was preparing for him, and the days passed quickly and joyously in the company of Liban and Labra and Fand. And it seemed to him as though Erin were but a dark unquiet land beside the clearness of Moy Mell, the Fairy-land of all Delights.

At length one night he could not sleep ; not all the warbling of the fairy-birds from the branches of the tree and from the eaves, nor yet the sound of minstrel's strains could soothe him into slumber. For he re-membered Ulster and his duty to his king, and Emer and the feast she was to make for him, and all his warrior deeds which were departing from him, and he felt he must needs forsake the Land of all Delights and go back to his work in Erin once again.

In the morning he called Fand, and told her he must go that day, for he knew not what troubles might be happening to Ulster while he was away, or what was become of Emer, his wife. But Labra and Fand besought him to stay yet awhile, and they called the musicians and bid them chase away the sudden gloom of Cuchulain, and they brought out the playing-games, hurley and chess, and raced the horses to please him, and they harnessed the steeds of the chariots for his delight. But even for all this Cuchulain would not stay. For he said, " My warrior-strength is passing from me as I rest in idleness, my vigour is decaying. Let me then go, for I am not as the little dogs that play about their mistresses' feet; I am a Hound of war and conflicts to stand before the foe, and do battle for my country and my king."

And Cuchulain sang this lay :

" No pup am I to play about the feet of ladies fair,
   But where the hounds of war are loosed you'll find me ever there ;
   No mongrel whelp to watch the fire or crouch beside the hearth,
   I stand beside the fords, I scare the champion from his path.

" My bark is not the yelp of curs cowed to the heels by fear,
   But the deep bay of winded hounds chasing the leaping deer ;
   No swathes of wool shall bind my wounds, no cushioned couch
      have I,
   Amidst the carnage of the slain I and my kind shall lie.

" No silky coat of well-combed hair, smooth 'neath the children's
      hand,
   But a fierce mastiff, gaunt and grim, when strife invades the land ;
   Where fords are weak, where forts blaze red, where trumpets
      sound for war,
   The ' Hound of Ulster ' stands at guard, or drives the foe afar."

Then when Fand saw that nothing would content him, she bade him a gentle kind farewell; and all the youths and maidens came about him, sorrowing that he was so soon weary of their land. But Labra thanked him kindly and heartily for his help against the demon host and he bade Liban take Cuchulain safely back across the lake to Erin once again.

But, before he went, Fand lifted up her lovely witching face, and said, " Tell me some place where, at the end of a year from now, I may see your face once more. Never till now have I ventured forth from fairy-land; but, for your sake, for one brief hour I will come to the land of troubled mortal men. Give me a tryst."

Cuchulain was fain to deny her this, for he thought on Emer, and he dreaded her anger against Fand, if she should be aware of it. But when he saw the crystal-fair, witching face of Fand, and her ruby lips and eyes bright as stars on a summer's night, he could not say her nay; and he made a tryst with her on the Strand of the Yew-tree's Head, for a year and a day from then. And after that, they bade one another farewell.

So Cuchulain came home again, and Emer and Laeg and his friends greeted him right lovingly, and he told them that he had been in fairy-land, and of all its splendours and beauty he told them freely, but to Emer he said not anything of Fand.

Now when a year and a day were past, Cuchulain came to the place of tryst at the Strand of the Yew-tree's Head, and he and Laeg sat beneath the ancient yew-tree playing chess, while waiting for the coming of Fand. It chanced that, as Emer walked that way with her fifty maidens to take the air beside the shore, she beheld approaching a dignified lady, radiant as the clearness of a day in June, who came with a troop of maidens towards Cuchulain. Very swiftly and softly they moved across the plain, as though they hardly touched the sod, and all the land was filled with their brightness.

It appeared to Emer that they had come across the lake, yet no sign of skiff or boat was to be seen, and the unknown queen came where Cuchulain sat, and he rose up and made a glad gentle greeting before her, and she sat down by him, and they talked pleasantly and lovingly together.

When Emer saw this, she was filled with jealousy and anger against the fairy-woman, and to herself she said, "This, then, O Cuchulain, was the cause that kept thee so long in fairy-land, when I made that feast to which thou camest not."

And anger and dark revenge filled Emer's heart, and she turned to her maidens and said, "Bring me here sharp-bladed knives, for I myself will go softly behind them and I will kill the woman who talks with Cuchulain."

Then they went and fetched thin gleaming knives, and they hid them beneath their mantles, and went stealthily behind the place where Cuchulain sat. Now Cuchulain saw not what was going forward, but Fand knew, for she sat over against Cuchulain, facing the way that Emer came. She said to Cuchulain, "Emer thy wife comes here, with fifty maidens, and there are sharp knives hidden beneath their cloaks."

But he said, "Fear nothing, lady, I myself will speak to Emer, my own wife, and do thou wait here till my return."

But Emer came close to Cuchulain and cried, "Why dost thou do me this dishonour, O Cuchulain, to leave me for a fairy maid? The women of Ulster will contemn me if they think that Cuchulain loves another woman better than his wife; and what have I done to displease thee, that thou shouldst need to talk with her? Never have I left thee for any other, and well and truly have I loved thee from the day thou camest in thy chariot to the fort of Forgall the Wily, my father, till today; and for ever shall I love thee, and none other but thee alone."

Then Cuchulain said, "You wrong me, Emer, and you wrong this fairy-maid. No thought at all of harm have we, nor can any other be to me what thou hast been. Fair and pure is this maiden, and a worthy mate for any monarch in the world. Her race is noble, her mind is firm and gentle and full of lofty thoughts, no harm or evil will be found in her or me. Moreover, she is betrothed to a noble spouse, Manannan of the Ocean Waves."

"In very truth," said Emer, bitterly, for her heart was sore within her on account of the greatness of the love she bore Cuchulain, "it is ever so with men! All that is new is fair, and all that is old is of little worth; white is the last they see, and the others are but grey or black. Sweet is the thing they have not, but sour the fruit they hold within their hands! Once in peace and love we dwelled together and no one came between us, and in peace and honour we might dwell together again, O Youth, if but I were as dear to thee as once I was!" And great tears rolled down Emer's cheeks, and her grief weighed heavily upon her.

"By my word and truly," cried Cuchulain, "never wast thou more dear to me than thou art to-day, and dear shalt thou be to me for all my life."

"I think," said Fand, "that I had better go away, and return to my own country, for I am troubling you all

here." " Nay, nay," cried Emer, smitten with reproach when she saw the nobleness that was in the
fairy woman, " go not away, 'twere better I should go."

But Fand said, " Not so, indeed, from my own land
they call me to return. Take to thee thy man, O noble
Emer, no harm or hurt hath happened him with me.
Though in the Land of all Delights warriors and great
men sought my friendship, better to me than the affection of them all was the friendship of thy glorious spouse.
Need is there, now, that I should go my way, and leave
my friend to thee ; but though bright and dazzling is the
country of Moy Mell, some shadow hath fallen on it since
Cuchulain went away."

Then she lifted up her lovely face, and Emer saw that
tears like drops of crystal stood within her eyes.

Long years ago had Fand been betrothed to Manannan,
Lord of the Ocean and the Waves, a great and hoary
god. Ancient was he, for no man knew his age, and wild
and grey his hair, and all his brow rugged and·lined with
storms. Very kingly and majestic was his tread, but
men feared him, because of his strange, tempestuous
moods, and his shape-shifting, and his little care for
human life. For Manannan was ever restless, wandering
in distant lands, moving now this way, now that, and
visiting in turn all countries ; and years ago, as mortal
men count time, he had gone away and returned not,
nor did Fand even know where he was to be found. So
she thought he had forsaken her, and, when Cuchulain
came to fairy-land and she saw his youth and beauty,
her mind went out to him, for never had she seen before
a noble human man.

But Manannan knew within himself that Fand was
in sore grief, and he arose in haste to go and help her.

For, although he had tarried long in distant lands, daily he had news of Fand, and he learned all she was doing and when she needed him. So now he saw her trouble, for he it was who sent Cuchulain to fairy-land that he might test her love for himself; and swiftly over the waves he sped to go and save her. Invisible was he to mortal men, and he rode the white sea-foam as though it were a horse, for no need had he of any vessel, or of sail or oar; and as he passed by Fand, she felt his presence and looked up at him as he passed by. But for a moment she knew not that this was Manannan of the Waves, for his look of hoary age had gone from him, and the man she saw was young and strong, with a noble gentleness upon his face, like the sea on a calm summer's day.

For Manannan was a shape-shifter, and at one time he was terrible and cruel to behold, but at another he showed a kindly face, for he looked into the minds of men, and as he saw them, even so his own face reflected the thing he saw. Then Manannan said to Fand, " O Lady, what wilt thou now do ? Wilt thou depart with me or abide here with Cuchulain, if he comes for thee ? "

" By my troth," said Fand, " either of you two were a fitting spouse for me, and a worthy friend to stay with; and in neither of you do I see any one thing greater or better than is in the other; yet, O thou princely One, it is with thee that I will go, for I have been promised to thee for thy wife; thou hast no consort of worth equal to thine own, while Cuchulain has a noble spouse; therefore take me with thee, for Cuchulain needs me not."

Then Manannan stretched his arms to Fand, and drew her with him, and she followed him. And Cuchulain perceived her drawing away from him, but he knew not whither she went, nor could he see who was talking to her. And he cried out to Laeg, his charioteer, who had knowledge of fairy-land, " What meaneth this, Laeg, that I see ? Whither goeth Fand ? "

" She goeth with Manannan of the Sea," replied Laeg. " He is drawing her back to the Land of all Delights, but she is weeping as she goes."

Then Cuchulain uttered three sharp cries of sorrow and of grief, and he fled away from men into desert places, and would take no meat or drink, and he slept in the open rush-land beside the high-road to Tara.

Emer went then to Emain, and sought King Conor, and told him all that had happened, and that Cuchulain was out of his senses because Fand had gone away ; and she prayed him of his love for Cuchulain, and because of her love for him, to send to him men of skill and Druids who might bring him back to health. The king did so willingly, but when they came, Cuchulain fled from them, or sought to slay them, until at length he felt within himself a terrible thirst, and he craved of them a drink. In the drink they mingled herbs of forgetfulness, so that the memory of Fand slowly faded from him, and the remembrance of the time he had spent in fairy-land, and he came to his own mind again.

They gave soothing drinks to Emer also, for she was troubled, too, and stricken, and her natural joyousness had gone from her. But when Manannan heard in fairy-land of the trouble of Emer and Cuchulain, he came unseen of any man, and shook his cloak of forgetfulness between Fand and Cuchulain, so that from both of them the memory passed away, as though it had been a dream, and they thought of it no more.

N

CHAPTER XXII

Deirdre of Contentions

YEARS passed away, and the memory of their old feuds died down between Fergus mac Roy and King Conor mac Nessa. Fergus in his old age wearied for his home and country, and for the comrades of his youth. The private wars of Meave had little interest for him, and the tidings that came from time to time from his own province stirred in him a longing to be back. So at length he bade farewell to Meave, and with the most part of his followers he returned to Ulster, and settled in his own fort again. In order to keep his allegiance, King Conor gave him a position next himself, and in all outward things showed him honour, but all the while he watched him jealously, and Fergus knew well that the King would be glad to find a good excuse to shut him up in bonds or to put him to death. Conor feared his power with the people, and their pride and affection for him who once had been their king, and in his mind Conor knew well that he sat in Fergus' seat, and that many of the older chiefs would willingly have seen their rightful prince once more upon the throne. As old age came on him, Conor grew more wily and suspicious year by year, so that some men dreaded and some hated him, and few felt for him affection or true reverence. Yet among the youthful generation growing up, the reign of Fergus and his mighty deeds were but a

tale told by their fathers of their own youthful days;
and though they looked with awe upon his mighty
stature and his massive form, Fergus seemed to them
more like a giant of the ancient time, or like a hoary god,
than like a being of human kind as they were, feeling the
needs and passions of a man.

Ulster was now at peace, and quietly the days rolled
by. Once more the sound of laughter rang out from
the playing-fields. New boys, grown out of babyhood,
played the old sports, lads brave and manly as those of
other days; but older men, passing, would shake their
heads and wipe away a tear, for still the shadow of the
tragedy that met the boy-corps at the ford hung over
them. And many a mother wept at night remembering
a bright boy, her pride and darling, swept away contending for Cuchulain and for Ulster against the
warriors of Meave.

From time to time, in days of peace, the chiefs of
Ulster, each in his turn, made a feast for Conor and the
nobles in his company, the famous Champions of the
Red Branch. In his turn, Felim, son of Doll, the chief
of the King's story-tellers and his close friend, made such
a feast for Conor.

For a whole year had Felim been preparing for the
coming of the King. He built a noble banqueting hall
close to his house, and sleeping rooms for the King's
followers, and stables for their steeds. From all the
country round the farmers brought butter and cream,
fresh curds and cheeses, cakes and wheaten bread.
Cattle and sheep and swine worthy of the royal banquet
were brought in, and fruits and onions, honey and strong
ale were stored in plenty in Felim's vats and store-
houses.

He gathered together singing men and singing women, musicians who played upon the fiddle and the harp, and the best tellers of stories that were to be found in all the country-side.

On the day appointed, the King set out in state from Emain, with the Champions of the Red Branch in his train.

Fair was the day and bright when Conor and his followers set out, each in his chariot drawn by two spirited steeds, each decked in his festal array, in mantles of rich crimson, blue or purple, fastened with massive brooches of pure gold, wondrously chased and set with stones of price brought out of distant lands. Upon their heads their helmets of bright bronze shone in the sun, and on their spear-points the sunlight danced so that they seemed to move along beneath a flashing line of gold.

But as they neared the hall the sky grew overcast and black with clouds, and at the fall of night a wind arose and blew up clouds of heavy dust that dimmed their brilliancy, so that they reached the mansion of Felim besmirched and blown about and very weary.

Hardly had the chariot of the King drawn up within the court, than a roll of thunder, loud and terrible, resounded overhead, while floods of rain poured down, and a fierce tempest seemed to shake the building to its foundations. "An awful night is this," said Felim; "close to the doors and bid the singing men and women make bright cheerful music in the hall." But all in vain they tried to cheer the guests. Louder the tempest roared, and peal on peal of thunder, such as none of them had ever heard before, made all hearts quail. "No common storm is this," the monarch said, "I have forebodings that some ill will fall upon the province from this night." But Felim busied himself to push on the feast, and when all were seated at the board, with servers carving the great joints and wine poured out, a lull came in the storm, and Felim thought that all was well at last. But scarcely had the King begun to eat, when a swift messenger came running in. "O King," he proclaimed, "a child is born to Felim, a fine fair-fashioned girl; let Felim come and see his wife and child." But Felim said, "Be silent now, let not the feast be broken by your news. When once the feast is done and the King served, I'll come and see the child."

Beside the King sat Caffa, the first Druid of the province, an aged man. He heard the message, and up-rose. "A child is born to our host, O King, while we are present here. I will go forth and by the stars find out her destiny, whether to Felim and his wife comes joy or woe with this girl's birth." "Go forth," the King replied, "not less than this is due to our good host. Fair be the fate that will befall to him and all his house because this child is born."

Then Caffa went far out beyond the house, and at the outer rath he stood awhile, trying behind the drifting clouds to read the stars. The quarter of the moon he calculated carefully, and in what constellations the wandering stars, the planets, lay. In his old books and tablets, carried within the folds of his wide flowing robes, was gathered all the ancient wizard's lore, the wisdom of his craft. Closely he scanned the lines, and with unusual care he drew the horoscope. And now and then he started, as though things surprising to himself were found therein.

So long he lingered, that, when at length he closed

his tablets made of soft wood and written o'er with runes, and turned him to the house, the King and all his company had quite forgot the child, and loud uproarious laughter rang throughout the hall, and sallies of keen wit and merry song as the full horns of mead and ale passed round from hand to hand. So at the door a moment Caffa stood ; and in his face was dreadful warning, and a look so strange, that all the laughter died away, and silence, sudden and complete, fell on the company.

" Well," said the King, and laughed, though fear smote on his mind, " we hope the omens prophesy good luck ; we drink a horn of mead to the maid's good health ; may she thrive, grow fair and marry well, and to her parents bring no harm or ill."

" Not to her parents will this child bring ill, but to the province, and to Ulster's king and chiefs. Fair she will be, so fair that queens will soon grow jealous of her beauty, and kings will wage red war to gain her hand. I see her, tall and stately as a swan or as the sapling of the mountain-side ; her cheek the ruddy foxglove puts to shame, her skin is white as winter's driven snow. Like the soft hyacinth is the deep, liquid blue of her sweet eyes, and teeth, like pearls, gleam between crimson lips. Like to a crown of gold her clustering hair, gathered in rolls about her shapely head. She walks apart, alone, like a fair flower hidden within a dell, yet all around her and where'er she comes are tumults and the sounds of rolling war, and broken friendships and black treachery. I see that she is destined to a king, but something comes between her and her fate. Beware, O King ; this maid is born for ill to Ulster, and the downfall of the Red Branch and its noble Champions."

Up-sprang the Heroes of the Red Branch then, and one

and all cried out that if upon the province ill must fall because of this one babe, 'twere better far to put the child to death while she was young, and rid the land of her. But the King held them back. "Bring the babe hither," he said, "and let us see this harbinger of ill."

Then came the babe all swathed in white and lying, soft and fair, within her nurse's arms. And when the infant saw the lights and heard the sounds of singing, she was pleased, and puckered up her baby face and looked up at the King and crowed and smiled. At this the King was moved to gentleness ; he rose up from his seat and took the babe out of her nurse's arms and loudly he proclaimed before them all: " The prophecies and omens of the seers I do most strictly honour and believe. No man can fly from fate, nor can man set aside his destiny. The mandates of the gods of earth and air and fire, the Unchanging Elements, must be fulfilled. Yet will I not believe that any good can come of an ignoble act. No man or hero of a noble mind for his own good would slay a helpless babe, neither then for the good of Ulster shall this foul, cowardly deed be done. The child shall live, and if she prove as fair as Caffa says, one part at least of his grim prophecy shall be fulfilled, for I will take the girl as my own wife when she is come to marriageable age, and so she shall be wedded to a king. And here I do declare to one and all, I take this child under my special charge and make myself responsible for her. I bring her up in my own way, and he who lifts his hand against the child must after reckon with the king himself."

Then Fergus, Conall Cernach, and the rest arose and said : " The King's protection is a circling wall through which no man may break. We, the Champions of the Red Branch and thy own chiefs, do well observe and will fulfil your will. Even though trouble happen through her life, the child shall live." So said they all. Then Caffa said: " Alas! Alas! O King, you and your chiefs will live to rue this day. Great woes are bound up with the destiny before this little maid, and all the world will hear of them and weep. A child of sorrow is this child, and 'Deirdre of Contentions' is her name." " So be it," said the King, " I like the name; when Deirdre is of age to foster with a nurse, bring her to me."

CHAPTER XXIII

The Up-bringing of Deirdre

AS soon as she was weaned, King Conor took the child away from her own parents, as was the custom in those olden days, and put her out to foster with a nurse, Levarcam, a wise and skilful dame, who told the King from day to day how Deirdre fared. And for the first seven years Deirdre grew up within the royal household, petted and loved by all, and she was richly fed and robed in silk, and nourished like a princess, for all in the palace knew that this young lovely child was destined to be mated with their king. Often she spent her days upon the playing fields, and watched the boy-corps practising their sports, and joined their games and laughed with glee like any other child. Thus happily and gaily passed the years for Deirdre, till one day when she was playing ball among the little lads, the King came down to watch their play. He saw how like a flower Deirdre grew, half like the opening daisy, pink and white, half like the slender hairbell on its stem, graceful and delicate; and though he was an old man, and had been a widower for now many years, and the child but a babe of seven years, a sudden jealousy smote at his aged heart. He saw the girl surrounded by the lads, who tossed the ball into her little lap or into her small apron held out to catch it as it fell. And every time she caught it, her ringing childish laugh broke out, and all the boys cried,

"Well, caught, O Deirdre; bravely caught, our little Queen!" For to them all, it was well-known that this small child was kept by Conor for himself, to share his throne and home; so oft in play they called her "Little Queen."

Then Conor called his Druid Caffa to him, and he said, "Too long we leave this child at liberty among the chieftain's sons. She must henceforth be kept apart and quite forget that there are younger men than you or me. If she grows up among these lads, most certainly the day will come when she will wish to wed some chief of her own age. See, even now, the lads bend to her will; she rules them like a queen indeed, and gladly they obey her. When she is grown to maidenhood, small chance for me, an aged man, when comes the time to woo."

"The King woos not," said Caffa, "he commands, and none dare disobey." "Still I would rather have a willing bride," the King replied; "I want no girl to be my royal mate who craves and hankers for some other man among my subjects. She shall come to me of her own free will, because she knows no other man but me. She shall not even know what kind of thing a man may be, for I will shut her up apart from men, and, save yourself and me, she shall not ever see a manly face." "The King commands," said Caffa, slowly, "and it must be done as he desires. But yet I fear the maid will pine in her captivity. The bride you wed will be a lily pale as death, and not a maiden in her blooming loveliness."

"She shall have space and air and garden-ground," the King replied, "only she shall not ever see a human face, save yours and mine, and nurse Levarcam's."

So for the girl he built a place apart, far off from Emain in a lonely dell, surrounded by a wood. A simple

stately house was reared, surrounded by an orchard of
rare fruits. Behind the house a garden and a piece of
barren moor, and through the wood a gently-flowing
stream that wandered amid carpets of bright flowers.
And all seemed fair enough, but round the place he built
a mighty wall, so high that none could climb it, and a
moat ran round within. Four savage man-hounds sent
by Conor were on constant guard, watching on every
side by night and day, so that no living thing could enter
or pass out, save with the knowledge of Levarcam.

And for a time the child was happy, for Levarcam,
the wise woman, taught her all she knew. She taught
her how each bird sings to its mate, each different note
of thrush or cuckoo or the soaring lark ; she taught her
of the plants that spring towards heaven, their roots
deep hidden in the yielding soil, and of their names and
uses, and the way they fructified and sent out shoots, and
of the fruits they bore. And in the solemn night, they
went abroad and watched the motion of the stars, and
marked the wandering planets how they carved out their
own path among the rest, and all the changes of the moon
the maiden knew, and how to calculate the time of day
by shadows on the grass. There was no bird upon the
spray, nor herb among the plants, nor star in heaven,
but Deirdre had a name for each and all.

And ever and anon, King Conor came and sat with her
and talked, and brought her gifts to while away the time;
and because the days were long and passed one like the
other without any change, she liked his coming, and
would call him " Father," and make tales for him, and
sing her songs and show the little garden she had made
herself alone.

And Deirdre grew up tall and stately as the sapling

of the forest, and lithe as the green moorland rush that bows before the wind. Of all the women of the world was Deirdre the gentlest and best, lovely of form and lovely in her mind; light as the hind that leaps upon the hill, and white and shapely as the snowy swan. But though they tended her, and fed her with the best, the maiden drooped and pined. And on a day Levarcam said, "What ails thee, girl? Why is thy face so pale, thy step so slow? Why dost thou sigh and mope?" And Deirdre said, " I know not, nurse, what ails me; but I think I should be well if once again I saw the boys upon the playing fields, and heard their shouts, and tossed the ball with them."

" Fie, fie," replied the nurse, " 'tis seven full years since on the green you played at ball. A child of but seven years were you at that time, and now full fourteen years have come and gone, and you are growing into maidenhood." " Seven bitter years," said Deirdre, " since I beheld the joyous playing field, and saw the sports, and marked the manly face of Naisi, noblest and bravest of the corps of boys."

" Naisi, the son of Usna ? " asked Levarcam, much surprised. " Naisi was his name, he told me so," said Deirdre ; " but I did not ask whose son he was." " He told you so ? " Levarcam asked again. " He told me so," said Deirdre, " when he threw the ball, by a mis-cast, backward, across the heads of the group of maidens who were standing on the edge of the green, and I rose up among them all, picked up the ball, and gave it back to him. He pressed my hand and smiled, and promised he would see me oft again ; but never since that day, that fatal day, when Conor brought me to this lonely place, have he or I beheld each other more. Bring

Naisi here, O nurse, that I may once again behold his face, so bright and boyish, with its winning smile; then shall I live and laugh and love my life again."

" Speak not like this, O Maiden," exclaimed the nurse. "To-day the King comes for his visit. We are in winter now, but in the budding of the spring, he takes you hence to Emain, there to claim you as his wife."

" The king no doubt is kind," the girl replied, " and means me well, but he is old and grey, and in his face is something that I do not like. I think he could be cruel, and that if any man stood in his way, he would not hesitate to lay a trap to catch him, as Caffa snared the little mouse that ran about my room and kept me company. Yet will I go with him to Emain, for I think that somewhere among the people of the court, I shall find Naisi out."

" Hush, hush," the nurse replied, " Naisi is now a little boy no longer, but the foremost of all Ulster's younger chiefs, the hero of the Red Branch, and the favourite of the King. Speak not of Naisi to King Conor, or mayhap some harm will come to him." " Then will I never speak his name, or tell of him," the girl replied, " though in my dreams I see him every night playing at ball with me; but when he flings the ball for me to catch, 'tis ever the same thing. King Conor comes between and seizes it, and throws it back at Naisi. So can I never catch and hold it in my hands, and I am vexed and weep. But last night, O good nurse, King Conor flung the ball craftily at his head, and Naisi fell all red and stained with blood, like that poor calf that Caffa slew, thinking that I could eat it for my food. The little tender calf that played with me! Upon the winter's frosty floor I saw its blood, all crimson-red upon the driven snow,

and as I looked I saw a raven that stooped down to sip
the blood; and, O dear nurse, I thought of Naisi then,
for all his hair, as I remember it, was dark and glossy
like the raven's wing, and in his cheeks the ruddy glow
of health and beauty, like the blood, and white his skin
like snow. Dear nurse, dear nurse, let me see Naisi
once again, and send the King away." "Alas! alas!"
Levarcam said; "most difficult indeed is thy desire,
for far away is Naisi, and he dare not come within this
fort. High is the wall and deep the moat, and fierce
the blood-hounds watching at the gates." "At least,"
said Deirdre, "procure for me from Caffa that I may
once in a while wander without the fort and breathe the
open air upon the moor; this wall frowns on me like
an enemy holding me in his grasp and stifling me, surely
I die e'er long within these heavy walls. But on the
moor, where no man comes (if you must have it so),
I'd see at least the grouse winging its flight, and hear
the plover and the peeweet call, and pluck the heather
and the yellow gorse in summer time. O nurse, dear
nurse, have pity on your child." When Levarcam saw
the misery of the maid, she feared that Conor would
upbraid her with neglect because her cheek grew pale,
and her young joy seemed gone; and so that night she
spoke to Caffa, and he said, "I think no harm could
come if we should let the maiden walk out upon the wild
hillside. No human creature, save a stray hunter
following the deer, or a poor shepherd garnering his
sheep, or some strange homeless wanderer, e'er sets his
foot upon this lonesome moor. Far off are we from any
human habitation; and the maid droops, indeed. Let
her go out, but keep her well in sight; to climb the hill-
top and to roam the heather moor as spring comes on,

will bring fresh colour into her pale cheeks, and fit her for the wooing of the king."

So from that time, Deirdre went out upon the upland moor, and soon she knew each nook and stream and bit of forest-land for miles around.   She learned the zig-zag flight of the long-billed snipe, she knew the otter's marshy lair, and where the grouse and wild-duck made their nests.   She fed the timid fawn, wild, trustful as herself, and made a dear companion of a fox that followed her as though it were a dog ; and once, while Levarcam stayed below, she climbed the dizzy height where golden eagles had built their nest upon the mountain's crest, and smoothed the eaglets with her own soft hand.   And so she grew in health, and all her spirit came to her again, and when King Conor came to visit her, he thought that in his dreams and in the long life he had passed among the best of Erin's women, he had never seen or dreamed of a girl so lovely as this blood-drop of the moor. Eagerly he began to reckon up the days until, her fifteenth birthday being passed, he should bring her down to Emain, and take her as his wife.   But of her walks he knew not, only Caffa and Levarcam knew.

CHAPTER XXIV

The Sleep-Wanderer

ON a wild wintry night while things were so, there came into the neighbourhood a hunter of wandering game, who had lost his course and his companions. The man was tired with travelling among the hills all day, and in the dark cloudy night, with the mist rising round him from the hills, he laid him down outside the garden within which Deirdre dwelt, and fell asleep. Weak he was with hunger and fatigue, and numb with cold, and deep sleep fell upon the man. Sleep-wandering came upon him then, and he thought that he was close beside a warm hollowed-out fairy mound, and in his dreams he heard fairy music, soft and sweet. In his sleep he called aloud that if there were any one at all in the fairy mound, they would open the mound and let him in, for the sake of the Good Being.

Now Deirdre had not slept that night, and she had arisen and with her nurse had moved about the grounds to seek for warmth of exercise. Just as they turned to go back within the house out of the chill and heavy mist, Deirdre heard the faint feeble voice of the weary man outside the gate. " Nurse-mother, what is that ? " she asked and stopped. Levarcam knew it was a human voice, but she replied, " Only a thing of little worth, the birds of the air have gone astray, and are seeking one

another; let them hie away to the forest of branches";
and she tried to draw Deirdre towards the house. Again
sleep-wandering came on the man, and he called out again
and louder than before, that if there were any in the
fairy mound, for the sake of the Being of the Elements
they would arise and let him in.

"What is that, nurse-mother?" said the girl again.
"Only a thing of little sense, the birds of the woods are
gone astray from each other, and are seeking to come
together again. Let them hie them away to the forest
of branches."

The third time came sleep-wandering upon the hunter,
and he called aloud that if there were any within the
mound, they would let him in for the sake of the God of
the Elements, for he was benumbed with cold and
parched with hunger.

"Oh! what is that, nurse-mother?" said Deirdre.
"Nought there is in that to bring gladness to thee,
maiden; it is but the birds of the air who have lost one
another in the woods; let them hie away into the forest
of branches. Neither shelter or home will they get from
us this night." "Oh! nurse-mother, it was in the name
of the God of the Elements that the bird asked shelter
of us; and oft hast thou told me that anything asked
of us in His name should willingly be done. If thou
wilt not allow me to bring in the bird that is benumbed
with cold and sore with hunger, I myself will doubt thy
teaching and thy faith. But as I believe in thy teaching
and thy faith, as thou thyself didst explain it to me, I
myself will let in the bird." So Deirdre turned back
to the gate and drew the bar from the door, and let in
the hunter. She brought him into the house, and placed
a seat in the place of sitting, food in the place of eating,

o

and drink in the place of drinking, for the man who had come home.

"Go on and eat thy food, for indeed thou art in need of it," said Deirdre.

"Well, I was in truth needful of food and of drink and of warmth when I came to the door of this home," said the hunter, "but these are all gone from me now that I behold thee, maiden." Then Levarcam was angry with the man, and spoke sharply to him : "It is too ready on thy tongue the talk is, O man, with thy food and with thy drink. It would be better for thee to keep thy mouth shut and thy tongue dumb in return for the shelter we are giving thee on a cold winter's night."

"Well," said the hunter, "I may keep my mouth shut and my tongue dumb if it suits thee, but by thy father's two hands and thine own, there are some others of the world's men who, if they but saw this blood-drop thou art hiding here, it is not long that they would leave her here with thee."

"What people are those and where are they ? " said Deirdre, eagerly. "I will tell thee that, maiden," said the hunter. "There are three heroes of the Red Branch, Naisi, Ainle, and Arden, sons of Usna, brothers, who, if they saw thee, would bear thee hence to some other place than this."

"What like are these three brothers of whom you speak ? " cried Deirdre, and all her face blushed to a rosy red. "Like the colour of a raven their dusky hair, tossed back from each high, shining brow; their skin white as the plumage of a swan, their cheeks like to a red-deer's coat, or like your own cheeks, maiden. They swim and leap and run as strong and stately as the salmon of the stream, or as the stag upon the dappled hill, 'twixt sun and shade; but Naisi, when he stands upright, towers a head and shoulders above all the men around him. Such are the sons of Usna, noble maid."

But Levarcam interfered: "However be those men of whom you speak, off with you now and take another road that comes not past this way. Small is my gratitude for all thy talk, and well for her who let thee in hadst thou died of thy cold and hunger at the door, and never come within for food and drink."

The hunter went his way; but he bethought himself that if he told the sons of Usna of the lovely blood-drop he had seen, they might free the maiden out of Levarcam's hands, and do a good deed to him also for telling them that there was such a damsel as Deirdre on the surface of the living dewy world. So he told his tale to Naisi and said to him that there dwelt, far away on the distant moor, shut in between high walls, the loveliest maiden that ever was born in Erin, and that none lived beside her but an aged nurse and an old Druid, so that Deirdre was like a tender flower over-shadowed by two ancient branchy trees, that hid her from the air and sun.

When Naisi heard that, he said, "Who is the maid and where is she, whom no man hath seen but thee, if, indeed, seen her thou hast?" "Truly I have seen her," said the hunter, "but no one else could find her save I myself should guide him."

Then Naisi said that he would go; but Arden and Ainle tried to dissuade him, for they said, "What if the girl should be the maid the King hath destined to himself?" But from far-off to the mind of Naisi there came a memory of a young child, scarce seven years old, whom on the playing-fields he once had seen and promised to see again, but who had disappeared that very day, and never from that day to this had he set eyes upon the girl. So all his brothers could devise served not to turn him from his purpose; and at dawn of the next day, amid the early carolling of birds, in the mild morning dawn of fragrant May, when all the bush was white with hawthorn-bloom, and dew-drops glistened from every point of sapling, bush, and plant, they four set out, going in search of the retired place where Deirdre dwelt.

"Yonder it is, down on the floor of the glen," the hunter said, when at the fall of eve they stood upon the mountain-brow above the house, so well concealed in trees that many times they might have passed it by and never known that any house was near. "I care not for myself to see again the woman who lives therein; sharp is her tongue, unwelcoming her words. I leave you then, good luck go with you, but if you will be advised, go not near the house. At every gate are blood-hounds, and Levarcam's bite is nigh as fierce as theirs."

From day to day the sons of Usna stayed among the hills that circled Deirdre's home. But for awhile Levarcam feared to let her charge go out, for soon would Conor come to claim her, and Levarcam thought, "If aught should happen or the girl should slip between my hands, small pity would King Conor have for me." But as time passed, and Deirdre pined again for open air and sunshine, and the walks she loved, and fretted for the fox that looked for her, and for her woodland company of beasts and birds, Levarcam once again took the girl abroad, and oft they sat upon the open hill and watched the sun go down, or brought their work and passed the long spring mornings on the heather, happy because the sunshine was so warm, the air so sweet, and all the world so fresh with herbs and flowers.

One day they long had sat thus drinking in the sun, and while Levarcam dozed and nodded with the heat and the fatigue of climbing up the hill, Deirdre from time to time would leave her side to seek some plant or follow a butterfly that passed across her path. Reaching the summit of the hill she saw three men whose like she never in her life before had set her eyes upon. They were not bent, like Caffa, or wrinkled, like King Conor when he came; nor were they dark and roughly clad, with shaggy beards, like the one hunter who had made his way to her abode. These men were young and lithe, straight as the pine and shapely as the stag. But one above the rest towered head and shoulders high, his raven locks thrown back, his blue eye scanning all the mountain for trace of fawn or deer. Beside them, in the leash, three noble hounds; and as they paced along the upland track, Deirdre sat mute in wonder, for in all her life never had she seen such goodly men as these. But suddenly, as they drew near, a flash of inspiration came upon her mind; she knew that these were Usna's sons, that he who overtopped the rest was Naisi, the boy who long ago had thrown the ball with her. The brothers passed her by, not seeing her seated above them on the hill. But all at once, without a moment's thought, Deirdre sprang up, and gathering up her dress, she sped as swiftly as a roe along the mountain side, calling out, " Naisi, Naisi, wilt thou leave me here ? " Now Naisi had rounded the bend of the hill, and he could not see the maiden, but Ainle and Arden saw her bounding after them, and no thought had they but to get Naisi away, for they knew well that this was Deirdre, and that if Naisi once set eyes on her, nothing in life would prevent him from carrying her off, the more especially, since Conor was not yet married to the girl. So when Naisi asked, " What is that cry that came to mine ear that it is not easy for me to answer and yet not easy for me to refuse ? " the brothers replied, " What but the quacking of the wild ducks upon the mere ?   Let us hasten our steps and hurry our feet, for long is the distance we have to traverse, and the dark hour of night is coming on." They went forward quickly, but when Deirdre saw that they were lengthening the space between themselves and her, she called again piteously, " Naisi, thou son of Usna, is it leaving me alone thou art ? " " What cry is that which strikes into my very heart ? " said Naisi.   " Not easy is it for me to answer, but harder yet is it to refuse." " It is but the cry of the grey geese in the air, winging their flight to the nearest tarn," said the brothers again; " let us hasten now and walk well, for long is our path to-night and the darkness of night is coming on." They set out to walk faster than before, and farther yet was the distance between themselves and Deirdre.   Then Deirdre flew with the swiftness of the winds of March across the bend of the mountain, and reached a place above them on the cliff, and called again the third time, " Naisi, Naisi, Naisi, thou son of Usna, wilt thou leave me here alone ? "   " The cry I hear strikes sweetly on mine ear, but of all cries I ever heard, this cry makes deepest wound within mine heart," said Naisi, and he stopped short.

" Heed not the cry," his brothers said, " it is the wail of the lake-swans, disturbed in their nesting-place; let us push on now, and win our way to-night to Emain

Macha." "Three times came that cry of distress to me," said Naisi, " and the vow of a champion is upon me, that no cry of distress shall be passed by unheeded. I will go back now and see whence comes that cry."

Then Naisi turned to go back, and on the hill above him he saw Deirdre, standing on a rock with her arms outstretched, and all her hair blown backward by the wind, and her fair face flushed all with red, part with her running, part with a lovely shame, and changing as the aspen shimmering in the summer's breeze. And Naisi knew that never in his life had he seen anything one-half so fair, or any blood-drop like the living blood-drop here, and he gave love to Deirdre such as he never gave to any other, or to a dream or vision, or to a person on the whole world's face, but only to Deirdre alone.

And Deirdre came close, and to him she gave three loving kisses, and to his brothers each a kiss ; and Naisi lifted her and placed her on his shoulder, and he said, " Hitherto it is you, my brothers, who have bidden me to walk well, but now it is I who bid the same to you."

That night they carried Deirdre to their own home, and sheltered her there for many days. But the news reached Conor that Deirdre was flown, and that it was the sons of Usna with whom she went, and in his fury he sent out armies, and hunted them from place to place, so that they traversed all Ireland, fleeing before the King. And when they found there was no rest for them in Ireland, Naisi determined to forsake his native land and to flee to Alba, for there he had made wars and had carved out for himself a kingdom as great as the kingdom of Conor in Ulster. So he and Deirdre, with his brothers and a great band of followers fled to Alba, which is to-day called Scotland, and they made their home on Glen

Etive in Alba, and thence Naisi ruled over the territories he had taken from the King of Alba, and he made wars, and became a powerful prince. And joyous and gladsome were he and Deirdre in each other's company, and great was the love and affection they gave one to the other.

CHAPTER XXV

The Wiles of King Conor

BUT all this while the cunning, cruel heart of Conor was planning his revenge. For though he was an old man with grown-up sons of middle age, he had begun to feel affection for the child who had been sheltered by his care, and who looked to him as her protector and her friend. And after all the years that he had waited for the girl, to have her plucked away beneath his eyes just when she was of age to be his wife, aroused his bitter wrath and jealousy. Deep in his heart he plotted dark revenge, but it was hard to carry out his plan, for well he knew that of his chiefs not one would lift his hand against the sons of Usna. Of all the Red Branch Champions those three were loved the best; and difficult it was to know which of the three was bravest, or most noble to behold. When in the autumn games they raced or leaped or drove the chariots round the racing-course, some said that Arden had the more majestic step and stately air; others, that Ainle was more graceful and more lithe in swing, but most agreed that Naisi was the princeliest of the three, so dignified his gait, so swift his step in running, and so strong and firm his hand. But when they wrestled, ran or fought in combats side by side, men praised them all, and called them the " Three Lights of Valour of the Gael."

When his plans were ripe, King Conor made a festival

in Emain Macha, and all his chiefs were gathered to the
feast. The aged Fergus sat at his right hand, and Caffa
next to him; close by sat Conall Cernach, a mighty
warrior, still in his full prime, and by his side, as in old
times, Cuchulain sat. He seemed still young, but of an
awesome aspect, as one who had a tragedy before him,
and great deeds behind; and, for all that he was the
pride of Ulster's hosts, men stood in dread before him,
as though he were a god.

Around the board sat many a mighty man and good
prime warrior seasoned by long wars. But in the hall
three seats were empty, and it was known to be the
king's command that in his presence none should dare to
speak the names of Usna's banished sons.

This night the King was merry and in pleasant humour,
as it seemed. He plied his guests with mead and ale
out of his golden horns, and led the tale and passed the
jest, and laughed, and all his chiefs laughed with him,
till the hall was filled with cheerful sounds of song and
merriment. And when the cheer was bravest and the
feast was at its height, he rose and said: "Right
welcome all assembled here this night, High Chiefs of
Ulster, Champions of the Branch. Of all the kingly
households in the world, tell me, O you who travel
much and see strange distant lands and courts of kings,
have ye in Alba or in Erin's realms, or in the countries
of the great wide world, e'er seen a court more princely
than our own, or an assembly comely as the Red Branch
Knights?"

"We know not," cried they all, "of any such. Thy
court, O High King, is of all courts on earth the bravest
and the best."

"If this be so," said wily Conor, "I suppose no sense

of want lies on you; no lack of anything is in your
minds?"

"We know not any want at all," they said aloud;
but in their minds they thought, "save the Three Lights
of Valour of the Gael."

"But I, O warriors, know one want that lies on us,"
the King replied, "the want of the three sons of Usna
fills my mind. Naisi and Ainle and Arden, good
warriors were they all; but Naisi is a match for any
mighty monarch in the world. By his own strength
alone he carved for him and his a princely realm in
Alba, and there he rules as king. Alas! that for the
sake of any woman in the world, we lose his presence
here."

"Had we but dared to utter that, O Warrior King,
long since we should have called them home again.
These three alone would safely guard the province
against any host. Three sons of a border-king and used
to fight are they; three heroes of warfare, three lions
of fearless might."

"I knew not," said King Conor craftily, "you wished
them back. Methought you all were jealous of their
might, or long ere this we should have sent for them.
Let messengers now go, and heralds of the king to bring
them home, for welcome to us all will be the sight of
Usna's sons."

"Who is the herald who shall bear that peaceful
message?" cried they all. "I have been told," said
Conor, "that out of Ulster's chiefs there were but three
whose word of honour and protection they would trust,
and at whose invitation Naisi would come again in
peace. With Conall Cernach he will come, or with
Cuchulain, or with great Fergus of the mighty arms.

These are the friends in whom he will confide; under the safe-guard of each one of these he knows all will be well."

"Bid Fergus go, or Conall or Cuchulain," the warriors cried; "let not a single night pass by until the message goes to bring the sons of Usna to our board again. Most sorely do we need them, deeply do we mourn their loss. Bring back the Lights of Valour of the Gael."

"Now will I test," thought Conor to himself, "which of these three prime warriors loves me best." So supper being ended, the King took Conall to his ante-room apart and set himself to question cunningly: "Suppose, O royal soldier of the world, thou wert to go and fetch the sons of Usna back from Alba to their own land under thy safeguard and thy word of honour that they should not be harmed; but if, in spite of this, some ill should fall on them—not by my hand, of course—and they were slain, what then would happen? what wouldst thou do?"

"I swear, O King," said Conall, "by my hand, that if the sons of Usna were brought here under my protection to their death, not he alone whose hand was stained by that foul deed, but every man of Ulster who had wrought them harm should feel my righteous vengeance and my wrath."

"I thought as much," said Conor, "not great the love and service thou dost give thy lord. Dearer to thee than I are Usna's sons."

Then sent he for Cuchulain and to him he made the same demand. But bolder yet Cuchulain made reply: "I pledge my word, O King, if evil were to fall upon the sons of Usna, brought back to Erin and their homes

in confidence in my protection and my plighted word,
not all the riches of the eastern world would bribe or
hinder me from severing thine own head from thee in
lieu of the dear heads of Usna's sons, most foully slain
when tempted home by their sure trust in me."

" I see it now, Cuchulain," said the king, " thou dost
profess a love for me thou feelest not."

Then Fergus came, and to him also he proposed the
same request. Now Fergus was perplexed what answer
he should give. Sore did it trouble him to think that
evil might befall brave Usna's sons when under his protection. Yet it was but a little while since he and Conor
had made friends, and he come back to Ulster, and set
high in place and power by the King, and well he knew
that Conor doubted him ; and such a deed as this, to
bring the sons of Usna home again, would prove fidelity
and win the King's affection. Moreover, Conor spoke
so guardedly that Fergus was not sure whether the King
had ill intent or no towards the sons of Usna. For all
he said was : " Supposing any harm or ill befall the sons
of Usna by the hand of any here, what wouldst thou do ? "

So after long debate within himself, Fergus replied :
" If any Ulsterman should harm the noble youths,
undoubtedly I should avenge the deed ; but thee, O
King, and thine own flesh and blood, I would not harm ;
for well I know, that if they came under protection of
thy sovereign word, they would be safe with thee.
Therefore, against thee and thy house, I would not raise
my hand, whatever the conditions, but faithfully and
with my life will serve thee."

" 'Tis well," the wily king replied, " I see, O royal
warrior, that thou lovest me well, and I will prove thy
faithfulness and truth. The sons of Usna without doubt

will come with thee. To-morrow set thou forward; bear the King's message to brave Usna's sons, say that he eagerly awaits their coming, that Ulster longs to welcome them. Urge them to hasten; bid them not to linger on the way, but with the utmost speed to press straight forward here to Emain Macha."

Then Fergus went out from the King and told the nobles he had pledged his word to Conor to bring back the sons of Usna to their native land. And on the morrow's morn Fergus set forth in his own boat, and with him his two sons, Illan the Fair and Buinne the Ruthless Red, and together they sailed to Loch Etive in Alba.

But hardly had they started than King Conor set to work with cunning craft to lure the sons of Usna to their doom. He sent for Borrach, son of Annte, who had built a mighty fortress by the sea, and said to him, " Did I not hear, O Borrach, that thou hadst prepared a feast for me ? " " It is even so, O King, and I await thy coming to partake of the banquet I have prepared." And Conor said, " I may not come at this time to thy feast; the duties of the kingdom keep me here at Emain. But I would not decline thy hospitality. Fergus, the son of Roy, stands close to me in place and power; a feast bestowed on him I hold as though it were bestowed on me. In less than a week's time comes Fergus back from Alba, bringing the sons of Usna to their home. Bid Fergus to thy feast, and I will hold the honour paid to him as paid to me."

For wily Conor knew that if his royal command was laid on Fergus to accept the banquet in his stead, Fergus dare not refuse; and by this means he sought to separate the sons of Usna from their friend, and get them fast into his own power at Emain, while Fergus waited yet at Borrach's house, partaking of his hospitality. " Thus, thought the King, " I have the sons of Usna in my grasp, and dire the vengeance I will wreak on them, the men who stole my wife."

CHAPTER XXVI

The Sorrowful Death of Usna's Sons

AT the head of fair Loch Etive the sons of Usna had built for themselves three spacious hunting-seats among the pine-trees at the foot of the cliffs that ran landward to deep Glen Etive. The wild deer could be shot from the window, and the salmon taken out of the stream from the door of their dwelling. There they passed the spring and summer months, Usna's sons of the white steeds and the brown deer-hounds, whose breasts were broader than the wooden leaves of the door. Above the hunting-lodge, on the grassy slope that is at the foot of the cascade, they built a sunny summer home for Deirdre, and they called it the ' Grianan,' or sunny bower of Deirdre. It was thatched on the outside with the long-stalked fern of the dells and the red clay of the pools, and lined within with the pine of the mountains and the downy feathers of the wild birds ; and round it was the apple-garden of Clan Usna, with the apple-tree of Deirdre in its midst and the apple-trees of Naisi and Ainle and Arden encircling it.

And Deirdre loved her life, for she was free as the brown partridge flying over the mountains, or as the vessels with ruddy sails swinging upon the loch.

But in the winter they moved down to the broad sheltered pasture-lands that lay on the western side of the loch near the island that was in olden days called *Eilean Chlann Uisne* or the Island of the Children of Usna, but is called *Eilean nan Ron* or the Isle of the Seals to-day; and there they built a mighty fortress for Deirdre and the sons of Usna which men still call the *Caisteal Nighean Righ Eirinn* or the Castle of the Daughter of the King of Ireland, and thence they made wars and conquered a great part of Western Alba and became powerful princes.

One sultry evening in the late autumn, Deirdre and Naisi were resting before the door of her sunny bower after a day spent by the brothers in the chase. Below, their followers were cutting up the deer, and as they brought in the bags of heavy game, and faggots for the hearth, the voice of Ainle singing an evening melody resounded through the wood. Like the sound of the wave the voice of Ainle, and the rich bass of Arden answered him, as together the two brothers came out from the shadow of the trees, gathering to the trysting-place of the evening meal.

Between Naisi and Deirdre a draught-board was set, but Deirdre was winning, for a mood of oppression lay upon Naisi and his thoughts were not in the game. For of late, at evening, his exile weighed upon him, and little good to him seemed his prosperity and his successes, since he did not see his own home in Ireland and his friends at the time of his rising in the morning or at the time of his lying down at night. For great as were his possessions in Alba, stronger in him than the love of his kindred in Alba was the love of his native land in Erin. He thought it strange, moreover, that of those three who in the old time loved him most, Fergus and Conall Cernach and Cuchulain, not one of them had all

P

this time come to bring him to his own land again under his safeguard and protection.

So, as they played, Deirdre could see that the mind of Naisi was wandering from the game, and her heart smote her, as often it had smitten her before when she had seen him thus oppressed, that for her sake so much had gone from him of friends and home, and his allegiance to his king, and honourable days among his clan. Wistfully she smiled across the board at Naisi, but mournful was the answering smile he sent her back.

" Play, play," she said, " I win the game from you." " One game the more or less can matter little when all else is lost," he answered bitterly. But hardly had the unkind words passed from him, the first unkindness Deirdre ever heard from Naisi's lips, when far below, across the silent waters of the lake, he caught a distant call, his own name uttered in a ringing voice that seemed familiar, a voice that brought old days to memory.

" I hear the voice of a man from Erin call below," he cried, and started up. Now Deirdre too had heard the cry and well she knew that it was Fergus' voice they heard, but deep foreboding passed across her mind that all their hours of happiness were past, and grief and rending of the heart in store. So quickly she replied : " How could that be ? It is some man of Alba coming from the chase, belated in returning. No voice was that from Erin ; it was a Scotchman's cry. Let us play on."

Three times the voice of Fergus came sounding up the glen, and at the last, Naisi sprang up. " You are mistaken, damsel ; of a certainty I know this is the voice of Fergus." " I knew it all the time, whose voice it was," said Deirdre, when she saw he would not be put

off. " Why then didst thou not tell us ? " Naisi asked.
" A vision that I saw last night hath hindered me,"
replied the girl. " I saw three birds come to us out of
Emain from the King, carrying three sips of honey in
their bills ; the sips of honey they left here with us, but
took three sips of our red blood away with them."

" What is thy rede of this vision, O Damsel ? " Naisi
asked. " Thus do I understand it," Deirdre said ;
" Fergus hath come from our own native land with peace,
and sweet as honey will his message be ; but the three
sips of blood that he will take away with him, those
three are ye, for ye will go with him, and be betrayed
to death." " Speak not such words, O Deirdre," cried
they all ; "never would Fergus thus betray his friends.
Alas ! that words like this should pass thy lips. We stay
too long ; Fergus awaits us at the port. Go, Ainle, and
go, Arden, down to meet him, and to give him loving
welcome here." So Arden went, and Ainle, and three
loving kisses fervently they gave to Fergus and his sons.
Gladly they welcomed the wayfarers to Naisi's home,
and led them up ; and Naisi and Deirdre arose and
stretched their hands in welcome ; and they gave them
blessing and three kisses lovingly, for old times' sake, and
eagerly they asked for tidings of Erin, and of Ulster
especially. " I have no other tidings half so good as
these," said Fergus, " that King Conor waits for you to
give you welcome back to Emain, and to the Red Branch
House. I am your surety and your safeguard, and full
well ye know that under Fergus' safeguard ye are sure
of peace." " Heed not that message, Naisi," Deirdre
said ; " greater and wider is your lordship here, than
Conor's rule in Erin."

" Better than any lordship is one's native land,"

said Naisi; "dearer to me than great possessions here, is one more sight of Erin's well-loved soil."

"My word and pledge are firm on your behalf," said Fergus; "with me no harm or hurt can come to you." "Verily and indeed, thy word is firm, and we will go with thee."

But to their going Deirdre consented not, and every way she sought to hinder them, and wept and prayed them not to go to death. "Now all my joy is past," she said; "I saw last night the three black ravens bearing three sad leaves of the yew-tree of death; and O Beloved, those three withered leaves I saw were the three sons of Usna, blown off their stem by the rough wind of Conor's wrath and the damp dew of Fergus' treachery." And they were sorry that she had said that. "These are but foolish women's fears," said they; "the dropping of leaves in thy dream, and the howling of dogs, the sight of birds with blood-drops in their bills, are but the restlessness of sleep, O Deirdre; and verily we put our trust in Fergus' word. To-night we go with him to Erin."

Gladsome and gay were the three brothers then; they put all fears away from them, and set to prepare them for their journey back to Erin's shores. And early the next morning, about the parting of night from day, at the delay of the morning dawn, they passed down to their galley that rocked upon the loch, and hoisted sail, and calmly and peacefully they sailed out into the ocean. But Deirdre sat in the stern of the boat, and her face was not set forward looking towards Erin, but it was set backward looking on the coasts of Scotland. And she cried aloud, "O Land of the East, My love to thee, with thy wondrous beauty! Woe is me that I leave thy lochs and thy bays, thy flowering delightful

plains, and thy bright green-smooth hills! Dear to
me the fort that Naisi built, dear the sunny bower
up the glen; very dear to my heart the wooded slope
holding the sunbeams where I have sat with Naisi."
And as they sailed out of Glen Etive she sang this song,
sadly and sorrowfully :—

> " Farewell, dear Alba of the free,
> Beloved land beside the sea,
> No power could drag me from my home,
> Did I not come, Naisi, with thee
>
> Farewell, dear bowers within the Glen,
> Farewell, strong fort hung over them,
> Dear to the heart each shining isle,
> That seems to smile beneath our ken.
>
> Glen da Roe !
> Where the white cherry and garlic blow,
> On thy blue wave we rocked to sleep,
> As on the deep, by Glen da Roe.
>
> Glen Etive !
> Whose sunny slopes these waters lave,
> The rising sun we seemed to hold,
> As in a fold, in Glen Etive.
>
> Glen Masaun !
> Love to all those who here were born !
> Across thy peak, at twilight's fall,
> The cuckoos call, in Glen Masaun.
>
> Farewell, dear Land,
> From Alba's strand I ne'er had roved
> Save at the call of my beloved,
> Farewell, dear Land ! "

The next day they reached the shores of Ireland not
far from the fort of Borrach.   And as they landed there,

messengers from Borrach met Fergus, saying, " Borrach hath prepared a feast for the King, and it is the King's command that the honour of this feast be given to thee. Come therefore and spend this night with me ; but the King desires to hasten the sons of Usna that he may welcome them, and he bids them press onward to Emain this very night."

When Fergus heard that, sudden fear and gloom over-shadowed him, lest in very truth Conor had evil designs towards the sons of Usna. " It was not well done, O Borrach, to offer me a feast in Conor's stead this night, for I was pledged to bring the sons of Usna straight to Emain without delay." " It is the King's command," said Borrach ; " needs must a true vassal obey the King." Still was Fergus loth to stay and he asked Naisi what he ought to do about this. " Do what they desire of thee, O Fergus," said Deirdre, " if to partake of a banquet seems better to thee than to protect the sons of Usna. However to me it seems that the lives of thy three friends is a good price to pay for a feast."

" I will not forsake them," said Fergus ; " for my two sons, Illan the Fair and Buinne the Ruthless Red will be with them to protect them, and my word of honour, moreover, with them ; if all the warriors of Erin were assembled in one place, and all of one mind, they would not be able to break the pledge of Fergus."

" Much thanks we give thee for that," said Naisi, for he saw that Fergus feared to fall foul of Conor more than he cared for their safety ; " never have we depended on any protection but that of our own right hands alone ; we will then go forward to Emain Macha, and see there if the word of Fergus will be sufficient to protect us."

But Deirdre said: " Go not forward to-night ; but let

us turn aside, and for this one night take shelter with Cuchulain at Dundalk; then will Fergus have partaken of his feast, and he will be ready to go with you. So will his word be fulfilled and yet your lives will be prolonged." "We think not well of that advice," said Buinne the Ruthless Red; "you have with you the might of your own good hands, and our might, and the plighted word of Fergus to protect you; impossible is it that ye should be betrayed." "Ah! that plighted word of Fergus'; the man who forsook us for a feast!" said Deirdre. "Well may we rely on Fergus' plighted word." And she fell into grief and dejection. "Alas! Alas!" she cried. "Why left we Alba of the red deer to come again to Erin? Why put we trust in the light word of Fergus? Woe is come upon us since we listened to the promises of that man! The valiant sons of Usna are destroyed by him, the Lights of Valour of the Gael. Great is my heaviness of heart to-night! Great is the loss that is fallen upon us."

In spite of that the sons of Usna and their two friends went onward towards the White Cairn of Watching on Sliab Fuad; but Deirdre was very weary and she lingered behind in the glen, and sat down to rest and fell asleep. They did not notice at first that she was not with them, but Naisi found it out and he turned back to seek Deirdre. He found her sitting in the wood on the trunk of a fallen tree, just waking from her sleep. When she saw Naisi she arose and clung to him. "What happened to thee, O fair one?" said Naisi, "and wherefore is thy face so wild and fearful, and tears within thine eyes?"

"I fell into a sleep, for I was weary," she replied; "and O Naisi, I fear because of the vision and the dream I

saw." "Thou art too apt to dream, beloved," said
Naisi tenderly, "what was thy dream?" "Terrible
was my dream," said Deirdre; "I saw thee, Naisi, and
Ainle and Arden, each of ye three beloved ones, without a
head, thy headless bodies lying side by side near Emain's
fort; and Illan lay there too drenched all with blood, and
headless like ye three. But on the other side among our
enemies, fighting against us, was the treacherous Buinne
the Ruthless Red, who now is our protector and our
guide; for he had saved his head by treachery to thee."
"Sad were thy dream indeed," said Naisi, "were it true;
but fear it not, it was an empty vision grown out of weariness and pain." But Deirdre clung yet to him, and she
cried, "O Naisi, see, above thy head, and o'er the heads
of Ainle and of Arden, that sombre cloud of blood! dost
thou not mark it hanging in the air? All over Emain
lies the heavy pall; but on thy head and theirs red
blood-drops fall, big, dusky, drenching drops. Let us
not go to Emain." But Naisi thought that from her
weariness the mind of Deirdre had become distraught,
and all the more he pressed them onward, that she might
have rest and shelter for the night. As they drew near
to Emain, Deirdre said, "One test I give you whether
Conor means you good or harm. If into his own house
he welcomes you, all will be well, for in his own home
would no monarch dare to harm a guest; but if he send
you to some other house, while he himself stays on in
Emain's court, then treachery and guile is meant towards
you."

Now as they reached the Court of Emain, messengers
came out to meet them from the King. "King Conor
bids you welcome," said the men; "right glad is he that
you are come again to Erin, to your fatherland. But

for this one night only is he not prepared to call you as his guests to his own court. To-morrow he will give you audience and bid you to his house. For this one night, then, he bids you turn aside into the Red Branch House, where all is ready for your entertainment." "It is as I thought," said Deirdre, "King Conor means no good to you, I ween." But Naisi replied, "Where could the Red Branch champions so fitly rest as in the Red Branch House? Most gladly do we seek our hall, to rest and find refreshment for the morrow. We all are travel-stained, but we will bathe and take repose, and on the morrow we will meet the King."

But when they came to the House of the Red Branch, so weary were they all, that though all kinds of viands were supplied, they ate but little, but lay down to rest. And Naisi said, "Dost thou remember, Deirdre, how in that last game of draughts we played together, thou didst win, because we were in Alba, and my heart was here at home? Now are we back at last, and let us play again; this time I promise I will win from thee."

So with the lightsome spirit of a boy, Naisi sat down to play; for now that once again he was at home among his people and in his native land, all thought or dread of evil passed from him. But with Deirdre it was not so, for heavy dread and terror of the morrow lay on her heart, and in her mind she felt that this was their last day of peace and love together.

But in his royal court, King Conor grew impatient as he thought that Deirdre was so near at hand, and he not seeing her. "Go now, O foster-mother, to the Red Branch Hall and see if on the child that thou didst rear remains her early bloom and beauty, and if she still is lovely as when she went from me. If she is still the same, then, in spite of Naisi, I'll have her for my own; but if her bloom is past, then let her be, Naisi may keep her for himself."

Right glad was Levarcam to get leave to go to Deirdre and to Usna's sons. Down to the Red Branch House straightway she went, and there were Naisi and her foster-child playing together with the board between them. Now, save Deirdre herself, Naisi was dearer to Levarcam than any other in the world, and well she knew that her own face and form were upon Deirdre still, only grown riper and more womanly. For, without Conor's knowledge, she oft had gone to seek them when they stayed in Alba.

Lovingly she kissed them and strong showers of tears sprang from her eyes. "No good will come to you, ye children of my love," she said with weeping, "that ye are come again with Deirdre here. To-night they practise treachery and ill intent against you all in Emain. The King would know if Deirdre is lovely still, and though I tell a lie to shelter her, he will find out, and wreak his vengeance on you for the loss of her. Great evils wait for Emain and for you, O darling friends. Shut close the doors and guard them well; let no one pass within. Defend yourselves and this sweet damsel here, my foster-child. Trust no man; but repel the attack that surely comes, and victory and blessing be with you."

Then she returned to Emain; but all along the way she wept quick-gushing showers of tears, and heaved great sighs, for well she knew that from this night the sons of Usna would be alive no more.

" What are the tidings that you have for me ? " King Conor asked. " Good tidings have I, and tidings that are not good." " Tell me them," said the King. " The good tidings that I have are these ; that the sons of Usna, the three whose form and figure are best, the three bravest in fight and all deeds of prowess, are come again to Erin ; and, with the Lights of Valour at thy side, thine enemies will flee before thee, as a flock of frightened birds is driven before the gale. The ill-tidings that I have, are that through suffering and sorrow the love of my heart and treasure of my soul is changed since she went away, and little of her own bloom and beauty remains upon Deirdre." " That will do for awhile," said the King ; and he felt his anger abating. But when they had drunk a round or two, he began to doubt the word of Levarcam. " O Trendorn," said he to one who sat beside him, " dost thou recollect who it was who slew thy father ? "

" I know well ; it was Naisi, son of Usna," he replied. " Go thou therefore where Naisi is, and see if her own face and form remain upon Deirdre."

So Trendorn went down to the House of the Red Branch, but they had made fast the doors and he could find no way of entrance, for all the gates and windows were stoutly barred. He began to be afraid lest the sons of Usna might be ready to leap out upon him from within, but at last he found a small window which they had forgotten to close, and he put his eye to the window, and saw Naisi and Deirdre still playing at their game peacefully together. Deirdre saw the man looking in at the window, and Naisi, following her eye, caught sight of him also. And he picked up one of the pieces that was lying beside the board, and threw it at Trendorn, so that it struck his eye and tore it out, and in pain and misery the man returned to Emain.

"You seem not so gay as when you set out, O Trendorn," said the King; "what has happened to thee, and hast thou seen Deirdre?" "I have seen her, indeed; I have seen Deirdre, and but that Naisi drove out mine eye I should have been looking at her still, for of all the women of the world, Deirdre is the fairest and the best." When Conor heard that, he rose up and called his followers together and without a moment's delay they set forward for the house of the Red Branch. For he was filled with jealousy and envy, and he thought the time long until he should get back Deirdre for himself.

"The pursuit is coming," said Deirdre; "I hear sounds without." "I will go out and meet them," said Naisi. "Nay," said Buinne the Ruthless Red, "it was in my hands that my father Fergus placed the sons of Usna to guard them, and it is I who will go forth and fight for them." "It seems to me," said Deirdre, "that thy father hath betrayed the sons of Usna, and it is likely that thou wilt do as thy father hath done, O Buinne." "If my father has been treacherous to you," said Buinne, "it is not I who will do as he has done." Then he went out and met the warriors of Conor, and put a host of them to the sword. "Who is this man who is destroying my hosts?" said Conor. "Buinne the Ruthless Red, the son of Fergus," say they. "We bought his father to our side and we must buy the son," said Conor. He called Buinne and said to him, "I gave a free gift of land to thy father Fergus, and I will give a free gift of land to thee; come over to my side to-night." "I will do that," said Buinne, and he went over to the side of the King. "Buinne hath deserted you, O sons of Usna, and the son is like the father," Deirdre said. "He has gone," said Naisi, " but he performed warrior-like deeds before he went."

Then Conor sent fresh warriors down to attack the house. " The pursuit is coming," said Deirdre. " I will go out and meet them," said Naisi. " It is not thou who must go, it is I," said Illan the Fair, son of Fergus, " for to me my father left the charge of you." " I think the son will be like the father," said Deirdre. " I am not like to forsake the sons of Usna so long as this hard sword is in my hand," said Illan the Fair. And the fresh, noble, young hero went out in his battle-array, and valiantly he attacked the host of Conor and made a red rout of them round the house. " Who is that young warrior who is smiting down my hosts ? " said Conor. " Illan the Fair, son of Fergus," they reply. " We will buy him to our side, as his brother was bought," said wily Conor. So he called Illan and said, " We gave a possession of land to thy father, and another to thy brother, and we will give an equal share to thee ; come over to our side." But the princely young hero answered : " Thy offer, O Conor, will I not accept ; for better to me is it to return to my father and tell him that I have kept the charge he laid upon me, than to accept any offer from thee, O King." Then Conor was wroth, and he commanded his own son to attack Illan, and furiously the two fought together, until Illan was sore wounded, and he flung his arms into the house, and called on Naisi to do valiantly, for he himself was slain by a son of Conor. " Illan has fallen, and you are left alone," said Deirdre, " O sons of Usna." " He is fallen indeed," said Naisi, " but gallant were the deeds that he performed before he died."

Then the warriors and mercenaries of Conor drew

closer round the house, and they took lighted torches and flung them into the house, and set it on fire. And Naisi lifted Deirdre on his shoulders and raised her on high, and with his brothers on either side, their swords drawn in their hands, they issued forth to fight their way through the press of their enemies. And so terrible were the deeds wrought by those heroes, that Conor feared they would destroy his host. He called his Druids, and said to them, " Work enchantment upon the sons of Usna and turn them back, for no longer do I intend evil against them, but I would bring them home in peace. Noble are the deeds that they have wrought, and I would have them as my servants for ever." The Druids believed the wily King and they set to work to weave spells to turn the sons of Usna back to Emain Macha.

They made a great thick wood before them, through which they thought no man could pass. But without ever stopping to consider their way, the sons of Usna went straight through the wood turning neither to the right hand or the left. " Good is your enchantment, but it will not avail," said Conor; " the sons of Usna are passing through without the turning of a step, or the bending of a foot. Try some other spell." Then the Druids made a grey stormy sea before the sons of Usna on the green plain. The three heroes tied their clothing behind their heads, and Naisi set Deirdre again upon his shoulder and went straight on without flinching, without turning back, through the grey shaggy sea, lifting Deirdre on high lest she should wet her feet.

" Thy spell is good," said Conor, " yet it sufficeth not. The sons of Usna escape my hands. Try another spell."

Then the Druids froze the grey uneven sea into

jagged hard lumps of rugged ice, like the sharpness of swords on one side of them and like the stinging of serpents on the other side. Then Arden cried out that he was becoming exhausted and must fain give up. " Come thou, Arden, and rest against my shoulder," said Naisi, " and I will support you." Arden did so, but it was not long before he died ; but though he was dead, Naisi held him up still. Then Ainle cried out that he could go no longer, for his strength had left him. When Naisi heard that, he heaved a heavy sigh as of one dying of fatigue, but he told Ainle to hold on to him, and he would bring him soon to land. But not long after, the weakness of death came upon Ainle, and his hold relaxed. Naisi looked on either hand and when he saw that his two brothers were dead, he cared not whether he himself should live or die. He heaved a sigh, sore as the sigh of the dying, and his heart broke and he fell dead.

" The sons of Usna are dead now," said the Druids ; " but they turned not back."

" Lift up thy enchantment," said Conor, " that I now may see the sons of Usna." Then the Druids lifted the enchantment, and there were the three sons of Usna lying dead, and Deirdre fluttering hither and thither from one to another, weeping bitter heartrending tears. And Conor would have taken her away, but she would not be parted from the sons of Usna, and when their tomb was being dug, Deirdre sat on the edge of the grave, calling on the diggers to dig the pit very broad and smooth. They had dug the pit for three only, and they lowered the bodies of the three heroes into the grave, side by side. But when Deirdre saw that, she called aloud to the sons of Usna, to make space for her between them, for she was following them. Then the body of Ainle, that was at Naisi's right hand, moved a little apart, and a space was made for Deirdre close at Naisi's side, where she was wont to be, and Deirdre leapt into the tomb, and placed her arm round the neck of Naisi, her own love, and she kissed him, and her heart broke within her and she died; and together in the one tomb the three sons of Usna and Deirdre were buried. And all the men of Ulster who stood by wept aloud.

But Conor was angry, and he ordered the bodies to be uncovered again and the body of Deirdre to be removed, so that even in death she might not be with Naisi. And he caused Deirdre to be buried on one side of the loch, and Naisi on the other side of the loch, and the graves were closed. Then a young pine-tree grew from the grave of Deirdre, and a young pine from the grave of Naisi, and their branches grew towards each other, until they entwined one with the other across the loch. And Conor would have cut them down, but the men of Ulster would not allow this, and they set a watch and protected the trees until King Conor died.

CHAPTER XXVII

The Fight of Cuchulain with his son Conla

WHEN Cuchulain was yet a youth in Shadow-land, living with Scáth, and learning feats of her, there had come from afar another woman-warrior to make war upon Scáth, a terrible, fierce princess named Aiffe, who had under her many mighty men. Sore was the war between them, and of Scáth's warriors a great multitude were slain and her two sons also fell in battle. Then Scáth called Cuchulain and persuaded him to go in embassage to Aiffe to induce her to make terms of peace and to withdraw her troops into her own country. Cuchulain went on that embassage, and he pleased Aiffe, and she said that she would return into her own country if he would go with her and tarry awhile, and aid her in her wars. So Cuchulain went with her and Aiffe delighted in him and they were wedded, and for a short time they were happy in each other's company, and waged wars together; but soon Cuchulain wearied of her, when he saw her cruelty and fierceness, and that nothing of a woman's gentleness was known to her. And though she besought him not to leave her, he bade her farewell, and returned to Scáth to finish his training, for the time drew near when he must go back to Ireland. When he bade Aiffe farewell, he told her that if a son should be born to him, she was to

Q

send him to Ireland at the end of seven years to seek his father. He gave her a golden arm-ring to keep for the child, and he said that as soon as the arm-ring should fit his wrist, the lad was to come. He laid upon her, too, three stipulations for the child. First, that he should be called Conla, but that he never was to make known his name to any; secondly, that if any man offered him single combat, he must on no account refuse; and thirdly, that he must never turn back from any journey that he had undertaken, no matter what perils stood in his way. Cuchulain prayed Aiffe also to send his son to learn feats of arms with Scáth, as he himself had done. And Aiffe promised him all these things.

Seven years passed away, when, one day in summer, the men of Ulster were holding an assembly beside the seashore, at the place that is called "The Strand of the Track." Their business over, they were amusing themselves along the beach, until they saw coming towards them over the waves a skiff of bronze, light and swift-moving, rowed by two golden oars. Within the skiff, as firmly as though he were on dry land, there stood a little lad playing at games of skill. At his feet was a heap of stones and in his hand a sling, and as the boat moved on, he would take a stone in his hand and fit it to the sling, launching it at the wild sea-birds that soared above his head in the deep, unclouded sky. So cleverly did he hit them that the birds fell at his feet unhurt, and he would throw them up again, and shoot another stone and so bring them down a second time alive. When he tired of this strange feat, he played the apple-feat upon his breath, sending little golden apples into the air, by the blowing of his mouth, so high that the eye could not discern them, first one and then the other until they danced and sparkled in the sun. Each golden ball was of a different size, and he would tune his voice to different notes, the balls dancing up and down, in answer to his singing, each to its own note. And the men of the Gathering watched him with surprise as he drew near.

"Alas!" said the King, who was passing by, "there is woe to the land to which that little boy comes. For, if a child like that can do such feats, of what sort must be the men of the land from which he comes? They would grind us all to powder if they came to fight with us. Let one of you go and speak with the boy, but let him not land on our shores at all." "Who shall go to meet him?" said they; for not one of them wished to approach the little boy, so greatly had his skill put them in dread. "Let Condere go," said the King, "he is ready in speech and wise in argument, and he will find excuses for us, why the stranger should not land." And Condere was content to go.

As the boy drew near the shore, he was about to leap upon the beach when Condere accosted him. "Stay," said he, "thou hast come near enough, good lad, for us to hear who thou art, and from what people and country thou dost come." "I make not myself known to any," replied the boy; "but, if there is a man here who would fight me, ready am I to meet him, for never have I turned back from any combat."

"Thou canst not land here," persisted Condere, "until thou hast made thyself known to us."

"Then needs must I return whence I have come, though it is not my wont to turn back from a journey," said the boy, and he made as though he would move away again. When Condere saw that, he was sorry, for

the child was fair and brave and had an open face, and
the high look of a prince upon him ; so he changed his
words quickly, and called after him, " Come back, come
back, brave boy ; no doubt the King himself will take
you under his protection, Conor the valiant son of Ness
shall be your guard.   Or Amergin the poet will take you
to his care, or Conall Cernach will be your protector ;
and he whom Conall shall protect is ever welcome to the
men of Ulster.   No one dare go against an unripe beardless boy when under Conall's safeguard ; for he himself
would avenge the deed.   Pay therefore the tribute of
the Bridge, which all who come from far must pay to
Ulster ; then will the men of Ulster make welcome to you
here."

" Kindly hast thou spoken," said the lad, " nor do I
doubt that thou dost mean me well ; yet, not to seek
protection of Conall the Victorious, nor of Amergin your
poet, nor even of the king himself, did I seek out this
land ; nor yet to hear myself dubbed, ' an unripe beardless boy,' did I come hither.   If therefore thou wilt
don thy arms, and come to meet me in single combat
at the Bridge, thou there wilt get thy answer ; though
the might of a hundred were in thy arms, no tribute
will I pay, unless in fair fight I first be overthrown."

But when Condere saw the spirit of the lad, he grew
afraid, for though he was an orator and spoke brave
words, he had no mind to face the boy in fight.   " Well,
well, my boy," thought he, " I will let some better
warrior than myself go and speak with thee in words of
war, since words of peace do not suffice thee."

Then the King commanded that warriors of good
renown should go down and speak to the boy in the
battle-speech of arms and combat.   And a goodly com-

pany of men went down to withstand the stranger. When
the little lad saw that, the power of a full-grown fighting-
man came upon him, and he donned his arms, and one
after another as they came to the waterside, he fell upon
them, and stretched them, dead or dying, on the beach.

"This must not be," exclaimed the King, "fetch
Conall Cernach here and let him make an end of this
presumptuous youth."

While they went for Conall Cernach, the little lad,
instead of sitting down to rest, betook himself straight
to his games again. One would have thought he had
no other end in life but to perfect himself in games of
skill, and that to bring a hundred foes into the agonies
of death was but an interruption to his game. When
Conall came above the cliff that over-looked the water's
edge, and saw the boy practising his feats, he stopped
awhile and watched him; but when he saw his cleverness,
and how the balls rose in the air upon his singing voice:
"One only other than this boy," he said, "can do a
trick like that, even Cuchulain, Ulster's Hound; and
indeed, I know not whether he can do it quite so well."
And Conall was astonished, but he would not let the lad
perceive his admiration or his fears.

"Thy play is pretty, my good boy," said Conall, as he
came down to meet him on the beach. "Dost thou find
it so?" said the child; "then I play now against
thee." With that he put a stone, larger than all the
others, in his sling, and shot it up into the air with the
force of a great thunder-bolt and with the noise of
thunder; and Conall was taken unawares and fell upon
his back with the suddenness of the commotion, as
though he had been dead. Before he could rise again,
the boy had leapt ashore and with the strap of his

shield he bound him where he lay, so that he could not move.

When the host of the Ulstermen saw Conall bound, a wail went up from them, for never since the day that Conall the Victorious first took arms had any man been able to overthrow him, though he had fought with the most famous warriors of the world. With one voice they cried, " Send for Cuchulain here, for the honour of Ulster is at stake before this child. Now that Conall lies bound in fetters, Cuchulain alone can retrieve our honour." And the King said : " It is well; send now for Cuchulain."

Cuchulain was in his own fort at Dundalgan when the messengers arrived. But he refused to go with them, saying, " Where Conall Cernach falls there is no hope for me ; bravest and best of all the warriors of Ulster is Conall the Victorious, and skilled in every feat of championship. Who then is this stranger who has come, and what is his name and lineage ? where has he learned arts to fright the men of Ulster ? " For in his own mind Cuchulain thought, " There is but one who can have learned those feats which Scáth teaches only to her most valiant pupils ; what if it be my son who comes ? " So, on that account, he was unwilling to go with the men.

But the messengers urged him, saying, " The honour of Ulster is at stake; the king also commands thee and thy people wait for thee. Wilt thou that Ulster be put to shame before her foes ? "

When Cuchulain heard that the honour of Ulster was at stake, he said, " Go on before me, I will but don my fighting-gear, and I will come." For he thought on Conall Cernach lying bound upon the beach, and he remembered their old love and pledge of ancient friendship; for they had sworn in youth that if either of the twain were in any trouble or peril, the other should go forth to his aid, wherever he might be, and thinking on this, he put on his fighting array, and took his massive broad-sword in his hand, and the terrible spear, the Gae Bolga, which no man could withstand, and that moved like a living thing upon the water to find its enemy.

But for all that, Cuchulain's heart was sad, for he thought on Aiffe, and on Scáth, and on the child that was to be born to him.

Then when the men of Ulster saw Cuchulain coming towards them, clad in all the panoply of war, and his shield and massive two-edged sword held in his hand, their grief was turned to gladness, and their weakness to power, and their fear to courage. And they cried, " Welcome Cuchulain, Welcome, Hound of Ulster! With thee the honour of Ulster is secure! Lo! thy comrade and thy lasting friend is bound before thy eyes; lo! the glory of Ulster is laid low. Welcome, Cuchulain!"

But Cuchulain came on slowly, and his head was bowed, for his mind was troubled within him, and he liked not the combat of that day. And he thought to put it off a while, so he stood and watched the boy, who was gone back to his games again. He took no heed of Cuchulain nor of the hosts; nor did any sign of weariness appear on him, though he had bound a hundred of the foe, and Conall the Victorious with them.

Then Cuchulain said: " You make delightful play, my boy. Who are you yourself? what is your name? what your nation and people, that we may know?" But the boy said: " I came not over-seas to tell my name or to give tidings of my people; never shall any man get such news from me. It is not to tell my name that I am come, but to get peaceful landing here; and if I get not peaceful landing in this place, I will give combat to any that resists me, for this is the condition that is laid upon me, that I should never turn back from any journey, and that I refuse not combat with any man that offers combat to me. Willingly would I now do battle and combat with thee, O noble warrior, save that I like thy face and mien, and thy person is as the person of a prince of men, and not with good-will would I do hurt to thee. Moreover, thou hast brought with thee no strong comrade and warrior to protect thee from my blows."

Now when Cuchulain heard the little fellow talk like that, he laughed, and all the men of Ulster sent up one shout of mirth and of derision. "It would have been necessary for me to bring with me a tiny boy, or a wee baby in my arms," said the Hound, "if I were to fight without odds with thee. However, lad, no warrior or little boy can pass this bridge unless the toll be paid and unless the stranger tell his name and whence he comes. Therefore stand upon thy guard. And as I wish no harm to thee, come thou on shore and we will wrestle with each other." Then the lad left his currach, his little boat of bronze, and stood upon the shore. But when he came beside Cuchulain he reached not up to his knees. "This will never do," said the little fellow, "I cannot reach thy belt to wrestle with thee; set me up upon two stones that I may come on a level to fight with thee." Then Cuchulain helped him up on two large stones, and he thought to play with him gently, but the lad planted his feet so firmly on the rock that Cuchulain could not move him the smallest hair-breadth from his place ; while before ever he was aware of what was happening, the child had caught him, and thrust him backward between two standing pillar-stones, so that he was wedged between them, and could not free himself. And the men of Ulster groaned aloud when they saw their champion used like that.

" Come down to the water, now," said the boy, " and we will see which can pull the other under." And they went into the sea, and swam out a good space from the land, and they caught each other and each tried to hold the other down beneath the waves to drown him. And twice the stranger boy got the head of Cuchulain down and held him there, so that he was like to loose his breath, and to be suffocated in the sea.

Then all his fury and his red battle-anger came upon Cuchulain, because he was being made game of, and because his comrade and his ancient friend Conall was lying bound and helpless on the beach. He knew, too, that the honour of Ulster was at stake, and he could do nothing with this youth to hold it from dishonour. Therefore he loosed his belt that had in it the deadly weapon, from which no mortal could escape, and he set it on the water towards the stranger-boy, and the weapon moved of its own will across the waves of the sea, and it struck the lad and entered him, and the water of the ocean was stained with his blood.

" Now this was what Scáth never taught me," cried the lad, for he knew it was the Gae Bolga, from which he could not escape alive.

" Alas ! " said Cuchulain, " it is true " ; and he took the lad tenderly in his arms and carried him out of the water, and laid him down upon the beach. And as he carried him, he saw upon his wrist the golden ring that

he had left with Aiffe to give the lad, and he knew it
was his son. "Here is my son for you, O men of
Ulster," said Cuchulain, for they gathered round to see.
And when they heard that it was his own son that he had
slain for the honour of Ulster, a wave of grief and of
mourning went through the host, and they were silent
with shame and said no word, grieving for Cuchulain
and his son. Then Cuchulain said, "Alas! Alas! my
son," and he drew the Gae Bolga gently from his wounds,
and he sat down beside him and staunched the blood, and
he began to call upon Aiffe, that she might comfort and
support his son. But Conla said, "Grieve not, Cuchulain, Hound of Ulster, by whom the honour of Ulster
is avenged to-day. Call not on Aiffe, O my father, for
through her wiles it was that I came hither to do combat
with thee; evil and cruel is that woman, and her ways
are evil; for it was to avenge herself on thee because
thou hadst left her that she sent me hither, that I might
bring thee to death or die myself in the attempt. I am
Conla thy son, indeed; yet, until to-day, has no man
known my name; as thou didst lay command upon me,
never have I refused combat to any man, nor have I
turned back from any journey, or revealed my name
to any. And now, O Father, first of Heroes, it is well
for me that I have fallen by thy hand. No shame it
is to fall by the hand of the Guardian of Ulster, but to
have fallen by a lesser hand, that, O Father, would have
been unworthy thee and me. And yet it is woe that I
must die so young, for had I been but five years beside
thee, I would have vanquished the champions of the
world for the honour of Ulster and for thy honour, and
I would have made thee king of the world as far as the
walls of Rome. Since I must needs die, and my strength

is passing fast away, lose not this little space in grief, but point me out the heroes of Ulster of whom Scáth used to tell, that I may take leave of each before I die."

Then the heroes of Ulster drew near, and Cuchulain named them all, and Conall Cernach amongst them, and the boy put his arms round the neck of one hero after the other, and kissed them, and then once more he put his arms round the neck of his own father, and with that he died.

When Cuchulain saw that his son was dead, he laid him on the earth, and he stood up, and a burst of anguish like the breaking of a heart came from him. And he cried aloud : " The end is come indeed for me :

> " ' I am a man without son, without wife,
> I am the Father who slew his own child,
> I am a broken, rudderless bark,
> Tossed from wave to wave in the tempest wild ;
> An apple blown loose from the garden wall,
> I am over-ripe, and about to fall.' "

Then the men of Ulster came about Cuchulain and tried to comfort him, and they raised the body of Conla on a shield, as it is wont to do with heroes, and they made for him a noble grave, and buried him there, with a pillar-stone to mark the spot, and his name and his deeds written thereon. And all Ulster wept for him, and the King commanded that for three days no merriment or feasting should take place within the borders of Ulster, as is wont to be done on the death of a king.

CHAPTER XXVIII

The Hound at Bay

YET all this while Cuchulain's foes drew closer round him, watching their opportunity, and the land was filled with smoke and flame, and omens foretold that the Hound was at bay at last, and that the King of the Heroes of Erin was doomed to die. For though Meave entered not again into open war with Ulster, never had she forgotten the disgrace put upon her armies by Cuchulain, in that he alone had beaten and held back her troops during the whole winter's length, slaying and destroying her chosen men. His kindness to her in her weakness she soon forgot, or if she remembered it, it was made bitter by the laugh of Fergus; she felt humiliated that she, the mighty warrior queen, and leader of her forces, had stooped to ask help from the hands of her enemy. So she awaited the moment of revenge.

Throughout all Ireland she sent messengers to stir up strife against Cuchulain, so that he was harassed and pursued on every hand; nor did he ever sleep a night in peace. To all those men whose fathers or brothers or sons Cuchulain had slain she whispered of revenge, and glad and pleased she was when one and another fell upon him unawares or led a raid into the country of Murthemne, to burn and spoil the land. Above all, she stirred up Luga, son of Curoi, prince of Munster, and

Erc, the son of Tara's royal king; and these awaited but a chance to fall upon Cuchulain unawares.

But worst of all, she sent a brood of monstrous, ill-shaped sprites, half-women, half-goblins, in their forms and minds, to learn throughout the whole wide distant world some secret way to bring Cuchulain to his death. Monstrous they were, for but one single eye was in their foreheads, and their right legs and left arms were lopped off at the stump. They did not move along the earth like men, but on the broad back of the whistling winds and wrapped in magic clouds of their own making, they sped o'er land and sea.

Hideous and frightful were they to behold, and hideous were their thoughts and their designs. When they drew near, a poisonous ill-wind preceded them, and all the sky was dark with venomous clouds about them and above, so that although they saw them not, men shrank with fear and felt but ill at ease. These creatures then she sent through the wide spaces of the universe to learn all cruel magic arts that hurt and trouble men. And for five years they wandered through the earth, until they reached the fearful realm where Vulcan forged his weapons in the fire.

The secret of all poisonous herbs they learned, the use of every charm that spoils men's lives and drives them to despair; they learned to raise a magic stormy sea upon dry land, in which men might be drowned; and out of forest twigs and fluttering leaves they learned to form a host of fighting-men and armed them with the spiked thorn of the thistle leaves or with the black-thorn's barb.

From Vulcan's hand three cruel spears they took, their names, 'Wind,' 'Good-luck,' and 'Cast';

three swords of magic power, too, they got, the 'Wounder,' and the 'Hacker,' and the 'Hewer.' "By these three spears or these three swords the splendid Hound shall die," was Vulcan's word; "each one of them shall kill a king of Erin, and among those kings will be the mighty king of Erin's hero-chiefs, the triumphant, heavy-smiting, noble youth, whom men call "Ulster's Hound."

Then with a fierce and cruel glee those hideous children of the storm bade Vulcan and his crew farewell, and on the rough and whistling blast that blows keen from the east, they rose on high and made their way to Erin's coasts, alighting on the plain before the fort of Meave. She, rising early on the morrow, looked forth out of her bower, and saw them resting, each upon one leg perched on the rampart's top. Her five-fold crimson mantle flung about her, straightway she stepped forth and made them welcome, and with a cruel joy she heard their news. The venomed spears and hard-wrought swords she took into her hands, and waved and brandished them to try their power, but though from point to hilt she bent them back, no sign of crack or failure could she find. "Well-tempered swords are these, indeed," she cried, "by these my deadly foe shall fall at last."

Then straight to Ulster she sent forth the brood of ill-formed goblin women. "Seek out Cuchulain where he lies," she said, "and on him try your spells. Set right before his face your magic tide of ocean-waves that he may rush into the flood and come thus to his death; or, if that fail, tempt him with magic troops and armed battalions made out of puff-balls or of fluttering leaves and armed with sharp and prickly thistle-spikes. Thus lure him forth, for I have heard it said that Emer and her women hold him with their gentle wiles within his own strong fort, till he be healed of all his pain and wounds. Tempt you him out into the open plain, and there his foes will find and speak with him and utterly and for ever strike him down. My hosts are there, and Luga's hosts and Erc's. Give to each one of them your magic spears, that he may not escape. Thus shall the strength of Ulster fall at last! Thus shall our vengeance come! Within the space of three short days bring in his head to me."

So with deep wiles Meave laid her cruel plans, plotting Cuchulain's death; Murthemne and Cuchulain's country she filled with war-bands, marching through the land wasting and marauding, and they burned the villages and the forests of the plain, so that the whole region was a cloud of fire about them. Now the friends of Cuchulain, and Emer, his dear wife, had taken the hero away with them from his own home at Dun Dalgan to a secret glen in Ulster, that is called the Glen of the Deaf, because no sound of war or tumult reached it, where was a pleasant summer palace retired from mankind. There they entertained him with sweet music and pleasant tales and games of chess, to hold him back from rushing to meet the foe; and they took from him his chariot and his weapons, and turned his chariot-steeds out into the fenced green, for they knew that if he should go forth at this time, he must surely fall. But the hero was restless and unhappy, and save that he had plighted his word to Emer and to all his friends he would not have entered the Glen. For Emer's sake and theirs he went with them to the lightsome summer palace, and sat down with the poets and artists and the women-folk to listen to sweet beguiling music and tales of ancient deeds to while away the time.

Everywhere throughout the Province the horrid brood of mis-shaped children sought him, but they found him not, neither in Dun Dalgan nor in Emain, nor in his own country of Murthemne's Plain; but at last one of them soared up to the very clouds of heaven and surveyed the whole wide land of Ulster, and from a hidden forest glen she heard the sound of joyous revelry and the high, shrill voice of women's laughter, and the cheerful noise of a great company keeping festival together.

Then she transformed herself into the shape of a black raven, and swooped down and perched above the seat on which Cuchulain sat. And it seemed to Cuchulain that he heard words, inciting him to go forth.

" Dun Dalgan is burned," they said to him, " and all the province is laid waste ; the war-bands and the hosts of Meave have ravaged all the land, and everywhere but smoke and flames are seen. Arise, O Hound, arise ! "

But to the rest it seemed as though the raven croaked, and they laughed loud to hear the bird of ill-omen croaking in the house. Cuchulain sprang to his feet to rush forth ; but, as he rose, his mantle caught beneath his feet, and he was thrown backwards on his seat. Once more he rose in haste and red with shame, but the great kingly brooch that fastened his mantle, being loosened by his fall, dropped on his foot, and dropping pierced his skin. " Alas ! alas ! " he cried, " even my mantle warns me of ill-luck ! " And Emer said, " 'Tis even so ; heed now the warning of a friend. Let this pass, Cu ; for three days stay with us, and then in peace thou mayest go forth to fight. For three days only have the Children of the Blast their fatal power. Not for thyself or thine own safety do we thus entreat, but for the sake of Ulster and her king. For Ulster is destroyed if Cuchulain falls. For three days then abide." And for the sake of Ulster Cuchulain stayed, though heaviness and shame sat deep upon him, and in his heart he longed to go. And wearily he sat down again to play his game of chess.

For that night the Wild Women of the Blast went back, and they waited until another day was past, but towards the fall of night the horrid brood of mis-shaped children betook them to the Glen. On the swift magic wind of their own making they soared aloft, and at the very entrance to the Glen they lighted on the ground. There they began to work their noisome spells. Out of the light wee puff-balls and the rustling forest leaves they formed great lines of fighting-men, all armed with battle-weapons of the hooded sharp-spiked thistle-stalks. All round the lightsome, pleasant house the army stood, in marshalled band on band, and all the country rang with battle-shouts and cries of war and trumpetings, and loud pealing laughter, and the taunts of strong men when they mock at cowards.

In the palace Cuchulain caught the uproar and the mocking laughter of the phantom fairy hosts. He started up and would have rushed madly from the hall, but those around him stayed and hindered. " Close fast the doors," they said, " if for this one day and to-morrow we can keep him fast, the magic evil spell is past." And Emer came to him and said, " This one day yet abide, O dear one, noblest of the whole world's race, my one and only love. These are but shows and phantoms that thou hearest wrought by the sprites to lure thee to thy doom. To-morrow, or the next day, or the next. comes Conall Cernach back from travelling.

R

Alone, thou fallest; with him thou art a match for any host. For Ulster's sake and ours, and for thine own, abide."

Then at this thing Cu felt a mighty shame; his soul was filled with storms of anger and reproach. "Alas! alas!" he cried, "henceforth there is no cause to guard my life. My span is ended, my honour is destroyed. Better for me than all the gold and riches of the world, if I had died before there fell on me this shame. In every tongue this noble saying is recorded, "Fame outlives life"; but by your urgency I keep my life, when all my fame and honour is destroyed. Come death, come life, to-morrow I go forth."

And gloomily and sadly he sat down, nor would he play or listen to the music of the bards, or hold sweet converse with the women, but all that night, till break of day, he tried and proved his weapons, and his spears and sword he polished lovingly, and he sent Laeg out to catch his chariot-steeds and bring them to the green beside the house. And his heart revived within him when he heard without the neigh of the Grey of Macha and the Black Steed of the Glen.

But the foul Children of the Blast were disappointed and dismayed because they could not tempt Cuchulain out. And all that night they sat in council, devising plans to snare him. "We have but one day more," they said, "before our power is lost. To-morrow then and verily, we lure him forth."

Before the morning's sun was well arisen, on the blast of the swift moaning wind of their own making, and all unseen, they came around the glen. Then they put forth their magic spells and round the house they made the likeness of a mighty sea that wave on wave rolled ever

nearer to the pleasure-house, threatening to overwhelm
it as it stood. Amid the women's talk and loving
laughter, and the sweet music of the harps and singing
men, Cuchulain heard the lapping of the waves, and the
low distant ocean's roar, and whistling of the wind upon
the sea. Then he rose up and seized his weapons in his
hand, and for all Emer and the rest could do, he rushed
forth from the house. And madness came upon him
when he saw the rolling billows rising ever towards
the house, and all the land covered with mist and spray;
and he called Emer, and would have lifted her up above
the waves to carry her in safety through the billows.
But Emer and the rest could see no waves, only the green
waving grasses of the pleasure-field, and nought they
heard save the soft rustling breath of spring that whispered through the leaves. And Emer said : " Little
Cu, O my first love and darling of all earth's men, never
until this hour have I or any of thy women-folk put
hindrance in thy way in any exploit or battle-raid that
thou didst desire. Though oft we wept, and many a
time we thought thou never wouldst return, we never
held thee back. But now for my sake, my own chosen
sweetheart, go not forth. No sea is that thou seest upon
the green, but only waving grasses and the fluttering
leaves. Heed not the magic noisome spells of those thy
enemies, but one day more abide. Then never till the
end of life or time will we restrain or hold thee back
again." But Cuchulain said, " Emer, restrain me not;
I see the horses of Manannan riding on the waves; I
hear Manannan's fairy harp play gently o'er the billows;
Manannan's ancient face I see beckoning me o'er the
main."

Then Emer knew that the hour of Cuchulain's fate

was come, and that nought of all that ever they could do would avail to turn him back. For the seer had prophesied that when Cuchulain should see the horses of the ancient Ocean god upon the waves, and when he should hear Manannan's harp play sweetly, the hour of his fate was come, and he must e'en go back to Shadowland.

Then she herself called Laeg to prepare his chariot and harness his horses, and to set his fighting-gear in order, that not by phantasies or magic wild imaginings, but as a chariot-chief and champion facing his foes he might go forth to die; and she brought out his helmet and set it upon his head, and placed his mighty shield within his hand, that he might die as a hero should.

And when Cuchulain saw his chariot standing ready for him, and Laeg therein awaiting him, and the noble steeds pawing the ground, the phantoms of his brain passed away from him, and his warrior strength and joyousness of mind came back, and he donned his armour with good-will and gladness, and made to spring into the chariot. But for the first time since the day when they rose out of the magic lake, the steeds obeyed not his hand, but started from him and turned the chariot round, evading him. And when Laeg drew them back, and Cuchulain prepared to spring again into the chariot, they fled away before him. "How now, how now is this, good steeds?" said Laeg; "full oft before ye two came bounding at your master's call, nor ever turned away. Ill deed is this of thine, for never upon any former day did he and I need help from you as now we need it. Presage of evil is this freak of thine!" This when the Grey of Macha heard he stood quite still, the Black Steed by his side, and they let Cuchulain mount into the chariot; but even as he sprang to take his seat, his weapons all fell down about his feet; to him a grim fore-shadowing of ill. He saw, moreover, that from the horses' eyes and down their cheeks coursed tears of dusky blood.

Yet for all that he stayed not, but without farewells or partings of any kind at all, joyously he set forth towards Murthemne's Plain, to meet the hosts of Meave. But when the cruel Children of the Blast saw the imprisoned champion go forth and take the level road across the plain, up to the highest heavens they rose aloft with wild shrill cries and shriekings of delight, and through the air upon the whistling wind they sped before him, hastening to arouse the hosts of Meave to meet him in their strength. Before Cuchulain's eyes they raised a vision of battle-troops and marshalled lines standing round Emain, with chariots, steeds and weapons in great plenty. He saw the city red and dark with flames, and heard the shouting of the foe as Emain sank in ashes. That vision passed away, and then another came before his mind. He saw Dun Dalgan, his own home, aglow, like Emain, in the ruddy flame. He saw the women flying from the flames, with hair dishevelled, and with streaming eyes. He heard the crashing of the blazing walls, as inward one and then another fell. He saw the foe behind with swords upraised, slaying and cutting down the women as they ran. Then he saw Emer, his own loving wife, standing alone upon the outer wall, scanning the distant plain. She raised her hands and called on him for help, and down her face ran torrents of salt tears. Then he could see behind her, creeping slowly on, a fierce relentless warrior of Meave's host. And with one spring he saw him seize her hair, the soft long locks Cuchulain loved to touch, and backward with his cruel pitiless hand he drew her head, and with a single blow he sheared it off, flinging it in disdain out o'er the rampart's wall, and trampling her fair body under foot. When he had seen that deed, Cuchulain groaned, and sped along the plain with greater haste.

Then passing o'er a stream they saw a maiden stooping on the brink, as though she washed and rinsed the garments of the slain. Slender and white her body and her hands, but all the waters ran with crimson blood, and still she washed, and wept, and wrung her hands, and all her yellow hair hung down in tresses slowly dropping blood. Sharply and quick, without a word or pause, Laeg turned the chariot when he saw the girl, and made as though to flee. "How now?" said Cu; "what dost thou, Master Laeg? What spoils are these the maiden wrings and washes in the stream? and who and what is she?" "She is the Watcher of the Ford," Laeg cried, "the daughter of the goddess of grim war. She wrings the garments of the slain, or those about to die. Dost thou not see that they are thine own garments that she washes out to-day; that it is thine own sword that runs with blood, dying the river red? Alas! alas! while there is time, let us now turn and flee."

"Dear comrade, it is well," the hero said, "I may not turn me back from this my hour of vengeance on the men of Erin, revenge for all the ill that they have wrought on us. What though the fairy woman wash my spoils? great spoil of arms, of armour and of gear, is that which by my spear shall shortly fall and lie there drenched in blood. None knows it better than I know myself that in this coming onslaught I must fall; whether I stay I am devoted to death, or whether I go, the span of my life is run out. No more then hinder or delay my course, for sad as you may be to see me go to Death, even so glad and cheerful I myself go forth to meet my fate. Let me but once more thus avenge my country's wrongs, and gladly and with joy I give my life."

So he turned again and faced the enemy, and all his gloom and heaviness passed from Cuchulain, and the delusions of the gruesome fairy folk troubled him no more. Cheerfully and free from care he rode on towards the host, and from his forehead, brighter than the sun, shone out the Hero's Light. Right terrible and beautiful he stood, his mighty sword uplifted in his hand, his eyes beneath his helmet flashing fire. And when they saw him coming thus alone, a shout of triumph rose from all the host, and mounted to the very clouds of heaven.

CHAPTER XXIX

Fame outlives Life

THROUGHOUT that day the battle rolled and raged. No time to eat or drink Cuchulain gave, but from the dewy morn to fall of night he wrought upon his foes death-dealing blows, cutting them down as hailstones crush small flowers. And though he was alone against a host, they fled in terror from his path, so like a god of battles and of war the hero seemed. In his first onset men and horses, hounds and charioteers gave way before him, as the corn gives way, bowing before the scythe; and all around his path the bodies of the slain were piled. Throughout the day, they rallied once and then again, but still they could not take him whole or strike him dead. From off his helmet and the armour Scáth had given, their weapons broke and shattered in their hands; no sword would wound, no spear would pierce his skin. His chariot-steeds, like horses god-possessed, trampled their men to death; the fire breathing from their nostrils consumed all who ventured near. Thus through the hosts from side to side Cuchulain urged his steeds, and all his way was heaped and piled with dead. Twice seemed it that the victory was his, but at the last, the warriors rallied and held him back. Then, at the third time, the Wild Women-Goblins of the Blast, who watched the fight, screaming above the slain, swooped down. Into the hands of Luga and young Erc, but late ascended Tara's royal seat, and into the dread hand of dark Curoi, they placed the venomous spears of magic might brought out of fairy-land. "The time is come," said they; "take these and strike; with each of these three spears a king shall fall."

Together those three foes drew near, and first Curoi threw his weapon, aiming it at Cu. But from his mantle once again it swerved, missing its mark. But glancing off from him, it pierced the Grey of Macha, pinning the gallant creature to the ground.

Cuchulain, when he saw his steed transfixed, without a thought for his own safety, bounded from his chariot, and stooped to draw the weapon from the wound; but for all he tugged and pulled, he could not get it out. While he was bending down to help his steed, Erc, the young king of Erin, flung the second spear, hoping to kill Cuchulain. It touched his hip and wounded him, but fell upon his charioteer, inflicting a mortal wound. "Alas, my little Cu," cried Laeg, "by this wound now I die; never before in any fight or foray that we have faced together have I been wounded past thy guard!"

"Not past, but through me went that spear," Cuchulain said, "see, I am hurt by it. My blessing with thee, Laeg, and leave me now, ere faintness falls on thee; seek shelter far beyond the host, thither will I in safety lead the way. If haply thou shouldst escape and live so long, back to Dun Dalgan make thy way, where Emer of the waving hair still looks for my return. My blessing take to her and my dear love; tell her I love her yet, and had I lived, not all the women of the whole globe's space would e'er have lured or drawn my love from her. Tell her again, tell Conor and tell Conall, how for their sakes I wage this awful fight, tight closed in grips with all the hosts of Meave. 'Tis Ulster's honour and mine own I avenge. Let Emer weep awhile that I am dead, and mourn my loss ; surely she will not live when I am gone. Yet for their bitter weeping and their tears, the dead return not to their friends who mourn. My blessing take, O Laeg ; no chariot-chief had ever man so faithful and so true. My word I swear upon my weapons here, all Erin's hosts shall hear how I avenged thy loss. In grief and gloom we part ! Thou goest and Emer goes ! No more as in old days from foreign lands in gallant glee shall I return to her."

Thus to each other, in heaviness and grief, the hero and his servant bade farewell. Yet for awhile, so long as he could stand, from a low hillock Laeg looked on and watched the fight. Then (for the Black Steed followed him, and would not turn away) upon the back of his own chariot-horse he took his way straight to Cuchulain's home.

But after his farewell, the hero turned him back into the fray, and on his foes he took a fierce revenge. No sword or armour could withstand his blows. On every side he seemed to be at once, now here, now there, dealing death-bearing wounds. Before him, and on every side, the men of Erin fled, while, like the avenging god of war, Cuchulain pressed behind.

Then when the cruel Children of the Blast beheld the rout, one of the three limped to where Luga stood, and ugly was her face, and black her scowl. " Why fling you not the spear we brought to you ? A king will fall by it if it is thrown."

" I heard you say a king would fall before, when Erc

and Curoi flung their venomed spears. Yet Cuchulain lives," Luga replied.

" And so it was," she said ; " the King of Erin's steeds, the King of Erin's charioteers have fallen by those spears. One King lives yet, and by your spear the King of Erin's heroes is to fall."

Then Luga flung the spear. Straight, vehement, and true the aim he took, and over all the heads of all the host it rose and fell, piercing Cuchulain to the very earth.

Then out of sudden fear the host stood back, seeing Cuchulain fall. No shout went up, but silence deep and awful seized the host. They ceased to fly and turned, but none of all of them advanced to aid or slay the wounded man.

In a wide circle as they turned they stood each leaning on his spear, and in the empty space, near where Cuchulain fell, in silence Luga stood to watch the hero die. Thus all alone, without a single friend, the king of Erin's mighty heroes lay, dying upon the plain. Slowly Cuchulain rose in mortal pain, and stooped to drag the weapon from the wound ; but he could not, for it broke off at the head, leaving the metal fastened in the flesh. And as he tugged, the red blood trickled slowly to his feet and made a stream that ran away along a furrow of the plain. Cuchulain saw an otter that crept up from the rushes on the margin of the lake. Stealthily the creature drew towards him, attracted by the blood, and in a timid way began to drink. It vexed Cuchulain when he saw the cringing beast drinking his blood while he was yet alive, and he ceased tugging at the buried spear-head, and made shift to stoop and pick up the fallen shaft and fling it at the beast. At that a raven came fluttering down and hesitatingly drew near, and dipped its beak into the hero's blood; but in the slippery stream its claws were caught and so the bird upset. When he saw that, Cuchulain laughed aloud, and well he knew that laugh would be his last.

For, even as he laughed, Death's mists and swoonings fell on him. He closed his eyes, and when at length he opened them again, the warrior-host had moved, drawn nearer to the place where he was lying still; but such an awe was on them that in that mighty ring of warrior-hosts, armed all with clanking weapons and with arms, no sound was heard; they stood as silent as a nurse might stand within the dark sick-room, to watch the champion die.

Then came a mighty thirst upon the wounded man. "Fain would I go," he said to them, "and quench my thirst beside the loch."

"We give thee leave to go," they said, "but only if thou come again to us."

"If I come not to you again myself, I bid you come for me," the hero said.

So he gathered himself together and went slowly to the loch. And he drank his drink and washed himself, and came forth to die, calling upon his foes to come and meet him.

Now his eye lighted upon a tall pillar-stone that was beside the loch in the midst of the plain. And he drew himself to the stone, and leaned his back against it, and with the girdle that was about his breast, he bound himself to the stone, standing up facing the men of Erin. And in his hand he grasped his naked sword and held it up aloft, and in his other hand he took his shield, and placed it close beside him on the ground. For he said, " I will not die before the men of Erin lying

Cuchulain comes at last to his Death

down nor sitting on the ground, but I will die before them standing up." 'And the Grey of Macha found him where he stood, and came up, dragging the spear that still held in his wound ; and it laid its head upon Cuchulain's breast, weeping great dropping tears of dusky blood. And all about his shoulders hovered carrion birds, yet still the host dared not venture nigh, for the hero's light shone from his forehead, and they knew not whether he were alive or dead.

Then went Luga near to see if he were yet alive, and as he came beside him, the great sword fell from the dying Champion's hand, and struck the hand of Luga, and smote it off, so that the sword and hand fell to the ground together. Cuchulain heaved a deep and troubled sigh, and with that sigh his soul parted from his body. Yea, with the greatness of that sigh the pillar-stone was split, as may be seen to this day. Men call it still the Pillar of the Hero's dying Sigh.

CHAPTER XXX

The Red Rout

DAILY upon the ramparts of Dun Dalgan Emer of the beauteous hair looked out and waited for Cuchulain, for nought of Laeg's grim tale, that he was dead or dying on the Plain, would take hold on her mind. But still and evermore he came not home.

Upon a certain day, far off she saw a single horseman coming towards the fort, upon a horse that wearily and weakly moved along, dropping red blood at every step. Weary the horseman seemed, and in his hand he bore a rod made out of osiers of the stream, and on it hung the gory heads of lately slaughtered men. Then trembling and affright fell on the queen. Full well she knew the horse that dripped with blood, the Grey of Macha, Cuchulain's chariot-steed, but on his back another rider sat. " 'Tis Conall the Victorious," she exclaimed, " he rides Cuchulain's horse. With evil news he comes to me this day. The tale is true that Laeg told, Cuchulain in his blood lies on Murthemne's Plain, dying or dead. Woe that another rides Cuchulain's steed! Woe that the Hound of Ulster draws not near. Full many a day in triumphant pride by this same path he hath come home to me! Full many a day along this beaten way in gallant glee he hath gone forth to war!" Sadly and sorrowfully drew Conall near and greeted Emer. And Emer said, " What gory heads are those thou bearest on the withe ?

How and in what fight didst thou come by them ? "
" These are the heads of those who slew thy hero and
my friend !   Alas ! that I in distant lands was wandering
when Cuchulain died.   Too late I came to save him, if
perchance he still might shun the hour of his death ;
but not too late my promise to redeem and to avenge his
fall.   See here upon the withe is Luga's head, and here
the head of dark Curoi mac Daire, and here is Erc's, the
fair young lad who stained his youth with blood, the
blood of Ulster's Guardian and its Hound.   These and
the others I bear here with me in token of my duty well
performed, my promise kept.   Where'er men speak the
praise of Ulster's Hound and tell his deeds, there also
shall they speak of the Red Rout of Conall Cernach, in
vengeance of his death ! "

Then trembling Emer said, " One head I see not here
upon the withe ; yet in thy bosom surely thou hast yet
one head for me.   I see fair hair, O Conall, bring it forth ;
give back to me my lover and my friend."

Then Conall said : " Listen, O Emer, to the tale I tell.
When round the men of Erin in my wrath and battle-
fury I had passed, cutting and hewing down their chiefs
and leaders and their mighty men, close up to Tara's
wall I made my way, seeking for Erc, who fled before
my steps surrounded by his chosen counsellors.   Passing the playing-fields without the fort, I saw men playing
hurley with a head, a human head in place of hurley-
balls, a human head yet fresh and wet with blood.   My
own blood froze within my veins !   It was the head of
Ulster's Hound they struck and flung from hand to
hand !   And at the shame of it methought its cheeks
blushed hot and rosy red.   Even as I came the head
was struck ; it bounded up, and nobly took the goal.   A

shout went up from all those reckless men.   ' So, so, the Hound of Ulster wins again ; good man, good man, we hit him under once and took his head from him, but he would take revenge upon us now.'

"' Revenge,' I cried, ' revenge he'll find indeed,' and at that word into their midst I sprang, dealing on every hand death-bringing blows.   Like corn before the mower's scythe, or like grown grass beneath the feet of many hosts, I hewed them down.   Harsh cries went up, for all unarmed they fell, helpless and with no power to withstand, and Erc came out upon the green, and stood there in dismay.   I held Cuchulain's head on high in my left hand.   ' Thy head to match with his,' I cried, and ere he raised a sound his head was rolling at my feet. I picked it up and hither came to seek thee, gentle queen."

Then Emer, white as death, and trembing as a rush that bows before the onward-flowing stream, put forth her hands, and said, " Give me Cuchulain's head." But when with reverence Conall placed within her hands Cuchulain's head, a cry of sorrow and of grief rang out from Emer's lips, and pierced the souls of all who heard it in the fort.   She bent to kiss the head, and at that moment her sad heart broke within her breast, and o'er Dun Dalgan's rampart Emer fell, her fair hair mingled with the hair of Cuchulain, her mantle rent and torn, and all her lovely face splashed o'er with blood.   Gently and reverently they raised her up, and bore her, with the head still clasped within her arms, to where the body of Cuchulain lay.   There on Murthemne's plain they buried them, two lovers and two friends within one tomb, husband and wife.   And when the grave was digged and filled again, the Grey of Macha roamed away ; through all the fields and furrows of the plain, through all the glens and hills in Erin's bounds he seemed to search and closely scrutinise, as though to find some being he had lost. But when he found him not, back to the lonely loch among the reeds, where first Cuchulain found and mastered him, he came again; and with one bound he leaped into the very centre of the loch, and so appeared no more. This witnessing, the Black Steed neighed in mournful wise, and went back to the glen in Donegal, and no man dared to seek or follow him, nor ever found they trace of him again.

But to the three times fifty queens who wept for him, the soul of Cuchulain, radiant and noble as in life, appeared once more; and on the ramparts of Emain by night, old warriors tell how, when men are asleep, the spirit-chariot of a spirit-chief, clad in his battle armour as of yore, moves round the walls, guarding the outer ramparts from the foe; and all men sleep in safety, for the Hound of Ulster wakes.

And as, with slow and stately pace the chariot moves, drawn by two noble horses, white and black, a chant goes up upon the midnight air, not like the pagan chants of other days, but sweet and gentle as a summer-song, and with a note of triumph in its sound, telling the coming of a hero-chief, who shall be called the Christ, and who will bring great peace and rest to men. And when that song is heard, rising with its sweet strain o'er all the fort, the fires of war and hate are softened in the chieftains' hearts, and women smile upon their little babes and hug them to their breasts. And all, the young and old, set forward minds to welcome the new time when wars shall cease, and peace shall come to men.

S

Notes on the Sources

"Táin bó Cuailnge."   The two oldest versions of the long tale of the "Táin bó Cuailnge," or "Cattle-Raid of Cooley," from which the main part of Chapters ii.-vi. and ix.-xix. of this book are taken, are those found in the old vellum manuscripts known as the "Leabhar na h-Uidhre" (L.U.), compiled about the year 1100 in the monastery of Clonmacnois on the Shannon, and preserved in the Library of the Royal Irish Academy, Dublin, and that occurring in the Book of Leinster (L.L.), preserved in Trinity College, Dublin, the larger portion of which appears to belong to the twelfth century.   A version found in the Yellow Book of Lecan corresponds closely to that in L.U., and seems to contain an even earlier text.   The text of this older version is in course of publication in Ériu, the journal of the School of Irish Learning in Dublin, and a translation has been made of it by Miss W. Faraday (Grimm Library Series, vol. xvi.).   The lengthy L.L. version has been published with a German translation, and copious notes and glossary, by Dr Ernst Windisch, 1905.

Among the later versions of parts of this long tale, is a copy found in the British Museum (marked Add. 18748) 1800 A.D., which coincides in the main with that of the Book of Leinster.   A translation of large portions of this manuscript was contributed by Dr Standish H. O'Grady to the present author's

" Cuchullin Saga in Irish Literature " (Grimm Library, vol. viii.).

The story of " The Education of Cuchulain " in Alba or Scotland, with the amazon Scáth, originally formed part of the tale of " The Wooing of Emer," but separate accounts exist of these adventures. For the details of Chapter vii., I have drawn partly upon the incidents contained in the longer version of " The Wooing of Emer," and partly upon two late manuscripts found in the British Museum (Egerton, 106 and 145). These have since been edited by Dr Whitley Stokes in the Revue Celtique, vol. xxix.

" The Wooing of Emer." This story is taken from Dr Kuno Meyer's edition of the tale found in Stowe MS. 992, and first published by him in the Archæological Review, vol. i.

The story of " Cuchulain's Visit to Fairy-land," usually known as " The Sick-bed of Cuchulain " (our Chapters xx., xxi.), is adapted from the accounts as given in the only two copies known to exist of it, one found in L.U. and the other in a fifteenth-century manuscript in Trinity College, Dublin. It was first published by O'Curry in Atlantis, vols. i. and ii., and later Dr Windisch edited the tale in Irische Texte, vol. i. An English translation will be found in Leahy's " Heroic Romances of Ireland," vol. i.

The story of " Deirdre," usually called " The Tragical Fate of the Sons of Usnach," is one of three favourite titles that for the last two hundred years at least have been known as "The Three Sorrowful Tales of Erin," the other two being "The Fate of the Children of Lir" and "The Fate of the Children of Tuireann." There is, however, no connection or similarity between these tales. The story is found in numerous versions dating from the twelfth century down to the present day, and it has undergone much modification in the course of repetition. It is still a popular story in the Highlands of Scotland, and all round Loch Etive and its neighbourhood are the remains of forts and sites bearing the names of the unfortunate lovers.

No single version contains the entire story, and I have therefore been obliged to combine the accounts given in various versions belonging to different ages, slightly altering the arrangement in order to fit them together. In the chapter called "The Sleep-Wanderer," and in the account of "The Death of the Sons of Usnach," I have drawn largely on a very beautiful and poetic Gaelic folk-version taken down by Dr Alexander Carmichael from the lips of an old man of eighty-three years of age, John Macneill or "Iain Donn" of Barra, and first published by him in the Trans. of the Gaelic Society of Inverness, vols. xiii., xiv. It has since been republished under the title of "Deirdre."

Some suggestions I have also taken from a modern manuscript found by Dr Douglas Hyde in the Belfast Museum, part of which was printed by him in Zeit. für Celt. Phil., vol. ii.

But the main body of the story follows the mediæval version, which has been printed repeatedly, one of the best recent editions being that of Dr Whitley Stokes in Irische Texte, 2nd series, pt. 2.

In the oldest version, that found in the Book of

Leinster, Deirdre is made to survive the sons of Usnach, and is forced to come into Conor's house ; but she will neither eat nor smile, and finally she puts an end to her intolerable existence by springing from a chariot and dashing her head against a rock. This version is much ruder and more barbaric than any of those belonging to a later period.

" The Tragical Death of Conla (or Conlaech), Son of Aiffe." Apparently the oldest form of this story, which is the Irish parallel to the Persian story of "Sohrab and Rustem," is that found in the Yellow Book of Lecan, recently edited by Dr Kuno Meyer in Ériu, vol. i. pt. 1 ; Mr J. G. O'Keeffe gives another ancient version in the same journal. The story is usually told in verse, and is still alive in Gaelic-speaking parts of Ireland and in the Highlands of Scotland. Miss Brooke has published one of these poetical forms in her " Reliques of Irish Poetry," 1789.

" The Tragical Death of Cuchulain." The incidents connected with the death of Cuchulain, and immediately preceding and following it, are chiefly taken from, or suggested by, two good but comparatively recent manuscripts in the British Museum (Egerton, 132, and Add. 18947) dating from the early eighteenth and the nineteenth centuries respectively. They contain the cycle of events known as " The Great Defeat on the Plain of Murthemne," " The Death of Cuchulain," " The Red Rout of Conall Cernach," " The Lay of the Heads," and " Emer's Death." Portions of the material from the first of these two manuscripts were translated for my " Cuchullin Saga " by Dr S. H. O'Grady, but these five stories as a consecutive whole have not yet been published.   An older (L.L.) version of Cuchulain's death was published by Dr Whitley Stokes in Revue Celtique, vol. iii.

Murthemne, or Cuchulain's country, formed part of the present Co. Louth, and a great pillar stone is still pointed out by the people as the place of Cuchulain's death, a split in the side having been caused, according to living tradition, by the dying sigh of the hero.

The poem on p. 141 is reprinted by kind permission of Mr T. Fisher Unwin.

Lightning Source UK Ltd.
Milton Keynes UK
UKOW021154050213

205850UK00004B/67/P